PENGUIN BOOKS

RAJESH KHANNA

Yasser Usman is a journalist by tribe, a television producer by creed and a film commentator by caste. He has been a recipient of the prestigious Ramnath Goenka Award for excellence in journalism and the NT (News Television) Awards thrice over. A master's in environmental science, he remembers more films and songs than classroom theories. He has worked for over a decade in leading TV news organizations and is currently with ABP News (formerly Star News). He is also a bilingual columnist for Dearcinema.com and News Today. An IIMC New Delhi alumnus, he lives in Delhi NCR and is ever available on www.yasserusman.com.

D1564961

RAJESH KHANNA

The Untold Story of
India's First Superstar

YASSER USMAN

Foreword by SALIM KHAN

PENGUIN BOOKS

PENGUIN BOOKS
Published by the Penguin Group
Penguin Books India Pvt. Ltd, 7th Floor, Infinity Tower C, DLF Cyber City,
Gurgaon 122 002, Haryana, India
Penguin Group (USA) Inc., 375 Hudson Street, New York, New York 10014, USA
Penguin Group (Canada), 90 Eglinton Avenue East, Suite 700, Toronto,
Ontario, M4P 2Y3, Canada
Penguin Books Ltd, 80 Strand, London WC2R 0RL, England
Penguin Ireland, 25 St Stephen's Green, Dublin 2, Ireland
(a division of Penguin Books Ltd)
Penguin Group (Australia), 707 Collins Street, Melbourne, Victoria 3008, Australia
Penguin Group (NZ), 67 Apollo Drive, Rosedale, Auckland 0632, New Zealand
Penguin Books (South Africa) (Pty) Ltd, Block D, Rosebank Office Park,
181 Jan Smuts Avenue, Parktown North, Johannesburg 2193, South Africa

Penguin Books Ltd, Registered Offices: 80 Strand, London WC2R 0RL, England

First published by Penguin Books India 2014

ISBN 9780143423614

Typeset in Adobe Garamond Pro by Eleven Arts, Delhi
Printed at Thomson Press India Ltd, New Delhi

A PENGUIN RANDOM HOUSE COMPANY

True, I have fallen down and that hurts . . . If I'd enjoyed moderate success, it would have been easier to adjust to . . . But falling from that height has bruised me and left me internally bleeding. The hurt is much more because I fell from Mount Everest.

—Rajesh Khanna

CONTENTS

ACKNOWLEDGEMENTS

To begin with I would like to thank Shazi Zaman, who encouraged me to put my ideas to words and showed me the path forward.

Salim Khan, for opening his heart and door to me.

Hanif Zaveri, Bhupesh Raseen and Ashish Kumar Singh, for being ever helpful.

The late Sushama Shelly, whose meticulously maintained archives and articles proved to be a starting point in my research.

Namita Gokhale, for graciously allowing us to use the photographs from her magazine, *Super*.

Malvika Verma, Puneet Sharma, Vijay Lokapally, Suparna Sharma, Kanika Vohra, Faizal Islam, Ajmal Malik and all those senior journalists who have provided a helping hand and valuable insights for this book.

Vishal Gaurav and Ajay Khullar, for being fellow footmen in the journey.

Kunal Gaurav, whose house in Mumbai became my house during my many visits to the city for my extensive research.

The various co-stars of Rajesh Khanna, film-makers, technicians as well as the old spot boys, who shared their memories (but who wished to remain unnamed). They added significant layers to the account of the life and times of Rajesh Khanna.

Meenakshi Jauhari Chawla, for being my first reader and giving me her invaluable feedback.

The incredible team at Penguin, with a special shout-out to Udayan Mitra, Renu Agal and Ambar Sahil Chatterjee.

My father, M. Usman, from whom the writer in me germinated; my mother, Haseeba; and brother, Sahir, for their unconditional support, always.

Pervez Jamal and Shabnam Faridi, for their love and encouragement.

And lastly, my wholehearted thanks to my wife, Nazia Erum, for taking care of everything, for giving me perspective whenever I faced a block, for patiently listening when I forced repeated narrations on her. I would not have truly come so far without you by my side.

And my little daughter, Myra, whose share of time I gave to this book. But she still reserved her best smile for me . . . unconditionally.

FOREWORD

By early 1970, both Rajesh Khanna's career and mine gathered momentum, almost around the same time. When Javed Akhtar and I first met Rajesh Khanna, he was already proclaimed a superstar, and two of his films *Aradhana* and *Do Raaste* had been released. Then we worked together for the first time in G.P. Sippy's *Andaz*. It was during the production of this film that we got to know each other better. We would discuss several new story ideas with him, and we gradually became good friends. We were also neighbours in Bandra and used to meet almost daily. When his star was in the ascendant, I was a regular part of the gatherings at his bungalow, Aashirwad. I got to know him at close quarters. But even after years of getting to know him, he remained a particularly baffling man—not someone you could easily categorize as just good or bad. He was different from everyone.

In those days, the film industry was much smaller in size than it is today, but it was no less competitive. The industry was ruled by actors like Dilip Kumar, Raj Kapoor, Dev Anand, Shammi Kapoor and Rajendra Kumar. With them around, it was no mean task for any new actor to find a niche and be recognized. Rajesh didn't just make a name for himself, but in a short span of time took his stardom to a new peak. From 1969–75, I saw his superstardom at close quarters and I have no hesitation in stating that the heights of stardom he reached have never been achieved by any other star in the world of Hindi cinema. His success was exemplary.

Today, my son Salman Khan is a big star. Crowds cluster daily in front of our house to catch a glimpse of him. People often come to me and say that they haven't seen such a craze for any star before this. But I tell these people that just a small distance away from here, on Carter Road, I have witnessed many such sights in front of Aashirwad. And I have never seen that kind of mass adulation for any other star after Rajesh Khanna.

Rajesh Khanna's fans ranged from six to sixty years of age. Girls were passionately excited about him. I too had a hand in writing his career's biggest hit film, *Haathi Mere Saathi*. I remember I had gone with him for this film's shooting to Madras and many other locations in Tamil Nadu, where huge crowds would gather on hearing that Rajesh Khanna had arrived. This was a surprise because Hindi films weren't that popular there. The Tamil film industry itself was robustly successful and had its own big stars, but it was the charisma of Rajesh Khanna which could transcend the barrier of language. Remember, this was purely his charm and charisma at work, because it happened in an era when there was no television, no twenty-four-hour FM radio stations or big PR agencies.

But then in four or five years his career started to slide a bit. Just like there was no singular reason for his stupendous success, there wasn't any one particular reason for the descent of his career graph. The tension in his family life, the behaviour of people in the industry towards him and, to an extent, the fact that he was not doing anything new . . . there were many such reasons. But I feel that fate also played its part. And when his films started flopping, he didn't look within to evaluate what was going wrong and where. He started blaming others. He used to feel that there was some conspiracy against him.

You would be amazed to know that a superstar like him was an introvert, a shy person, and that often he wasn't even able to express himself properly. I was also witness to his great hospitality. He was a large-hearted man and loved hosting feasts. And if he felt someone was a good man, he would go all out to please him. I know that he gave houses to members of his staff and, on occasion, he was even known to gift cars. I recall he once gifted a car to his friend Narender Bedi. Then slowly his star faded, but I feel that in his heart he could never accept this.

Many books have been written on the big stars of the film industry. Most of these have been on stars who came before Rajesh Khanna, like Dilip Kumar, Dev Anand, Raj Kapoor and Shammi Kapoor, or on star who followed Rajesh Khanna, like Amitabh Bachchan. In his time, Rajesh Khanna was a one-man industry, and one can say that it was not the films which were hits, it was Rajesh Khanna who was the biggest hit.

It is not easy to write a rigorously researched book on the life of an artist. As time passes, the memories of those who knew the artist start fading. It is necessary to talk to them and glean glimpses of the artist's personality, which can then be documented. Why was someone the way he was? His acting, films and life—all are part of the history of cinema about which one needs to write.

As part of his research for this book, Yasser Usman has talked to many such people who knew Rajesh Khanna up close and personal or had worked with him. Apart from this, the author has beautifully recreated his life and times through old interviews of the actor, his producers and directors, the experiences of his co-stars and the fruit of rigorous research. Yasser writes with such flair that it brings to life the story of Rajesh Khanna in a manner as gripping as one of his major films. The book conjures some memorable images of the superstar—in some, Rajesh can be seen blinking his eyes in his own characteristic way and flashing his beautiful smile; in others, one sees him as a star of a later era, struggling with anonymity and loneliness.

We often forget when we talk of film stars or public figures that they are also mere human beings who also make mistakes, face failure and are scared of losing their successful run professionally, like everyone else. This book talks about Rajesh Khanna's superstardom and his talents as an actor, but it also delves beneath the surface to talk of both his good qualities as well as his weaknesses as a human being. Overall, the writer has been able to bring out the many dimensions of Rajesh Khanna with great finesse. Lots of people claim to know him. Nobody really knew Rajesh Khanna, but this book comes the closest to understanding him.

Often, books or articles written about the real lives of famous personalities either praise them to the hilt or are deeply critical of them, and so they end up becoming unidimensional. But Yasser's book is different. He writes with a lot of empathy for his subject and substantiates his facts with thorough research, all the while writing with great panache. The result is a deeply engaging and balanced account of Rajesh Khanna's life. Especially towards the end, the way in which Yasser examines the factors that shaped Rajesh Khanna's personality clearly shows his command over language as well as his rigorous training as a journalist.

I had never imagined that if one unravelled a person's life so many layers would emerge, and these layers give so many dimensions to one's personality. When writing a film script, I used to pay special attention to these things while creating new characters, but when I read this book I feel that, really, truth can be stranger than fiction. A person whom I knew as a living, vibrant being now appears to me through a different prism, and I can see new facets of his life in this book.

I am sure that as you read this book you will smile at some places, while your eyes will be moist with tears at others. In a sense the experience will be similar to the one you used to have when you watched a very successful Rajesh Khanna film. This book has tried to bring alive an era of the Hindi film industry to which even I have been a witness. I believe that this book is an important document of writing on cinema, which will, in times to come, become part of film history. I congratulate the author, Yasser Usman, for his tremendous effort.

Mumbai, 24 August 2014   Salim Khan

INTRODUCTION

Rajesh Khanna passes away at 69 years

ABP News bureau
Wednesday, 19 July 2012

Mumbai: Yesteryear superstar Rajesh Khanna passed away on Wednesday afternoon after a prolonged illness. He is survived by his estranged wife Dimple Kapadia and two daughters Twinkle and Rinke. Film actor Akshay Kumar was his son-in-law.

His funeral will be held at 11 am on Thursday, family sources said. Latest reports suggest that all his family members have gathered at his Bandra house and the house has been cordoned off by police officials.

The actor is hailed as India's first superstar after 15 consecutive solo superhits between 1969 and 1972. His demise brought back memories of the charmer, lover and hero that he was to his family, fans and well-wishers. For them, his magic will remain forever.

I was in Mumbai at the time. Working with the national news channel ABP News (formerly Star News), I was shooting for a special show in Kamalistan Studios (also called Kamal Amrohi Studios) in Mumbai on 18 July 2012, when I got a call informing me that Rajesh Khanna had passed away. Everyone was talking about it. Facebook and Twitter were abuzz with the news. In any case, the media had been constantly reporting on his terminal illness for several weeks by then, so the news of his death did not come as a total surprise. But the longer I thought about it, the more dispirited I felt. I suppose the news of a death—anyone's death— is always a bitter reminder of human mortality. And ironically, Rajesh Khanna was a movie legend who had been immortalized on celluloid. He was India's first superstar. But unfortunately, though his star burned bright, his success was short-lived.

I must admit I wasn't a huge fan of Rajesh Khanna. Sure, I loved him in films like *Anand*, *Aradhana* and *Namak Haraam*, where I'd always been floored by his innate charm and essential honesty. And of course, I knew about his superstardom and the stories about the mass hysteria he generated—girls pledging their love to him in letters written in blood; boys striving to imitate his hairstyle, mannerisms and gait; crowds who waited for hours to catch the merest glimpse of him, after which they screamed and wept for joy. But all this seemed remote to me, growing up as I did in the 1980s.

That evening, before the shoot got over, I received a call from our group editor, Shazi Zaman. Our channel was producing some special shows on the death of Rajesh Khanna, and he wanted me to take a closer look at the forgotten superstar's last few years and interview some people close to him for the same. Thus started my journey to unravel the enigma that was Rajesh Khanna.

Early next morning, 19 July 2012, I was sitting at the ABP News guest house in Vile Parle, watching the coverage as all the news channels got ready to cover Rajesh Khanna's funeral procession. On an impulse, I decided to be a part of it.

The procession seemed to be a massive affair, a ceremony befitting a king. The fact that it was raining only enhanced the sense of tragedy, as though the heavens were sharing in the grief of the crowds who followed the funeral procession. Mumbai had cleared its roads to make way for the superstar's final journey. As I walked shoulder to shoulder with his many fans, their sorrow acutely sharpened in the rain, I couldn't help but wonder how the city must have treated Rajesh Khanna in the early days.

I was struck by how many people in the procession did not seem to be a part of the film industry. They seemed to be lost in the memories of a bygone era—a time when they were young and very much in love; an era when Rajesh Khanna gave words and expression to that love in his own inimitable way. On that day, the final passing of their hero perhaps made them feel more keenly—that, like him, their youth would never return.

'I felt like saying a final goodbye to him,' said sixty-four-year-old Surjeet Singh Chaabra, an NRI from Vancouver, when I tried to speak with the people around me. I asked Surjeet if he had known the superstar personally, and he replied, smiling, 'Oh yes! I spent a lifetime with him through his films and songs. I was struggling in my life in the '70s, and he was a balm for everything sad happening in my life.'

I thought this was a bit too melodramatic and mushy, but as I spoke to more and more people, I found that many of them were equally emotional or sentimental in their responses.

A lady from Bengal claimed she was his biggest fan. She added, 'You will not be able to understand what he meant to me. Now times have changed. But back then, going for a Rajesh Khanna film was like going on a date with him! No matter whom he romanced on screen, I always felt that I was the one he was really in love with!'

Yes, I could not relate to her point of view, especially since I had never been witness to the zeitgeist of Rajesh Khanna's popularity in the 1970s. But, from the frenzy I personally witnessed that day at the funeral procession, it was clear that Rajesh Khanna was a giant in terms of the sheer magnitude of his fandom. This intense devotion from his fans made me all the more curious. What charm did this man possess that no one has matched before or since? What was it that made him such a phenomenal success? And how did he come to lose it all, spending the last years of his life in relative obscurity? What had transpired in the journey from superstar to forgotten star, a quirk of destiny that only his death could revoke?

Honestly speaking, Rajesh Khanna had almost been a long-running joke for the people of my generation. Movie folklore was dominated by many stories of his eccentricity, his temper tantrums, his seemingly absurd refusal to accept that his heyday was over as well as the inevitable comparisons to the mega-star Amitabh Bachchan. In fact, it was often said in jest that Rajesh Khanna's biggest problem in life was that he wasn't Amitabh Bachchan. However, Khanna himself claimed to be the 'reference point' for Amitabh Bachchan. Many said Rajesh Khanna could not handle his stardom while others said he couldn't handle failure. For many, he was the incandescent star who did epic films like *Amar Prem, Anand, Avtaar* . . . and for others, he was the ageing actor who did small-time television roles or some ridiculous films like *Wafaa* and *Jaana*. Some hailed him as the epitome of charm, others of arrogance. Some called him a man of humour, others of insecure spite. Contradictions, contradictions, contradictions. But what was Rajesh Khanna really about?

One could even see this sort of polarized opinion in the glowing tributes that poured in for more than two weeks after his death, saturating all forms of media—radio, print, television and even the Internet. While a good deal of it was all-out worship, some of it, if read closely, was dripping with sarcasm.

So as I set out to understand who Rajesh Khanna truly was— sifting between facts and opinions, gossip and myths—I realized that there would be no easy, clear-cut answers. What I discovered was a very intriguing individual: a man of great contrasts; a man who experienced both epic success and immense failure; a man of great talent and deep insecurities; a man determined to fight for his place in the sun; a man who ultimately distanced those closest to him. A star who was only too human.

I spoke with numerous people who had been part of Rajesh Khanna's dramatic life and career—some who had worked with him, some who had been close to him during certain phases of his life, and some who had extensively interviewed him as journalists. My inquisitiveness about him mostly drew apprehension from the people I spoke to. They always questioned my intentions. 'What exactly are you writing about him?' was the most common question thrown at me. People were curious about whether I was seeking to exalt Kaka (the name used to affectionately refer to Rajesh Khanna by those close to him) or denigrate him—it was as if they had not considered the existence of a third scenario: a balanced portrait of a complex and fascinating man.

Secondly, I found that most people do not like to talk ill of the dead. This is especially true for the Indian society. Hence, some important people who had worked with him or knew him closely just gave long interviews in which they diplomatically stated, in different ways, that Rajesh Khanna was a great man . . . a wonderful actor. When pressed further, they would say, *'Ab toh Kaka chale gaye . . . ab kya bolna?'* [Kaka is gone now . . . So what's left to say?] Or else they would request that I leave them alone. I tried wherever possible to speak to those people who were instrumental in his life. I even tried reaching out to his wife, Dimple Kapadia, but she remained unavailable whenever contacted. Such times obviously were disheartening for me. I am convinced that the testimony of these people would have resulted in a richer, more nuanced account of this important piece of cinematic history.

But luckily, there were always others who willingly opened the door for me into a different era, and it was a wonderful experience to see the Bollywood of the '60s and '70s come alive through their memories and insights. Nostalgia has its own infectious charm, and their reminiscences served as a time machine that transported me into another age: back when Bollywood was swinging to the hip, new tunes of R.D. Burman; when the sombre cinema of the 1950s had paved the way for movies that revelled in mischievous yet wholesome romance; when film-making was driven by passion and fandom was sincere; when actors were not closely guarded by public relations firms, and movie stars were synonymous with national heroes. This does not mean that those times did not have their own share of turbulence and strife, and I was constantly aware of this fact during my research.

A fighter to the end, Rajesh Khanna once said in an interview, 'I would love to live my entire life again and experience the same successes, same failures, same women and also the same heartbreaks.' I had once briefly met him long ago, but in no way was that meeting substantial enough for me to draw inferences about his life and personality. I strongly feel that this was, in a way, an advantage, because it allowed me to write about him without any preconceived notions. In my effort to fully understand the enigma that was Rajesh Khanna, I have attempted to tackle all the divergent facts and opinions about him in a manner that, I hope, pieces together a balanced, coherent story in all its three-dimensional complexity. In telling his story, I have also retained the original names of cities like Bombay (now Mumbai), Madras (now Chennai) and Calcutta (now Kolkata) as they were called at the time.

If one looks beyond his legion of fans around the country, reminiscing about the superstar, perhaps reverberating in the air is a story that had been left unfinished . . . untold.

This is that story.

PROLOGUE

The evening of 27 March 1973 in Bombay had an incandescent luminosity about it. Hordes of people had descended upon the streets leading from Carter Road in Bandra to the Kapadia residence in Juhu. A spectacular wedding procession had set out from Bandra along this route, heading towards the bridal home in Juhu. Houses lining both sides of the roads had spectators filling out on to the balconies and rooftops, jostling each other and craning their necks to catch a glimpse of this much-awaited *baraat*.

The cynosure of this wedding procession was the bridegroom, Rajesh Khanna, the reigning movie idol of those times, hailed by the film press as 'The Phenomenon'. Clad in a white sherwani, his face veiled by an ornate *sehra* of flowers that flowed from his turban, Rajesh Khanna rode high on a white mare, looking every bit the superstar he was born to be. And a superstar's wedding was bound to be anything but ordinary. The marriage party comprised a star-studded group, dancing and gleeful, that made its way through the streets of Bombay. For the cheering crowds, this was a momentous occasion that they would one day tell their grandchildren about. The actor who ruled their hearts as the

dominant romantic hero of the time was now fulfilling his own
romantic destiny in a real-life love story. It was like something
out of the very movies they thrived on—the kind that had made
Rajesh Khanna's success.

The news of Rajesh's marriage to Dimple Kapadia was the
talk of the town, and it wasn't surprising that the media was also
abundantly present, clamouring for ringside seats to the spectacle
before them. Film journalist Ingrid Albuquerque later recalled
how she 'went to his home, Aashirwad, and, with the rest of the
Bombay media, became part of the baraat'. There, she 'stared
with heartbreak and envy as Film Gossip Writing Queen Devyani
Chaubal put the Safa on his head.' Ingrid was a self-confessed
Rajesh Khanna fan with a big crush on the star. In her article 'In
Love and Death We Cry', she wrote, 'In what can be considered
an irony—the kind of ironies Hindi films thrive on—the first
time I was assigned the piece I was waiting for, it was to cover
Rajesh Khanna's marriage to Dimple Kapadia.'[1]

Ingrid might have seen irony in this situation, but it was true
that the news of the wedding had left numerous fans heartbroken.
And nobody was better aware of all this than the law-enforcers
deputed to ensure that pandemonium did not break loose that day.
The potential security hazard was enough to give any policeman a
nightmare. In any case, frenzied crowds were expected to swarm
the streets. To make things worse, there was a rumour doing the
rounds that a college girl had already committed suicide because
of the impending wedding. So it was imperative for the police to
see to it that nothing went wrong. 'On the day of the wedding
there were innumerable policemen lining the entire sea face,'
recalls film journalist and author Hanif Zaveri to me, 'as if they
feared that the nutty fans of Rajesh Khanna would jump into the
ocean. The wedding day was a mad, mad day.'

But on that day thoughts of these fans were perhaps far from
Rajesh's mind as he led his glittering baraat towards Dimple's

home. Maybe there was something else on his mind, because what happened next was rather unusual.

Now, Dimple Kapadia's residence in Juhu was on a straight and simple route from Rajesh Khanna's bungalow in Bandra. But instead of following the usual, pre-decided route, Rajesh decided to make a sudden detour midway and turned his baraat around. The procession was now headed towards the 7th Road, JVPD Scheme in Bombay.

Anyone even remotely aware of the film gossip of the time would immediately understand the significance of this new destination. This road housed the memories of a previously wounded relationship. On this road was the house of Anju Mahendroo, the bridegroom's ex-girlfriend of seven years with whom he had very recently broken up. The baraat, with great pomp and spectacle, 'deliberately passed' Anju's house 'on our way to the Kapadia residence in Juhu,' Ingrid Albuquerque later reported.[2]

It is virtually impossible that Anju Mahendroo would not have noticed the loud procession passing under her window. If Rajesh Khanna was seeking to avenge himself on an ex, he was certainly not subtle about it. If the gossipmongers were hoping for a juicy twist to the ceremonies, they were certainly not disappointed.

Rajesh Khanna's close friends, who were part of the baraat, were astounded. A senior film producer present there still reminisces, 'We were shocked. Everyone was thinking, "What has happened to Kaka? This is the happiest day of his life, why is he doing such negative thing?" . . . But Kaka had his own way of doing things.'

A senior film journalist who was close to Rajesh Khanna remembers the incident. 'Those who knew Rajesh Khanna were actually not surprised. When his ego was bruised, then he could go to any length for revenge.'

But Rajesh Khanna had everything that fame and fortune could offer. So why did he need to behave so ruthlessly and spitefully?

Was he lashing out at a past love because the relationship left him wounded? Was this an isolated incident, a sign of the turbulence that would later characterize his marriage? Or was it part of a larger pattern of behaviour, symptomatic of the deep-seated fears and insecurities that would one day erode the phenomenal success that he had won for himself?

Indeed, how does one even begin to fully understand this man? On the one hand, he could command nationwide devotion in an age when instant social media was non-existent and movie stars weren't promoted by a team of publicists. On the other hand, he was never able to nurture the same kind of adoration and love in his personal relationships.

To seek the answers, one must first unravel the incredible story of this fallen superstar—a story filled with all the drama, heartbreak, excitement and glamour that his best films are remembered for.

PART I

1949–65

Kitne sapne, kitne armaan, laya hoon main
Dekho na, dekho na

Hey . . . mera dil bhi ek mehfil hai
Tum bhi kabhi aao na, baitho na

(Song from *Mere Jeevan Saathi*, 1972)

Question: What is the most precious memory about your first love?

RK: When I first tried to kiss her, our noses collided.

CHAPTER 1

2, Saraswati Sadan,
Thakurdwar Naka,
Girgaum,
Bombay

This address was the residence of a little boy named Jatin Khanna—years before he would become the superstar Rajesh Khanna. Girgaum is an area in South Mumbai; its name is derived from the Sanskrit words *giri* (hill) and *grama* (village), referring to its location at the foot of Malabar Hill. The Thakurdwar area in Girgaum used to be a Marathi- and Gujarati-dominant congested middle-class locality. During his adolescent years, the commercial capital of India was beginning to grow into a metropolitan city. The first 'matchbox' skyscraper embraced the new Malabar Hill skyline. Bombay attracted migrants from all over the country with its promise of being the new financial capital, and by the mid-nineteenth century, Girgaum had become a hub for these immigrants. This sowed seeds of disaffection among the Marathi youth who felt threatened by this influx of 'outsiders'. The old tenants of the Saraswati Sadan building remember how Jatin would request them to speak to him in Marathi, so that he could pick up the language and become a part of the Marathi milieu.

In the first decade after India's Independence, Bombay's film industry grew rapidly as new avenues for garnering funds opened via both the government and external financers. Bombay cinema passed through its golden era in the 1950s, dominated by the likes of Ashok Kumar, Raj Kapoor, Dilip Kumar, Guru Dutt, Mehboob Khan, Bimal Roy, B.R. Chopra and the Anand Brothers, among others. Jatin grew up living next door to the legendary Royal Opera House, which was the site for many prominent theatre shows, film premiers and concerts. The Khannas lived in a two-bedroom corner flat on the third floor of Saraswati Sadan. The balcony of the flat overlooked Jagannath Sunkersett Marg, which runs from Chira Bazaar to the Royal Opera House. Jatin would often pass the large posters, lined up on its long compound wall, of the many memorable films screened there.

Records show that Jatin was the only child of Chunnilal and Leelawati Khanna. Chunnilal was a contractor supplying cotton cloth to the railways. A board saying *Chunilal Khanna & Co, Govt and Railway Contractor* hung on the second floor of Saraswati Sadan. Jatin was raised like a prince, and would address Leelawati as 'Chaaiji', a Punjabi word for an elderly, respected lady. It might strike many as odd that he addressed his mother in this unusual way. This was because Chunnilal and Leelawati Khanna were not his biological parents. They were, in fact, his actual aunt and uncle, who had adopted him as a young child before Chunnilal came over to Bombay from Amritsar in the wake of the Partition. This part of Rajesh Khanna's past is not widely known or written about. Perhaps he did not wish to talk about it.

I knew it was crucial to find out more. In the end, it took a lot of gumption and perseverance on my part to unravel the truth of what became of his real parents and the impact this had on young Jatin's psyche. As we will later see, this was going to hang over him like a cloud for the rest of his life, and would indelibly shape the man he grew into.

***

By the late 1940s, young Jatin was admitted into the prestigious St Sebastian Goan High School in Girgaum. Back then this school was popular among the upper middle classes in his neighbourhood. He befriended a classmate by the name of Ravi Kapoor, who later went on to be known as Jeetendra in the Hindi film industry.

Anil Baburao Chari, who used to live near the school, remembers the old days when Jatin and Ravi would come to school in their respective cars. 'At the end of a school day, they both would run out of the campus and buy ice cream, chikki and gola from the various hawkers across the road,' remembers Chari with a fond smile.

Jatin, or Kaka, was the apple of everyone's eye at home. His every wish and demand was catered to. He was given everything he asked for. As a result of all the attention lavished on him, Jatin got used to having his way. Prashant Kumar Roy, who later worked with him as his office assistant, fondly recollects, 'Chaaiji would often revisit the childhood memories. She would laugh and recollect that as a kid, he always behaved like a prince. On his return from school he would demand that Chaaiji be at the gates to receive him. And she would come running to receive her little prince. All his demands were always fulfilled by Chaaiji. She always remembered that he sulked a lot if things did not go his way.'

***

Jatin turned into a carefree and stubborn teenager. A close family member narrated this incident which was to be a turning point in Jatin's childhood and left a deep mark on him. Jatin was around ten years old. One day he went to his father's office. Chunnilal was busy in a meeting so Jatin went to sit in his cabin. There was an easy chair and a worktable inside the cabin, so he quickly made himself comfortable in his father's chair and became deeply engrossed in reading a comic book. Apparently, he used to loved emulating his father while sitting in his office. The chair was very comfortable and gave him a sense of importance.

But the young boy's enjoyment was short-lived, for at that moment his maternal uncle K.K. Talwar entered the cabin. Talwar was working with Jatin's father. Seeing Jatin sitting in his father's chair in his absence, Talwar questioned him angrily, 'Kaka, why are you sitting on this chair?'[1] The unexpected nature of the question and the tone unsettled Jatin. His uncle's anger and his question didn't make sense to him. His uncle further remarked, 'Before sitting on someone else's chair, make sure you deserve it.' Jatin felt stinging tears well up in his eyes. He did not know what his mistake was, but he felt the burden of an enormous folly. Scared and anxious, he quickly got up from his father's chair and rushed home.

At that age Jatin didn't understand his uncle's words, but they did hurt him immensely. Before this incident, no one at home had ever scolded him in this manner. He was not used to hearing the word 'no'. By the time he returned home, he was hurt and angry. Jatin wondered what his uncle meant when he said he must 'deserve' to sit in that chair. He had not dared ask his father for an explanation, but he asked his mother, 'What is "deserving" and why is it that a son cannot sit in his father's chair?'

In answer to this question, Leelawati Khanna responded in a way that remained etched in Jatin's mind forever. His Chaaiji sat him down and shared his father's story from struggle to success. According to his mother, Chunnilal started working as a supervisor while living in a chawl in Thakurdwar. He went on to become a railway contractor and then started his own business a few years later. He worked very hard to reach his current position, and this was precisely what made Chunnilal worthy of sitting in his chair. After all, everything they had was due to all the hardships that he had faced. Jatin continued to listen in amazement to this story of his parents' struggle. Finally Chaaiji conveyed the real message to him: hard work is what gives a man his real worth, and that it also gives him the right to claim and deserve all that he has worked so hard to achieve.

This became Jatin's first important lesson in life. Some of his close friends tell me that he never forgot this incident. He would fondly remember Chaaiji and often narrate this episode. Her message, that a man should be able to claim what he has worked for and thereby deserve the fruit of his labour, always stayed with him. After this incident he never sat on another man's chair again.

As the years went by, Jatin grew into a good-looking teenager. With age came new demands and desires. Jatin's first teenage crush was a girl named Surekha. She was a few years older than him and lived in the same building. This was sometime during the early 1950s. Years later, in an interview with the film writer Bunny Reuben,[2] Rajesh Khanna talked about his first love, and his first significant interaction with Surekha: 'I must have been about eleven or twelve, and she couldn't have been more than sixteen or seventeen.'

It was a glorious day. He was cycling in his building's compound, feeling rather chuffed about his brand-new bicycle. It was the latest model in the market, and it had taken a lot of persistence and grovelling before his parents could be persuaded to buy it for him. But his persistence paid off; he knew they couldn't say no to him for long.

He picked up speed. The cycle responded well—the pedalling was smooth, the chains well oiled. Round and round he went in the compound, enjoying the thrill. Then, suddenly, he lost his balance and fell down. It happened so quickly that there was little time to understand. He looked down to see a scratched knee that was bleeding. He hadn't felt the pain till he actually saw the blood. Fearing the worst, he started crying.

Heeding his call, a girl came running out of the building towards him. She was carrying a bottle of antiseptic and a swab of cotton. He recognized her as Surekha, the older girl who would often watch him playing around their building. He instantly stopped crying. How could he cry in front of a girl?

'I think that is the moment when I first fell in love,' he told Reuben. He recalled that Surekha tore some strips of cloth off an old saree to bandage his knee. And as she did so, she brought her face very close to Jatin's. 'Before I knew what was what, she kissed me lingeringly on the mouth . . . Blackout!'[3]

When he returned home that evening he avoided all eye contact with his Chaaiji and immediately retreated to his secret spot on the roof. Sitting there alone, he closed his eyes to reimagine the entire sequence again and again, recalling Surekha's large, light-brown eyes that 'seemed always to be smiling' at him, relishing the strange yet sweet tingle of first love.

He and Surekha were now drawn towards each other. They would meet quite often to play with their common friends or visit the nearby cinema. One afternoon, they went to watch a matinee show with a group of friends. But all Rajesh remembers of that day is sitting next to Surekha in the darkened theatre, his hand held in hers. He remembers being aroused by the way she stroked his hand. He goes on to say that, at one point during the film, she even deftly guided his hand to her bosom.

The relationship left him confounded. He had no clue what was happening to him. But it felt amazing to meet Surekha and spend time with her. He had started feeling a dire need to tell her everything about school, his friends, his family, his joys and his sorrows. Immediately after school every day he would dump his school bag at home and run to meet Surekha to share his day with her. On one such day, he found a big lock hanging on the door of her house. He was short of breath, having run all the way from his own house. Confused, he inquired where the family was from a woman sitting nearby. He was completely unprepared for her reply.

'When Surekha turned eighteen they took her away to her native place and she was married off,' said Rajesh to Reuben. He never saw Surekha again, and the pain of parting plunged him into a deep and hellish grief. Rajesh also told Reuben of other youthful crushes in those years, but they did not seem to have the same intensity as his feelings for Surekha. In his own words, 'Even to this day I can never forget her for the effect she had on me.'

Having her wrenched away from his life when he was so young must have left him feeling horribly wounded. Who would Jatin have been able to talk to about this at the time? How would he have been able to explain this to himself or come to terms with it? Would he be able to love again without the fear of losing? One wonders if this was instrumental in fuelling his possessive streak when it came to the relationships in his later years.

CHAPTER 2

With Surekha gone, Jatin didn't have anyone to share his feelings with and this made him want to spend time alone. Whenever he missed her, he would go to the building terrace and spend time gazing at the Bombay skyline. Jatin was greatly fascinated by the airplanes flying high up in the sky. He would smile to himself as he watched them glide away, following them with his eyes until they could no longer be seen. In one such moment, deep down in his heart, he decided that he too would one day soar in the sky.

It was during these teenage years that the foundation was laid of his love for theatre. He once went to watch a play with his mother and was impressed by the various actors enacting different roles on stage. The very next day he grouped all his friends together on the building rooftop. He assigned a role to each of the boys, based on the play he had seen. It flourished into a fun activity—now any of the kids could play any role, adopt any character, become anything.

The rooftop became the first stage on which Jatin ever performed. The character he loved playing the most was that of a gypsy. It allowed him to live out his fantasies. He recounted, 'My favourite role, those days, was of a gypsy. I longed to get into colourful costumes, longed to paint my face, and mouth long dialogues. But more than anything, I loved watching plays. I never missed an opportunity of visiting the theatre. Slowly, however, as I grew older, films began to replace my passion for theatre.'[1] He loved the adulation the onstage actors received from the audience. Even if it was momentary, the admiration garnered and the opportunity to be the centre of attention remained etched in Jatin's mind. It was an empowering feeling—a chance to not only become whatever character he wished to play but also be loved and admired for it! It is tempting to speculate that this kind of love and admiration must have seemed far more appealing to Jatin after his gruelling experience of heartbreak. It might have seemed to him like the kind of love and adoration that could probably last for ever.

***

The 1950s were coming to an end. Bombay was changing and so were Jatin's aspirations. By the end of 1958, he was all of sixteen. For his college education, his father decided to send him to Pune. The Fergusson College in Pune was very famous and Jatin wanted to study there. But by the time he reached Pune, the admissions to Fergusson had closed. So, instead, he went to study at Wadia College, located in Pune's Camp area. In the college form for the BA course, he filled out his full name: Jatinder Chunnilal Khanna.

During his early days in Pune, Jatin stayed in the house of family friend Ramesh Bhatlekar. The Bhatlekars used to be neighbours to the Khannas in Girgaum, but had later shifted to Pune and lived in a house on Apte Road in the Deccan Gymkhana area. Jatin stayed with the Bhatlekar family for a few months. Ramesh Bhatlekar, now over seventy years old, still remembers young Jatin. In an interview with the *Times of India* in 2012, he said that Jatin was always a good-looking boy, even when he was young, and he also recalled Jatin's ardent wish to be an actor some day. 'We used to play together in Girgaum in Bombay . . . He always aspired to be an actor. Once he showed me a photograph of his and told me with innocent pride that he had sent it to Raj Kapoor, asking him for a role in his films.'[2]

Jatin was an average student and his love for drama and theatre took precedence over everything else. He could stay in Pune only for two years as he missed his beloved Bombay. In 1961 he shifted back to Bombay, where he was admitted to K.C. College for the third year of his BA degree. In many ways, it was a homecoming for Jatin.

***

Jatin felt he could breathe freely again in Bombay. There were no limits to his flights of fantasy here. He was young, rich, and his face shone with the luminescent glow of new aspirations.

Jatin was a free bird. He spent his days in college or near theatres, and would often spend his evenings by the beach. But his ambitions of being an actor were in conflict with his father's expectations of him taking over the family business.

Finally, one morning there was a face-off between reality and expectation. Like every other day, Jatin was getting ready to leave for college when his father confronted him. He asked Jatin, 'Going out, are you?'

'Ji,' answered Jatin in assent.

Chunnilal said, 'It's fine that you plan your holidays so well, and I hope that when the time comes, you will plan your career as carefully too. You will have to, some day, begin working, won't you?'[3]

Slowly nodding his head in agreement, Jatin left quietly. Very subtly, yet very clearly, his father had got his point across. It got him thinking. He had to do something. But what did he want to do? What did he want to be? Perhaps it was time to find the answer to these questions.

***

Jatin was keen on finding a way. A college friend was working at the INT Drama Company, where V.K. Sharma was the director. The writer and film director Sagar Sarhadi, who later wrote famous films like *Kabhi Kabhie* and *Silsila*, told me, 'The most important person in our group was my friend V.K. Sharma. He was from Uttar Pradesh—of short height, but extraordinarily talented. He used to write, direct and act in plays. Jatin considered him his guru.' Sarhadi smiles at the memory that initially no one, including him and V.K. Sharma, took this eager boy very seriously.

Every evening Jatin would arrive at the INT Drama Company for rehearsals and watch the actors preparing for their roles from a corner. He hoped that some day V.K. Sharma would notice him and hopefully give him his 'first break'. This went on for many months. One day an actor for the company fell ill. The show was scheduled to open two days later. Sharma was worried about finding a stand-in actor for the small role at such short notice. That is when his eyes settled on Jatin, who as usual was standing in a corner watching the rehearsals. He called Jatin and asked him, 'Will you do this small role?'

Jatin just nodded his head in affirmation. His heart was galloping at thunderous speed. After such a long wait, his patience was finally being rewarded and he was getting his first role. 'Within seconds, I had crossed over the boundary and was part of the world I had so far only dreamt of. But of course, it wasn't all that easy,' he later said.[4]

The play was called *Mere Desh ke Gaon*. It was to be performed in Nagpur a few days later at a state-level theatre competition. One of Jatin's close friends from those days was Haridutt, an actor working with INT. Haridutt played an important role in the same play. He told me, 'It was 3 May 1961. I still remember the date, because I won the Best Actor award for my role of a mentally retarded man. Jatin's role was a very small one. He played a doorman, but I remember he was shivering with nervousness.'

In the entire play Jatin had just one line to deliver: *'Ji huzoor, saab ghar mein hain.'* [Yes sir, the boss is in the house.] Jatin rehearsed a lot and memorized his line with earnestness. But as the performance drew near, Jatin started growing restless and fearful. Just the thought of being on a live stage for the first time and delivering a dialogue in front of a packed audience was making him nervous. At last the show started and very soon it was time for Jatin's scene.

Jatin felt a thousand pairs of eyes upon him, and the sound of his own heartbeat was drumming in his ear. In a sudden panic, he ended up mixing up his dialogue. He recalled later, 'Despite my best efforts, on the day of the show, I got nervous and goofed up my lines. I played a durwan in the play and had only one dialogue which was *"Ji huzoor, saab ghar mein hain."* Instead, I said, *"Ji saab, huzoor ghar mein hain."* [Yes boss, sir is in the house). The director was hopping mad at me. After the show, I ran away without meeting him or anybody else.'[5]

Haridutt remembers Jatin leaving the stage with tears in his eyes. On reaching home Jatin couldn't look at anyone. He straightaway went to his room, and upon seeing his own reflection in the mirror he looked away. He understood that he could run away from everyone, but not from his own self. In his very first attempt to fulfil his dream, he ended up feeling like a loser. He admitted later that the incident shook the very foundation of his self-confidence. Alone in his room, he started crying out loudly. Apparently, he also quickly downed many glasses of whisky to put himself to sleep. But that night sleep evaded him and even in his alcohol-induced state he could feel the pinch of defeat.

The next day his friends tried to cheer him up, but he wasn't able to come to terms with what he considered a humiliating defeat. He was so embarrassed of himself that he even stopped going for rehearsals. Haridutt recalls, 'He was very sensitive and took everything to heart. I used to tell him that these things happen, but he was very worried, because his father was constantly pressurizing him to join his business.' Jatin didn't even have the courage to look into his father's eyes. It was for this very dream that he had shunned his father's business. And now he couldn't even deliver a single line properly?

But, eventually, he returned to the play. Incidentally, the play went on to become one of the company's most successful plays. He started regaining his self-confidence. Sagar Sarhadi told me, 'We just knew him as a pleasant guy who likes to act. He acted in two plays written by me—*Mere Desh ke Gaon* and *Aur Shaam Guzar Gayi*—but initially we hardly gave any importance to him.'

But Jatin was adamant that sooner rather than later they would have to take him seriously. His evenings came to be centred on theatre circles. He was in love with the very air and ambience of the theatre. Every evening, all the theatre enthusiasts would get together and discuss new storylines and characters, apart from the latest news. Jatin loved all of this. Various new and creative ideas would take birth at such meetings inside cigarette-smoke-filled rooms. This entire process would fascinate Jatin no end.

His persistence bore fruit finally. He started participating in inter-college theatre competitions. Ramesh Talwar, a famous theatre and film director, recalls, 'He didn't get big roles in these plays, but still he wouldn't say no even to the smallest roles. My uncle Sagar Sarhadi wrote a play *Aur Diye Bujh Gaye*, and he played the role of an elder brother in it. It was directed by V.K. Sharma. This was the first role for which he was appreciated and even received an award in the college festival. The happiness on his face at that time was unparalleled.' Jatin also went on to act in *Andha Yug*, a play directed by theatre veteran Satyadev Dubey.

Even during this period of struggle, those who knew Jatin remember him for his special trait—his charming smile. Sagar Sarhadi recalls, 'The boy had charm. I remember there was a pretty girl Gauri, and all of us used to flirt with her. But the only person getting anywhere near her was Jatin. He had a boyish smile and heart-warming innocence. In theatre we could never see his charm, but the girls always used to like him. That charming smile did wonders.'

***

Jatin's self-confidence was on the rise. His dreams had grown wings. He now wanted to go beyond theatre and act in films. This was the time he would visit the offices of all the film producers to share his photographs.

Jatin knew that for the film industry he was no more than a mere struggler. While waiting for his first break in films, he concentrated his energies on improving his talent on the stage. During this time he got a call from theatre director B.S. Thapa. He wanted to direct a new play with Jatin in the lead role. Jatin was overjoyed at the news. Thapa called Jatin for a meeting to Gaylord restaurant the very next day.

Gaylord, located near Churchgate in Bombay, was very famous in those days as an upscale and sophisticated place. People associated with the film industry were often seen networking and holding meetings here. As a struggler, Jatin was also a regular at Gaylord. Among its usual patrons, he would often see actor Sunil Dutt as well as directors like J. Omprakash and Mohan Kumar.

When Jatin reached Gaylord the next day, he spotted a beautiful lady right outside. Jatin was struck by her allure: from the strong charisma of her face to her long mane of gorgeous hair. Entering the restaurant to look for the director, he was pleasantly surprised to find this lady seat herself next to B.S. Thapa. On spotting him, Thapa said, 'Come on in, Jatin, meet Anju Mahendroo, your heroine in the play.'

Jatin smiled and shook hands with her. Then the three settled into discussions on the new play.

CHAPTER 3

Rehearsals for the play began the very next day. The lead actors, Jatin and Anju Mahendroo, started working together and discovered a warm bonhomie between them despite their different backgrounds. While Anju was a contemporary Bombay girl with a modern upbringing, Rajesh came from a conventional Punjabi family. Anju had tried her hand at modelling and was now looking for a break in films. Her family already had connections in the film industry—her maternal grandfather, Rai Bahadur Chunnilal, co-owned the famous Filmistan Studio of Bombay; her maternal uncle was the illustrious music composer Madan Mohan. Coming from this milieu, she knew how the film industry functioned. On the other hand, Jatin was new to the industry and had little idea of its customs. This was a breeding ground for long conversations. An eager Jatin would spend hours talking to Anju. He was in complete awe of his new lady friend. They would discuss everything about their dreams and aspirations. And it was not long before they realized how much they enjoyed spending time in each other's company. The long hours spent in rehearsals every evening eventually blossomed into a deep friendship between the two.

The rehearsals for the play would be conducted either at Patkar Hall or sometimes at the old Bhulabhai Memorial Building. The latter was the venue of a life-altering event for Jatin. Some of his old friends from his theatre days still remember this incident. Geeta Bali, the famous actress of Hindi cinema, had her office in the premises of the building. Having started her film career at the early age of twelve, Geeta Bali went on to become a huge star in the 1950s and worked with almost all the leading actors of that era. People from the film industry would often come to meet her. Like the many strugglers queuing up outside her office, Jatin also tried to meet her many times. He would watch her famous guests come and go while his own hidden aspirations grew stronger—for no matter how much he kept it hidden from others, deep down he was convinced that acting in films was what he was destined for. Remembering those days, he said, 'Those were the days when I dreamt mad dreams: I dreamed of a time when, as an actor, I would try to reach out to people, and make their world a little more exciting and less lonesome.'[1]

Finally, one day, while Geeta Bali was leaving from her office, Jatin got a chance to meet her. It was a momentous meeting for him, but he couldn't muster up a single word in front of the actress. He had bumped into her by chance and her unexpected presence made his throat run dry. Seeing that he was tongue-tied, she asked, 'Are you an actor?'

Jatin couldn't come up with an answer and made an indecipherable head movement.

Geeta smiled and asked again, 'Do you want to be an actor?'

This time Jatin nodded gratefully in agreement.

'We are on the lookout for a new face for an upcoming Punjabi film . . .' and saying this, Geeta Bali then asked Jatin to leave his photographs and contact details at her office.[2]

But hope can be cruel. Out of nowhere hope arrived and suffused Jatin with happiness. He was so restless at the thought of his first break into films that he could not even pay attention to the rehearsals that day. In the changing room, looking at the mirror, he would have found himself at loggerheads with his inner turmoil. Knowing how difficult it was to get a break in the movies, he must have also felt a need to rein in his mounting excitement. Perhaps he played the devil's advocate and reasoned why this kind of hope was misleading, distracting, and couldn't be taken for granted. But despite trying to downplay his chances, hope would triumph over reason. In his enthusiasm, Jatin felt he was already Geeta Bali's next lead actor.

And so began the agonizing wait for the phone call from Geeta Bali's office. Days and weeks turned to months. Then one day he read in the newspaper that the Punjabi film Geeta Bali had mentioned had finally been announced. But Jatin Khanna's name was nowhere in the cast. He was heartbroken. In a fleeting moment the certainty of his career vanished. But the drama wasn't over yet.

The very next day he received a phone call from Geeta Bali's office. It was an invitation for the film's launch party. Ironically, Jatin was also invited to meet the man who had been selected over him—another actor from Punjab: Dharmendra.

***

The party was being hosted at Geeta Bali's residence, Blue Heaven. Well-known faces from the film industry were in attendance. Gentle music was playing on the lawns, while the place itself was aglow with lights and merriment.[3]

Geeta Bali watched the young man sitting quietly in one corner of the garden. He seemed to be feeling out of place, but did not have the look of a struggler. Instead, there was a certain pride and gravitas about him.

Jatin, however, was feeling quite anxious and lonely as he observed the ongoing party from his corner seat. What was he doing here, anyway? Why had he even been invited? He decided to leave the party midway.

The moment he stood up, he noticed Geeta Bali approaching him. Her wavy mane flowed loose upon her shoulders, her fiery eyes were trained on him. She remembered him well, for he seemed different from the usual film aspirants. He was not overly polite, apologetic or ingratiating—a far cry from the nervous young man she had encountered months earlier. Both his voice and the man had clearly left an impact.

She asked him, 'You are feeling unhappy, aren't you?'

He couldn't respond, but perhaps the glistening tears in his eyes were visible to her. Geeta Bali had herself struggled very hard to achieve her success. She knew that even the strongest willpower was not immune to the harsh blows of rejection, especially after one's hopes had been raised so high. And she had been partly responsible for raising his hopes. Jatin must have wondered whether she realized this, and whether she felt guilty about it.

'Look up,' she said gently.

Involuntarily, he turned to look at the sky above.

'The sky is filled with stars,' she said. 'One day you will shine too. One day, fame will be yours for the asking.'

He felt choked—somewhat consoled, but also strangely hopeless. He tried to acknowledge her kind words with a smile, but the tears he had been trying to hold back clouded his vision. Geeta's words re-instilled some self-belief into him. But he knew he still had a long way to go to achieving his dreams. He promised himself that the day he was able to achieve success, Geeta Bali would be the first person he would visit.

Sadly, this wasn't to be. Geeta Bali died before Jatin became Rajesh and achieved stardom.

CHAPTER 4

After his second encounter with Geeta Bali, Jatin went back to his theatre rehearsals.

Now, some of Jatin's close friends during this phase would, in later years, go on to work for him. Among these friends were Gurnam and Prashant Kumar Roy. Gurnam was active in theatre circles. He went on to become Jatin's confidant and manager. Prashant was one of Gurnam's friends who used to come to watch his plays often. This was how Prashant first came to meet Jatin. Later, he too worked for him as his manager/man Friday. Remembering the old theatre days, Prashant told me of an interesting incident.

There was an upcoming inter-college competition, and Jatin was playing an important role in a play directed by V.K. Sharma. He started practising vigorously for it, with singular attention. It was as if by immersing himself into the rehearsals, Jatin was trying to keep his mind off all the other negative thoughts clouding his vision.

Prashant told me that on the day of the play, there was an altercation with a rival college group before their performance. To take revenge, the group tried to sabotage their play by throwing banana peels and eggs at Jatin when he came on to the stage to perform. A fight broke out and the play was cancelled. Prashant recalls, 'Kakaji came out dejected and started crying in front of V.K. Sharma. He wept inconsolably, saying that he had worked so hard and they had ruined everything. He kept on lamenting that his dreams will never come true. We were also very angry at the turn of events, so we decided to hunt down the culprit. As far as I remember, the person who created the ruckus . . . his name was Pai.'

According to Prashant, they all decided to go in search of Pai and teach him a lesson. This was planned in a bid to console Jatin. Four of them trooped into a car: Jatin was driving, with Gurnam accompanying him in the front seat; Prashant and V.K. Sharma were in the back. It turned out to be a fruitless search, but the endearing support of his friends and the long drive itself helped soothe Jatin's nerves. Gradually everyone started joking around. They had dinner at the Khar station and then everyone went home. Before leaving, V.K. Sharma patted Jatin's back and said, *'Tu itna rota kyun hai? Roya mat kar. Sab theek hi hona hai anth mein.'* [Why do you cry so much? Don't be upset. All will be well in the end.]

Prashant remembers that Jatin was so overwhelmed by this gesture of his friends that he personally dropped everyone home and fondly remembered the incident for the rest of his life. But as far as his dreams of becoming an actor were concerned, there was still no light at the end of the tunnel.

***

However, very soon, a unique opportunity presented itself before Jatin. Some of the famous producers and directors from the Hindi film industry got together to form the United Producers Guild.

This group comprised big names from the industry—G.P. Sippy, Shakti Samanta and B.R. Chopra, among others. In association with the famous Times of India Group, which published *Filmfare* magazine, the guild organized the United Producers–Filmfare Talent Contest in the year 1965.

Today such contests are commonplace wherein the contestants showcase their talents in reality shows and celebrity judges grade them on their performance. The United Producers–Filmfare Talent contest was conceptualized along similar lines. While it did not get telecast on television as a reality show, it did have some of the leading names from the film industry on its jury board. The aim of the contest was to look for fresh, new talented actors for the film industry. The advertisement for this contest announced that the winners would get lead roles in the films produced by those in the United Producers Guild.

By this time, Anju and Jatin had become quite close. Jatin sought emotional support from Anju as she understood the conflict within him. She fondly called him Justin, while he addressed her as Nikki. It is said that Anju Mahendroo pushed him to apply for this contest.

Alongside thousands of hopefuls, Jatin also filled out the participation form. He got his best pictures clicked especially for the auditions. This time, fate was on his side and he easily got shortlisted for the final rounds. But as the time for the finals drew near, Jatin's nervousness scaled new peaks. Thus far, going by the pattern of his other auditions, Jatin always seemed to pass the initial stages easily enough, only to be rejected in the end. This made him wary of keeping his hopes high. In his mind, this was the last chance. The *do-or-die* chance.

Nervousness took its toll. Jatin walked around in a state of heightened anxiety, concealing his fears from friends and family. He withdrew into himself, speaking very little. He was not really preparing for the big day. His growing restlessness stemmed from a fear of failure. If he did not win this contest . . . would it mark the end of his dreams?

As the day of the finals came nearer, Jatin went to his favourite Irani hotel on his scooter and met his friend Haridutt. His friend inquired about his preparations for the final round. This was the very question he had been avoiding. Having it put so bluntly in front of him came as a cold shock. He confessed, 'What will become of me if I don't get through this competition? How will I ever face Chaaiji and Bauji again?'

Recollecting those moments, Haridutt recalls, 'The chips were down. I tried to cheer him up, but he kept quiet. He was my friend . . . His mood was still bad. So I took a one-rupee coin from my pocket and kept it in his palm saying, "There! I sign you for my next film as a hero!" Hearing this Jatin became very emotional and we hugged.'

During rehearsals, his other friends from the theatre encouraged him, but deep down he felt they did not believe in him as much as they said they did. He had not been able to achieve anything exceptional even in the theatre circuit. For a few moments he felt it was a useless dream he was pursuing. This thought made him even more nervous.

Days passed in nervous anticipation. Finally, it was the night before the final round of the talent hunt. I am going to give it a perfect shot, he told himself. He told himself that given that he had reached the final rounds, the judges must surely have recognized some talent in him. He looked at his reflection in the mirror. He changed his expressions and studied his face. He delivered some dialogues from one of his plays. He knew that the judges he was about to face were going to be some of the finest names in the film industry. He tried to imagine himself facing them and handling their questions with style and elan. He had collected lots of information about them. If he succeeded in impressing these people, then there was nobody who could stop him. The jury comprised the very same people whom he had tried to previously cold-call. He had left his photographs at their offices on numerous occasions, although he had not even been let inside the office premises by the security guards. Now all these people were going to be sitting together, judging his performance. All of them together. Waiting for him. He found comfort in this thought, and a strange smile played on his lips.

There were a few hours left for the sun to rise. Exhausted, he lay down on his bed and closed his eyes. Perhaps a silent prayer escaped his lips as a deep sleep finally enveloped him.

CHAPTER 5

Waking up early in the morning had never been a strong habit with Jatin. But this morning was crucial, and so he somehow managed to reach the office of the Times of India Group at the scheduled hour.

The contestants had been given chosen scripts beforehand, from which they were to read and perform. According to the script that had been provided to Jatin, he was to play a character who goes to inform his mother that he is in love with a dancer and wishes to marry her. Jatin tried to practise the dialogues, but found that he could not do it. Finally, his turn arrived, and he was called into a large hall. In front of him sat a host of well-known faces of the likes of B.R. Chopra, Shakti Samanta, J. Omprakash and G.P. Sippy. In later interviews, he dramatically described them as twelve to thirteen sombre-looking men—not a muscle in their bodies twitched, nor did they emit any sound. In fact, a beleaguered Jatin felt that they resembled the members of a firing squad, sizing up their prospective target.

He sat in front of the table where they were seated. They asked him, 'We had sent you a dialogue, did you memorize it?'

Jatin almost felt that they would take out a gun and fire at him. He replied, 'I know the dialogue, but I haven't been informed of the characterization of the person who is to narrate this dialogue. Is he the hero who is announcing to his mother that he plans to marry a dancer and make her the daughter-in-law of the house? You haven't told me whether this hero is rich, poor, a villainous character or a pleasant fellow . . . or is he from the middle class?'

Stunned at such an answer, B.R. Chopra thought the young man was trying to be over-smart. He said, 'You are from the stage, so make your own characterization. How will you convince the mother?'

Jatin replied that this is not a dialogue for a stage actor to mouth, so Mr Chopra asked him to choose his own dialogue. Jatin started to sweat nervously. He was anxiously wondering which dialogue would impress them the most. He closed his eyes for a few moments and his last few years in the theatre started to run through his memory. Which was the dialogue that he had prepared for the most? He could hear a thousand words at once. They echoed and bounced off the walls of his mind. Then, slowly, a dialogue started to take shape, a speech from one of his plays. As he later reminisced, 'I was hearing my own voice as if it were the sound of an engine pounding through a thick shrubbery of words: "Of course I am an artist. That's what I've always been struggling to be. Why would you want to hear my story? Yes, it was a terrible, back-breaking, uphill struggle that I had to put up with. My face was as ugly as my dreams beautiful . . ."'[1]

The words came to Jatin with heartfelt emotion and conviction. These were the words that laid the foundation of Jatin's career. 'A moment ago the silence was so thick you could cut it with a butter knife. Suddenly the firing squad cheered.'[2]

The battle had been won. He stood there numb, feeling nothing but disbelief. A glance at the faces of the judges seated in front of him gave Jatin the answer he sought. The day was indeed all his.

Veteran film-maker J. Omprakash tells me, 'I am one of those who selected him. He gave that wonderful speech and the instant reaction was: Let's select him. It was a long performance that revealed the tremendous potential needed, especially for an emotional actor. It moved the hearts of the panel members. We were always proud of our selection.'

Jatin's performance that day had been the fruit of his years of training in the theatre. It was the theatre that had taught him the nuances of understanding a character, and this very understanding was to shine through in the years to come.

The very next year a similar talent hunt was organized by a film magazine and thousands of aspiring actors filled out its forms. One of them was a young man named Amitabh Bachchan. But he couldn't make it to the shortlist.

CHAPTER 6

Jatin was at home the day the postman brought the winning letter from the United Producers–Filmfare Contest. Jatin didn't waste a second in tearing open the envelope and reading the contents of the letter. His eyes moistened. His vision blurred. He shut his eyes tightly and wiped away his tears. As his sight cleared, he felt he could see not only his immediate surroundings but also the good times ahead.

But to Jatin's bitter surprise, even after winning the talent hunt competition, the producers were not flocking to sign him on. He appeared in a few screen tests, but failed at them. Famous film columnist Devyani Chaubal recalled a meeting with the 'struggler' Jatin who went to the office of *Star & Style* magazine: 'He was brought to our office by photographer Biren Sarin. "Help an artist . . . poor fellow . . . he is struggling . . . he is the winner of a talent contest," Biren babbled. The visitor looked quiet . . . He had a faint spray of deep pimple-scars and penetrating dark eyes. In those days the eyes were not smiling or friendly . . . He never came to our office again and that is where he was different from the rest of the film aspirants.'[1]

Elaborating on Jatin's attitude as a struggler, Devyani also talked about subsequent meetings that happened at the Sea Lounge. Jatin would speak only of films and himself, making it clear he was from a well-to-do family, the only child, and did not really need a job. 'Missing from the conversation were the names of stars,' said Devyani. 'He never expressed a desire to be a "Kumar" or a "Kapoor". He reminded you of a typical Hindi film hero—an "Eklauta Laadla".'[2]

Meanwhile, Anju's career had started off with a small role in a big film *Jewel Thief*, with the evergreen star Dev Anand. Finally, after a long and patient wait, Jatin got his first 'break'. Producer G.P. Sippy asked to be shown shots of Jatin's screen test, after which he said to his son, 'Ramesh [Sippy], this one will make a great actor. Let's sign him up.' And so Jatin was signed for G.P. Sippy's *Raaz*.[3] At long last, he was a big-screen actor.

A few days later, Jatin was approached by famous director Chetan Anand to play the lead role in his upcoming film, *Aakhri Khat*. The lead actress of the film was Indrani Banerjee. The shooting schedule for the film was still some time away, while *Raaz* was to start filming immediately. Jatin played a double role in *Raaz*. Babita Shivdasani was his leading lady, and the film was directed by Ravindra Dave.

Having signed two films made Jatin exuberant with happiness. But this happiness lasted only till he was told of the shooting schedule for *Raaz*. The director informed Jatin that the shooting would commence every morning at 9 a.m., for which he needed to report to the sets at 8 a.m. A quick mental calculation told Jatin that this meant that he needed to wake up at 6 a.m. every day. This drained the colour from his face. Waking up early in the morning was next to impossible for Jatin. In his own words: 'Now, waking up early is just not my style. I am not an early bird. From childhood, I have always risen late. My mother wouldn't allow anyone to enter my room and disturb me. During school days, teachers called me "Late Latif", meaning latecomer. In college, it was kind of taken for granted that Jatin does not attend the morning lecture. I could not physically get ready so early. So when the director told me about attending shooting early in the morning, my heart sank.'4

***

The first day of shooting arrived. The whole unit was ready. The lighting was done. The cameras were set. The director was ready to roll camera and take the opening shots. Jatin was to report at the sets at 8 a.m., but it was 10.30 a.m. already and there was no news of his whereabouts. Nobody expected this from a new actor on the first day of his shoot.

Around 11 a.m. Jatin reached the sets in a hurry. Many senior technicians were outraged. Everyone stared at him. A senior team member smirked and taunted, 'If this is the way he is going to behave, he ought to pack up before he begins.' Any new actor should have been frightened and taken aback at such a comment. But, instead, Jatin grew angry and glared back at the man. He said in a defensive tone, 'In which case, to hell with the career and to hell with this film. My lifestyle cannot change for my career.'

The man was stunned into silence by Jatin's reply. In fact, the whole unit was surprised at this reaction. And so, on the very first day of the shooting, Jatin was stamped as 'Mr Arrogant'. In his heart Jatin knew that such an attitude could ruin his career. But he also knew that his response had been completely earnest. There was no way he could possibly promise to report for shooting at 8 a.m. every day. At that time he did not realize that this allegation of always being late would continue to haunt him for the rest of his career.

***

And then came another turning point in Jatin's career.

While the shooting of *Raaz* continued, Jatin decided to visit his father's office one day. There, he met his uncle K.K. Talwar, whom he respected very deeply—especially after the important life lesson he had given Jatin on "deserving" to sit in his father's chair. His uncle was now going to give him another wise offering: a new name.

K.K. Talwar was very proud of his nephew for now having entered the film industry on the strength of his own hard work and merit. The conversation between them turned towards the experience of Jatin's first shoot and the films he had signed. Much to Jatin's embarrassment, his uncle teased him about now being a star. His uncle then said, 'Your name "Jatin" doesn't seem to have the grandeur befitting a star in the making. It isn't impressive enough. I have also heard there is another new actor by the same name.' Jatin agreed with the logic. His uncle had probably already thought this over, for he added, 'I have thought of a new name for you. "Rajesh". You will henceforth be known as Rajesh Khanna and not as Jatin Khanna.'[5]

Jatin whispered this new name to himself, slowly, letting the sound of it roll off his tongue: 'Rajesh. Rajesh Khanna.' Perhaps for a moment he imagined his first film starting in a dark cinema hall, and his name appearing at the beginning of the credit roll: Rajesh Khanna. An enigmatic smile spread across his face.

As if reading his thoughts, his uncle said, 'Rajesh means "the king of kings". I pray that, like your new name, God takes you to the heights of fame, respect and riches.'

Jatin stared at his uncle. It was as if the older man had reinforced and strengthened his beliefs and goals. It was as if, in those few moments, a new man had been born inside him. Jatin was now Rajesh Khanna. The king of kings . . . *Rajesh*.

PART II

1965–71

Chand taaron se chalna hai aage
Aasmanon se badhna hai aage
Peeche rah jayega yeh zamana
Yahan kal kya ho kisne jaana

Zindagi ek safar hai suhana
Yahan kal kya ho kisne jaana

(Song from *Andaz*, 1971)

PART II

1965–71

Question: What were you in your previous life?

RK: An actor.

CHAPTER 7

Unlike his new name, Rajesh Khanna had not yet achieved the status of 'king of kings' but his general behaviour was not less than that of a king. As the shooting schedule for the film *Raaz* continued, so did his tradition of arriving late to the sets.

One of the shoots was in Himachal Pradesh's Kullu district. It was cold there and, as always, it was difficult for Rajesh Khanna to be ready early in the morning.

One evening, after pack-up, Rajesh invited a few technicians to his room for drinks. It was bitterly cold. Rajesh Khanna had a penchant for holding such evening get-togethers for the unit. As the night deepened, both banter and drinks flowed.

After a while, in walked the production-controller of the unit. He yelled at everyone at the sight of glasses in their hands: 'Don't you know that we have an early morning shoot?!' Then, looking at Rajesh, he said, 'And you . . . all this princely behavior doesn't suit an actor on his first film. You have come here to shoot, not to have fun.'[1]

Rajesh was furious at the way the production-controller had yelled at him. Nobody had ever spoken to Rajesh in that tone.

He retorted loudly, 'Look, this is not your set. This is my room. What I do after pack-up is not your problem but mine.'[2] The production-controller wasn't prepared for this. He had worked long in the industry and hadn't expected this newcomer to have the guts to answer back. He had heard of the 'Mr Arrogant' tag, but was now experiencing it first-hand.

In frustration, the production-controller picked up a plate and threw it on the floor. Equally furious, Rajesh shouted, 'You break a plate, and I'll break the table.' The argument escalated. Everyone else in the room tried to cool both of them down, but they continued to bicker as the matter had become a war of egos. Ultimately, Rajesh threatened, 'If this is how you will behave, I walk out of the film, this minute. All the expenses incurred due to my involvement—I'll reimburse on reaching Bombay.' Realizing that the matter would get out of hand, the production-controller left the room.

The next morning, however, everything was sorted out and forgotten. The shooting commenced without any hiccups and the schedule was completed.

***

Film-maker Chetan Anand wanted to make *Aakhri Khat* as a small-budget experimental movie after the mega success of his war film *Haqeeqat* (1964). The script revolved around the adventures of a toddler. The singer Bhupinder was signed on for the lead role; he had previously acted in *Haqeeqat*. But for some reason Bhupinder decided not to do the film and so the role was offered to Sanjay Khan. However, as luck would have it, the role finally went to Rajesh Khanna.

Aakhri Khat was the story of a fifteen-month-old toddler who gets lost in Bombay. As it was impossible to have such a small child perform from a script, Chetan experimented with a guerrilla-style shooting format. He would leave the toddler free to roam the city, and record his movements and expressions with hidden cameras.

With immense sensitivity, *Aakhri Khat* made a clear statement on the increasing loss of innocence in big cities, and Chetan Anand conveyed this message within the structure of a mainstream Hindi film. The screenplay was also not linear, unlike the films of that era. An interesting use of flashbacks was employed in order to maintain the suspense of the story, so that the facts were strategically unveiled. Although this film is hardly ever considered among Chetan Anand's prominent films—like, say, commercial hits like *Haqeeqat*, or else the critically acclaimed *Neecha Nagar* which won the top prize at the Cannes Film Festival in 1946— *Aakhri Khat* was perhaps his most experimental work, and one of his finest. The film was also rich in its musical offerings with melodies like 'Baharon Mera Jeevan Bhi Sanwaro' and 'Aur Kuch Der Theher' written by poet-lyricist Kaifi Azmi, and composed by ace composer Khayyam. In the beautifully haunting 'Rut Jawaan Jawaan', singer Bhupinder appears on screen too. Chetan's son Ketan Anand said, 'I feel his *Aakhri Khat* was a greater achievement, not only for him, but also for Indian cinema. It was a masterpiece and my father started with a bare outline of a script and a fifteen-month-old infant who he let loose in the city, following him with his camera.'[3]

In his role as the sculptor Govind, Rajesh Khanna gave a nuanced performance. Watching the film today, there is nothing to suggest that Rajesh Khanna is a first-time actor. Particularly impressive are the scenes at the police station, when Govind shouts angrily as a desperate young father trying to find his son, as well as the touching last scene, when Govind finally meets his child. He shines through as a confident performer. Although the story was centred on a fifteen-month-old child, the twenty-five-year-old Rajesh Khanna's performance oozed raw innocence which made him stand out and get noticed by the film-makers of the time.

This innocence was the special ingredient in his romantic image in later years. The gentle flutter of his eyelashes accompanied with a sweet smile, laced with a romantic dialogue went on to become his trademark move. A hint of the same can be seen in his first love song, 'Aur Kuch Der Theher'.

In an interview, Rajesh Khanna once said that the actress Waheeda Rehman was very impressed with his acting in *Aakhri Khat* and recommended his name for the film *Khamoshi*.

Aakhri Khat was India's official entry to the Academy Awards that year in the Best Foreign Language Film category. But for some reason, it couldn't reach the Academy entry on time. Released in 1966, *Aakhri Khat* became Rajesh Khanna's first official film, though he had first shot for G.P. Sippy's *Raaz*. Unfortunately, despite much critical acclaim, *Aakhri Khat* was a flop at the box office.

CHAPTER 8

Despite *Aakhri Khat*'s poor box-office performance, all was not yet lost. Not only did Rajesh Khanna's role in the film get noticed, but his association with an established banner resulted in other producers queuing to sign him up. He was being referred to as the 'new talent' found in a talent hunt. After *Aakhri Khat* and *Raaz*, Rajesh was signed for Nasir Hussain's *Baharon ke Sapne*, S.S. Balan's *Aurat*, and A. Subbarao's *Doli*. Although Rajesh Khanna had remained hitherto unknown during his theatre days, his luck took a fantastic turn right at the beginning of his film career. According to the contract of the talent hunt, the United Producers had to cast Rajesh Khanna in their films. Though most of these were small-budget films, landing a major role in them was a chance that not many newcomers ordinarily got. In most of these films the focus was either on the heroine, or on the songs and music. But with *Aakhri Khat* Rajesh Khanna had already shown his talent and flair despite the fact that the film had a heroine-oriented script.

Among his initial films, *Raaz* could have been an ideal launch pad for him. It was a suspense film, in which Rajesh had plenty of screen time as he was playing a double role. After the commercial debacle of *Aakhri Khat*, Rajesh Khanna pinned all his hopes on *Raaz*. But *Raaz*, released in 1967, was also a commercial disaster. And, unlike *Aakhri Khat*, it was panned by the critics. The direction had been below average and Rajesh Khanna appeared confused in both his roles.

With two flop films to his name, the film media started raising questions on the United Producer's decision of selecting Rajesh in the talent show. Rajesh was scared that everything would slip away. He later admitted in an interview, 'Some of my very early movies like *Raaz* and *Aakhri Khat* did nothing to eliminate these feelings. I was gawky, awkward, and tended to keep very much to myself. This was a period when I was groping in the dark.'[1]

***

In 1967, Rajesh Khanna started shooting for Nasir Hussain's social drama *Baharon ke Sapne*. The lead actress was a very popular star, Asha Parekh, who had an immense fan following of her own. A senior film journalist told me about an incident that took place during an outdoor shoot of this film.

After a shot, Asha Parekh and Rajesh Khanna were approached by a group of youngsters for autographs. While Asha received instant recognition, there was little attention given to Rajesh. He compensated by engaging some girls from the group in charming sweet talk. At that moment, one of the boys from the group commented, 'Oh, I didn't realize this guy is the hero . . . with his small eyes he looks like a Gurkha from Nepal.' The entire group started laughing at his comment.

The comment must have made Rajesh cringe. In hindsight, it seems absurd that someone could actually make a statement like that. In one of her interviews, Asha Parekh recalled that her mother used to ask her why she was working with a hero who has so many pockmarks on his face.[2] But success changes everything. Qualities that were once deemed a drawback for Rajesh Khanna during his early days in the film industry immediately become the reason for his winning formulae.

In the film *Baharon ke Sapne*, Asha Parekh was the bigger star attraction, with a more powerful role. But Rajesh Khanna's chocolate-boy looks and sensitive portrayal garnered attention and appreciation. The film had outstanding music by the young R.D. Burman. The three memorable gems written by Majrooh Sultanpuri, 'Aaja Piya Tohe Pyaar Doon', 'Kya Janoo Sajan Hoti Hai Kya Gham ki Sham' and 'Chunri Sambhal Gori' were all chartbusters. This movie also marked the beginning of the Rajesh Khanna–R.D. Burman association that was going to take the nation by storm in the years to come.

Ironically, *Baharon ke Sapne* met with the same dismal fate as Rajesh Khanna's first two films, as did S.S. Balan's *Aurat*. With four failures in one's kitty, any newcomer can become untouchable. But something strange was happening. Something that never happened before him, or has occurred since. Despite four huge flops, producers were still signing him on for their films as if reinstating a trust that seemed to come from nowhere. Among the new films he signed were Shakti Samanta's *Aradhana*, and Raj Khosla's *Do Raaste*.

***

Renowned producer-director B.R. Chopra was one of the film-makers who were a part of the United Producers group that selected Rajesh Khanna. His younger brother, Yash Chopra, also used to direct films for his banner, B.R. Films. At that time Yash Chopra was directing *Aadmi aur Insaan* with Dharmendra, Feroz Khan and Saira Banu as the lead star cast. The final schedule of the film was delayed as Saira Banu had injured her leg and was recuperating in London. Yash Chopra wanted to utilize the time left until her return.

Yash Chopra happened to watch a Gujarati play *Dhoomas* by the famous theatre personality Pravin Joshi. Pravin's brother Arvind Joshi—the father of actor Sharman Joshi—played the lead in *Dhoomas*. The play itself was an adaptation of Monte Doyle's English play *Signpost to Murder*. There was also a successful film made in Hollywood with the same name in 1964. The play is a taut psychological thriller, with the action taking place over the course of a single night. A runaway convict breaks into a bungalow to hide, terrorizing the girl who lives there all alone. But, in a clever twist, the innocent-looking girl entangles the convict in a web of deceit and murder.

Yash Chopra decided to make a film based on *Dhoomas*. Pursuant to discussions with his elder brother, B.R. Chopra, it was decided that they would make an experimental, low-budget film. Most importantly, there would be no songs in the film. Also, it would be completed in just one shooting schedule, on a single set, in one month's time. From today's standpoint, one does not realize how incredibly unusual this scenario was for a film in the 1960s. At that time, most films used to take at least a year's time to complete from the planning stage to its release, and songs were intrinsic to the movies as well. This challenge alone was enough to excite Yash Chopra. The film was titled *Ittefaq*.

Ramesh Talwar, Yash Chopra's chief assistant director in *Ittefaq*, told me, 'I joined B.R. Films during *Ittefaq*. It was completed within forty days. It was planned such that we were due to start shooting on 1 September 1969 and release the film on 10 October. It was shot on a single set.'

As they had to finish the film in one go, they needed a lead cast who had dates available for a month at a stretch. For the main male protagonist, B.R. Chopra suggested Rajesh's name. According to the talent hunt contract, B.R. Chopra had to make a film with him. Also, being new in the industry, Rajesh did not have any particular fixed image yet, and that suited the character for the film.

The lead female role was a negative character. Initially Raakhee was approached, but she had already signed Rajshri's *Jeevan Mrityu* and was bound by their contract. So Yash Chopra signed Nanda. Nanda had hits like *Jab Jab Phool Khile* and *Gumnaam* behind her. Yash Chopra wanted nobody to even suspect, while watching *Ittefaq*, that the heroine could be the murderer. Nanda's innocent face and romantic image was the perfect disguise required for this character.

The shooting started in September 1969. The set was built in the Rajkamal Studio in Bombay's Parel area. Every day the shooting started early morning and continued till late in the night. Surprisingly, Rajesh Khanna would come in before time every morning and rehearse for his scenes. Maybe it was the mounting pressure of four flop films that prompted this. Ramesh Talwar told me, 'He had perhaps come to realize that he was very lucky to be still offered roles from big banners. There was no question of coming late as we had to complete the film in a month. The portions that were shot during the day, Yashji used to go and get them edited the very same night. It was a wonderful experience. Even the work on the background music took place simultaneously.'

As an actor, *Ittefaq* was a big challenge for Rajesh Khanna. He rose up to the challenge and gave an inspired performance. He had many intense scenes to enact. He recalled, 'I worked very hard on my role. I'd carefully work out character traits, mannerisms, etc. There were times I'd wake up my director in the middle of the night, because there was something disturbing about the scene.' On watching the film now, he might appear overtly melodramatic, but melodrama was an essential part of the Hindi cinema of that era.

Before starting the shooting for *Ittefaq*, Rajesh Khanna had almost completed shooting for two other films: *Aradhana* and *Do Raaste*. Both the films were scheduled to release towards the end of 1969. But *Ittefaq*, which was splendidly finished in just a month, beat both the films and released before them on 4 October 1969. This song-less film stunned the audience who till now had been fed on the usual masala song-and-dance routine. Nanda was the star of the film, but Rajesh Khanna was praised by each and every film critic for his intense performance.

Ramesh Talwar recalled, '*Ittefaq* was a small-budget film and ran for fifteen weeks. It was praised everywhere. People in the film industry started saying, "Where was this actor hiding till now?" Audiences suddenly started liking Rajesh Khanna. The hope everyone had invested in him was rekindled.' With *Ittefaq* Rajesh Khanna tasted commercial success for the very first time. But no one had a clue that this was just the beginning.

CHAPTER 9

Producer-director Shakti Samanta had just shot his ambitious film *An Evening in Paris* extensively in Europe. The film had Shammi Kapoor and Sharmila Tagore in the lead roles. Despite being shot in gorgeous foreign locales, the film was a typical Bollywood film with its usual spectacle of songs and dances. In trade magazines and publicity material, the film's biggest USP was Paris and its beautiful locations. The music was a hit. But the film at best could only muster a lukewarm response at the box office. It didn't create waves as expected by Shakti Samanta.

After this disappointment, Samanta immediately wanted to start a new big-budget film *Jane Anjane* with Shammi Kapoor, who was very busy with other assignments. It is said that he had also put on a lot of weight and Shakti Samanta wanted him to lose some. So the project had to be postponed. Meanwhile, Shakti Samanta decided to make a *small* film—known as a 'quickie' in the industry. He wanted to finish and release the film in this transit period.

Film writer Sachin Bhowmick had narrated a story to Shakti Samanta which he had loved. This was a heroine-oriented subject and the entire story was told from her perspective. The storyline was very similar to the 1946 Hollywood film *To Each His Own*. Shakti Samanta named this film *Subah Pyar Ki*. The name was taken from the opening lines of the famous song 'Raat ke Humsafar' from his previous film *An Evening in Paris*. But after a few discussions on the script, Shakti Samanta realized that another name suited the film better: *Aradhana*.

***

Aparna Sen was Shakti Samanta's choice for the main lead. When he narrated the story to Aparna, she loved it and instantly agreed to doing the film. Now he needed two actors for the male leads—the husband and the son. The roles were not of much consequence as compared to the heroine's role. So it made sense to cast newcomers.

Shakti Samanta had watched the rushes of Nasir Hussain's *Baharon ke Sapne*. He had really liked the sensitivity of the young actor Rajesh Khanna. In fact, he loved him as one of the jury members of the finale of the Filmfare–United Producers talent hunt. He too was thus obliged to sign him for a role in one of his films. In this case, Rajesh seemed fit for the role of the heroine's lover perfectly—that of a pilot who dies in the first half of the film.

Towards the end of 1968, when Rajesh Khanna got the call from Shakti Samanta's office, he was ecstatic. Though this was a female-oriented script and his role was not a very strong one, he was happy that he was getting the main lead in the film of a prestigious banner. Also, he had four flops to his name. So any new project was another new chance to make it big.

But problems started cropping up even before the shoot started. Shakti Samanta's son, film-maker Ashim Samanta, said, 'My father had a tough time casting for the role. Aparna Sen was almost finalized, but she opted out at the last minute.'¹ Apparently, she had left the film, citing date issues.

Thus started the quest for another lead actress. Shakti Samanta wanted an actress who could play a glamorous girl in the first half and then handle the heavy dramatic scenes in the latter part, where she would play an older woman. The actress had to carry the weight of the film on her shoulders. After a tension-filled evening of brainstorming, he thought about Sharmila Tagore. Samanta had launched Sharmila in Hindi films with *Kashmir ki Kali*. Post that, she was the heroine of his *Sawan ki Ghata* and *An Evening in Paris*, in which she had even donned a bikini. Incidentally, the bikini had created quite a furore, earning her the label of sex kitten. In stark contrast, the lead role in *Aradhana* was mostly very serious and non-glamorous. Sharmila said in a TV interview that by then she was engaged and was looking to change her image into that of a serious performer. *Aradhana* was the opportunity she had been waiting for.

At last the film was ready to roll. Rajesh was thrilled at the chance to work with Sharmila Tagore. Everything was ready and the shooting was due to start in a few days. But the film's fate again landed in the doldrums.

***

Shakti Samanta was invited by his producer friend Surinder Kapoor—the father of actor Anil Kapoor—to watch the trial show of his new film *Ek Shriman Ek Shrimati* starring Shashi Kapoor. It was normal practice among film-makers to take feedback from trusted friends before the film's release. Shakti Samanta settled down to enjoy the film, but by the time the film reached its climax, he was utterly distraught—the climax of the film was similar to that of *Aradhana*, shooting for which was about to begin in a few days! Asheem Samanta recalls, 'Dad was shocked to see that the climax was the same as *Aradhana*'s. It was possible, because both films were written by the same writer: Sachin Bhowmick. He made up his mind to scrap *Aradhana*.'

Shakti Samanta went back to his office in extreme tension. The quickie that he had decided to make and release in a few months' time had robbed him of his peace of mind. That same evening, writers Gulshan Nanda and Madhusudan Kelkar dropped by to discuss new story ideas. Samanta told them about his problem and they tried to calm him down. Gulshan Nanda said that there was still time to alter the script. But Shakti Samanta was not convinced. To instil confidence in Samanta, Gulshan proposed to offer him a new script, if he did not like the changes in *Aradhana*'s script. Gulshan had another script ready and Samanta could shoot that script with the same star cast. This interested Shakti Samanta and Gulshan narrated his other story: *Kati Patang*.

After the narration was over, Shakti Samanta was smiling. Relief was writ large all over his face. He immediately told Gulshan Nanda that he wished to make a film based on *Kati Patang*. Meanwhile, he agreed to discuss the alteration of *Aradhana*'s script with Gulshan Nanda. They worked the whole night, changing the second part of the script completely. 'Two of his finest films were created in that evening, within a gap of a few hours,' recalled Asheem. 'First, they reworked the second half of *Aradhana* in the next few hours and then they discussed *Kati Patang* at length.'[2]

During these discussions, Gulshan Nanda advised Samanta to have the same actor play both the roles of father and son in the film *Aradhana*, meaning a double role. Initially Rajesh Khanna had only the role of the father who was to die in the first half of the film, but with this double role his part became important in terms of screen time as well content.

Unknown to him, in a single night, Samanta had given birth to his two most iconic and predominantly heroine-oriented films.

What was even more unpredictable was the way the lead actor of these films was going to surpass all expectations.

***

There is an interesting story from the premiere of *Aradhana* in Bombay[3]—a sign, perhaps, of what lay ahead. The show was held at Opera House, one of the city's prestigious theatres, and Shakti Samanta had invited many well-known faces from the industry for this event. This was Rajesh's biggest film so far. His career depended on its success.

As the lead actor of the film, Rajesh stood near the entrance to receive and greet the guests. The night glittered with Tinseltown's biggest stars who had descended upon the theatre. Among them was the evergreen actor Dev Anand, who had enthusiastically shaken hands with Rajesh.

Dev Anand's style had a whole generation spellbound. Rajesh had met him once before on the sets of *Jewel Thief*. He had gone there to meet his girlfriend, Anju, who had a small part in the film. Today that same evergreen star had come to watch *his* film. Star-struck, Rajesh had not been able to say anything to Dev Anand. He only smiled wanly and noticed that the latter scrutinized him closely. Rajesh felt that perhaps Devsaab wanted to assess the talent possessed by this new actor who, after all, had been a discovery of Devsaab's elder brother, Chetan Anand.

The theatre was jam-packed. The show had started. He was suddenly aware of the heavy burden of expectations on him. His eyes were transfixed on the big screen. Halfway into the film, the song 'Safal Hogi Teri Aradhana' echoed in the hall. He felt as if the song was reiterating his emotions. But his attention wasn't on the film itself. Standing at one end of the dark hall, he was intently studying the faces of this glittering audience and gauging their reactions. How were they going to respond to his entry sequence?

Which scene drew the loudest applause? Will the industry accept him after this film? He was looking for answers to these questions in the faces of all those gathered there that night.

As he stood lost in his thoughts, his eyes trailed back to Dev Anand. From where he stood there wasn't much distance between him and Devsaab's seat. Devsaab was watching the film intently. Still lost in thought, he didn't realize when the film finished and the audience got up to leave. The atmosphere was upbeat. Many well-wishers from the industry came forward to congratulate him. Devsaab also came forward, smiled at him, shook his hands and said, 'Don't worry, go home and sleep in peace. You will go far in this film industry.'

CHAPTER 10

B ut it wasn't complete smooth sailing for Rajesh. November 1969, *Aradhana* was ready for release. The film got into trouble because the distributors were not sure the audience would accept a newcomer in the lead role. The selling point of the film was the attractive lead actress Sharmila Tagore, but in *Aradhana* she was playing the deglamorized role of an old mother.

On 4 November 1969, *Aradhana* was released at the famous Roxy cinema in Mumbai. The music of the film was already a big success. The film's storyline and treatment was a bit bold for those times. Surprisingly, during the first show, the reaction of the people was discouraging. This was in stark contrast to the reaction the film had received during its grand premiere. Sitting in the theatre on the first day to gauge the audience's reaction, Shakti Samanta was in for a shock. He walked out of the theatre, fearing that the audience had not accepted the film. *Aradhana* got a lukewarm response at its Delhi premiere too.

The collections started picking up with each show. As word of mouth spread, the film opened to full houses in Bombay a week later and went on to become a super-hit. There were serpentine queues at the ticket counters. But something unusual was happening in the theatres that screened *Aradhana*. Instead of the star Sharmila, who was the focus of the film, the eyes of the audience sitting in the dark theatre were magnetically drawn towards the new hero Rajesh Khanna. 'Before the premiere nobody even acknowledged my hi! or namaskar. But later everyone was looking for Rajesh Khanna asking, "Where is that boy?"'[1] said Rajesh in a TV interview.

Hitherto unknown, Rajesh had now obtained a new, original appeal. At every point in the film when Rajesh wasn't on screen, it was as though the audience felt a void. And whenever he was back in the frame, it seemed that the audiences had been waiting too long for his reappearance. It was sheer magic. The loving glances, the occasional tilt of the head, the shy smile, the flutter of the eyelids, the earnest voice, the suave hairstyle, the dashing pilot avatar—the audiences enthusiastically lapped it all up. There was a mesmerizing charm in his presence on screen. The audiences were unable to comprehend the effect this charm was having on them.

Rajesh Khanna was akin to a sort of intoxication, like wine— slow but strong, and ultimately overwhelming. He was known for having combined the best of the Dilip–Dev–Raj trio, while also offering audiences a whole new package. Describing his magic, senior journalist Rakesh Rao of *The Hindu* wrote, 'If the Hindi film industry remembers Dilip Kumar, Dev Anand, Shammi Kapoor and others for their *andaaz* [style], Rajesh Khanna was famous for his *adaa* [mannerism].'[2] It was this adaa that went on to become iconic and made Rajesh Khanna a household name overnight.

All this success might seem all too sudden to a reader not familiar with those times. But the public reactions were indeed sudden and unexpected . . . for the director, the crew, the film critics and, most of all, for Rajesh Khanna himself. 'Aradhana was meant to be Sharmila Tagore's film. It is destiny, however, that it became my launching pad,'[3] said Rajesh.

The fervour surrounding the film has been well documented in the years since and hence does not need much reiteration here. Senior journalist and editor of Bollywood News Service Dinesh Raheja told me, 'This was a phase when a pan-cultural phenomenon called Rajesh Khanna swept the film industry. It was as if one and all roads [sic] led to cinema houses showing Khanna's films. I still remember my elder brother Gopal wooing his girlfriend (who later became his wife) by playing the romantic anthem of the day, "Mere Sapnon ki Rani" so loudly in our eighth-floor balcony that she could hear it on her second-floor balcony of the opposite building.'

The song, 'Mere Sapnon ki Rani'—featuring Rajesh Khanna in an open jeep, pursuing a train—became the anthem for young boys and men. It is interesting to note that the song had been shot in Darjeeling without Sharmila. Her parts were shot in a studio later on and then spliced together with the other footage on the editing table. Yet, the way Rajesh Khanna carried himself in this opening song left the audience spellbound by his inimitable ease and flamboyance. It was unthinkable that such a star could have any flop films behind him. And so, in public memory, this became his first film.

Another iconic song was the erotically charged 'Roop Tera Mastana'. A buttoned-up Khanna perhaps seemed more of a virgin than the actress, and this probably appealed to even the more conservative female fans across the country. The sensual appeal of this very bold song, which was shot in a single take, was something that the audiences had never seen in a Hindi film before.

The winsome and cute boy-next-door personality, loaded with a disarming smile and a voice laced with honesty were all strategic in bolstering Rajesh's image as an irresistibly charming romantic hero. His voice wasn't a typically heavy baritone. But it had a softness and grace that tugged at your heartstrings. It left the audiences feeling convinced that Rajesh Khanna would fulfil the promises he'd made to his on-screen mother, sister, lover or friend. Perhaps this was the reason for his immense female-fan following. Every woman wished a lover, son or brother like Rajesh. From school-going girls to their grandmothers, virtually every female was a Rajesh Khanna fan in those days. He represented both the new generation's forward attitude as well as the diffident charm of the old school's cultural milieu.

While the audiences welcomed this new actor with open arms, critics suspected that Rajesh's mass appeal was temporary. Previously, there had been many actors who came with a bang from their first hits, but then disappeared with a spate of major flops. Rajesh Khanna said in one of his interviews, 'The *Aradhana* success did something vitally important to me. It taught me how important the masses are for the success of a star. It is their adulation, their love, their craze for you, which makes a struggling actor a superstar.'

Even after nearly one month of its release, *Aradhana* was still giving houseful shows at the Roxy cinema in Bombay and across all of north India. Around the same time, another film featuring Rajesh Khanna got released in a theatre very near to the Roxy. The theatre was Opera House and the film was *Do Raaste*.

Rajesh Khanna fans lined up for this new release. In fact some die-hard fans would watch *Aradhana* at Roxy and then proceed to watch *Do Raaste* at Opera House. This story was repeated in many different cities of India.

***

Based on a novel by Chandrakant Kakodkar, *Do Raaste* was directed by Raj Khosla. It was a family drama, in which seasoned actor Balraj Sahni played the elder brother and Rajesh his younger sibling. Despite the emotional and melodramatic story revolving around the family's many struggles, Raj Khosla wove his magic into the romantic subplot of Rajesh Khanna's and Mumtaz's characters. He was ably supported in this endeavour by music composers Laxmikant–Pyarelal and lyricist Anand Bakshi, and of course the new star Rajesh Khanna himself.

Do Raaste was a musical blockbuster. It had some of the biggest chartbusters of all time. 'Bindiya Chamkegi', 'Chhup Gaye Saare Nazare', 'Mere Naseeb Mein Ae Dost' and 'Yeh Reshmi Zulfein' ruled the charts of that era and are remembered even now. 'Yeh Reshmi Zulfein' was the only song that had a brooding Rajesh Khanna in a beard. This was because the song had been filmed while he was shooting for *Ittefaq*, in which he sported a bearded look. Therefore he appears clean-shaven in most of *Do Raaste* except for this song, a look his female fans loved despite it being a discrepancy in the character's appearance.

The chemistry between Rajesh and Mumtaz was electric. A *jodi* was made and the two became thick friends during the shooting of the film. The song sequences were shot in a stylish manner. Only one song 'Mere Naseeb Mein Ae Dost' was sung by Kishore Kumar, while the rest were Mohd Rafi chartbusters.

A second blockbuster in a row proved that the Rajesh Khanna fever was here to stay and was acutely infectious. The symptoms included ringing cash registers and fans—especially of the female species—becoming hysterical at the sight and, sometimes, mere mention of Rajesh Khanna. The fever was soon going to escalate into mass hysteria unlike anything that had ever been witnessed in the Hindi film industry.

The year 1969 was a milestone in Rajesh Khanna's career. In the same year, a lesser-known film *Saat Hindustani*, directed by Khwaja Ahmad Abbas was also released. It featured a new actor by the name of Amitabh Bachchan. Though he got the National Award for the best debutant, the film was a disaster at the box office.

CHAPTER 11

'A Superstar Is Born'—this was the headline of the cover story of a famous film trade magazine on 1 January 1970, written by film journalist and public relations officer Shabd Kumar. Thus Hindi cinema got its first superstar. Gossip columnist Devyani Chaubal from the magazine *Star & Style* popularized the term 'superstar' through her fortnightly column 'Frankly Speaking'.

Film critic and author Suparna Sharma, who is currently writing a book on Devyani Chaubal, told me that Devyani, known in film circles as Devi, already knew Rajesh Khanna through his girlfriend Anju's mother. Always dressed in a spotless white saree, with carefully puffed hair, she walked in the inner circles of Bollywood with the confidence of one who held great power within the film industry.

Devi started writing her column in the late 1960s, almost at the same time that Rajesh Khanna appeared on the scene. Both achieved instantaneous success. Seeing Rajesh's phenomenal popularity, Devi started featuring him regularly in her column. Journalist and anchor Sudhir Gadgil, who translated Devyani's column into Marathi for the Marathi weekly *Manohar*, often travelled with her during interviews. He told me about their meeting with Rajesh Khanna at his Thakurdwar house, 'It was immediately after *Aradhana*. Rajesh became a star overnight. Devyani went to meet him at Thakurdwar. I went with her. It was a corner flat of an old building where we met. She took his interview. To click his picture we called him out in the gallery of his building compound. He flashed his famous smile for our picture. I could see Devyani was completely charmed.'

Devi was famous for her 'poison pen' while writing about everybody else in the industry, but Rajesh ensured that his charm over her remained intact. He fed her with gossip which she wrote about in her inimitable style. And soon a symbiotic relationship formed. 'As a person he is a woman's delight—the father, the child, the lover . . .' wrote Devyani in one of her columns, praising Khanna.

***

It was as if Rajesh Khanna had turned into a philosopher's stone. Every film producer wanted him to touch his film and turn it into gold. There was a dominant Rajesh Khanna wave in the industry and he was signing films left, right and centre.

The Bombay of 1969 was struggling with various socio-economic issues. Corruption and unemployment were the twin epidemics bludgeoning the dominant middle class. Cinema remained the popular source of entertainment and an escape from life's many problems. But there was also a stagnancy of sorts in the dominant public icons, whether it was in politics, sports or cinema. In the film industry the trio of Dilip–Dev–Raj was still reigning. But while the star power of the trio was still something to be reckoned with, they were not doing anything fresh. The traditional goody-two-shoes image of Rajendra Jubilee

Kumar was repetitive, and the heart-throb of the youngsters rebel Shammi Kapoor had put on too much weight and looked aged in comparison to his young heroines.

By the new generation the trio was regarded more as their parents' favourite actors. The youth needed a new icon they could relate to. Someone who spoke their language and brought the energy and appeal of youth and yet reflected traditional value systems. An icon who could pave the way for new fashion statements, show the youth a fresh perspective on life and love and cater to their fantasies. Every era has seen the youth searching for such new fantasies and new icons. By the end of 1969, in Hindi cinema, one such fantasy was about to turn into a reality. The void for a fresh icon was ready to be filled. Author Avijit Ghosh wrote, 'Nobody really knows how an actor of average build, middling height and a face often sprayed with pimples hypnotized India. Maybe, he was the last gasp of innocence when India was getting angry about unemployment and price rise, a hyphen between the simplicity of the years gone by and the uncertainty of the future. Maybe, it was just written.'[1]

***

The year 1970 started with the release of two previously signed films: *Doli* and *Bandhan*. Directed by A. Subbarao, *Doli* was a social drama, and Babita, who debuted with Rajesh in *Raaz*, was again his heroine. It was a very average film, but in the storm of Rajesh Khanna's superstardom, even *Doli* did good business.

Bandhan was produced by G.P. Sippy and directed by Rajesh's close friend Narender Bedi. Unlike his previous films that projected a suave image of Rajesh, *Bandhan* had him playing a villager named Dharma. Written by new scriptwriters Salim–Javed, this was the second film in which Rajesh and Mumtaz starred together. What made it interesting was the casting of

Rajesh Khanna's real-life girlfriend, Anju Mahendroo. Until now the only time they had worked together had been in a play. There had been so much written about Rajesh and Anju in film magazines that the audiences were eager to see them together on screen. Many producers were of the view that if the audiences accepted them as an on-screen pair, they could be signed together for future projects.

But when the film got released, the whistles, claps and praises came for the pairing of Rajesh and Mumtaz. Anju Mahendroo had less screen time. *Bandhan* is not counted in the list of Rajesh's memorable films, but it was a high point in the graph of the Rajesh–Mumtaz jodi, which first shone in *Do Raaste*. The chemistry was magical and audiences went wild over the lead pair. The film was successful, but Rajesh and Anju could never make a successful film pair. Maybe the audience sensed something was missing. Years later, Rajesh Khanna explained it in an interview, 'The film had Anju Mahendroo, my first heroine too. The two of us had a fight over something as a result of which both of us behaved extremely unprofessionally while shooting together. Every time I said my lines, she looked in the opposite direction, and every time she said her dialogues, I looked away. This continued throughout the schedule and the hassled producer was utterly confused as to what was happening and why. Nor did we, frankly. For, if we did, we wouldn't have behaved in so juvenile a fashion. I know it all sounds foolish, but one cannot disassociate an incident from one's life, just because it was foolish or childish . . .'[2]

People who were close to Rajesh Khanna in those days tell me that such incidents between Rajesh and Anju had started taking place on a regular basis. With a five-year relationship behind them, they had settled into a comfort zone. This comfort zone came under immense pressure with Rajesh's overnight stardom. Suddenly, there were too many avenues demanding

Rajesh's attention and threatening Anju's share of time and attention.

Anju Mahendroo's neighbour in those times, senior film journalist Meena Iyer, told me that she saw Rajesh for the first time when he was dating Anju Mahendroo, who used to then live on the first floor of Lakshmi Nivas, near Iyer's house. Rajesh's car used to be parked outside Anju's house the whole night. Even after becoming a superstar Rajesh Khanna used to come to Anju's house like before. Meena Iyer was studying in senior school and most of her classmates were jealous of Anju. Meena Iyer said, 'After classes, the girls used to gather outside Anju's house to catch just one glimpse of the superstar. You must have heard or read about such incidents, but I witnessed it myself. The girls used to kiss his car that was parked outside Anju's house and put the dust from his car on their foreheads as sindoor. I have seen that happening myself.'[3]

The constant barrage of extreme attention and scrutiny on Rajesh's life, brought about by his sudden superstardom, affected not only him but all those near him—especially the new national heart-throb's girlfriend. Anju was swamped with media attention that was unexpected, and was something she wasn't prepared to handle. The much-in-love couple was regularly featured in the film magazines of the era like *Stardust* and *Star & Style*. Regular columns on their love life dwelled on various little details of their lives—from the parties they attended together to the events they were spotted at. Anju's position was most coveted. She was projected as the New Age dominating girlfriend. On a daily basis she had to handle fans and other women vying for her boyfriend's attention: from the endless trail of love letters to young girls falling at Rajesh's feet in front of her house. All this was perhaps unsettling for the relationship.

Anju recounted, 'He wanted me to fuss over him like all those others who are perpetually falling at his feet. I loved him.

I couldn't fawn over him. To me he was Jatin or Justin. A man I loved, not Rajesh Khanna, Superstar or The Phenomenon.'[4] Anju had not been able to make a name for herself in the film industry till now. She was still more of a model who occasionally acted in the theatre. As superstardom started eating into their space and time for each other, it is possible that their expectations from each other remained unfulfilled. Anju further said, 'As much as I could, I had submerged my individuality, my personality, my identity into his—to make him happy. He wanted me to give up modelling at a time when I was paid very highly. I did.'[5] But perhaps Rajesh wanted something else. Handling newfound success is a full-time job for anyone. And Rajesh was only all of twenty-eight at that time.

Any relationship needs time to adapt to such extreme changes. But for the next two years Rajesh Khanna's each and every day was booked by film producers. In his date diary there was no time marked for his close friends, his girlfriend . . . not even for himself.

CHAPTER 12

As the year 1970 wound on, Rajesh Khanna showed quick progression in his growth as an actor. His films thus far had established him as a star. Now he gave his audiences more variety to chew on. Director Asit Sen's two films *Khamoshi* and *Safar* displayed his intensity as an actor of calibre and a serious performer.

Khamoshi was based on a short story 'Nurse Mitra' by the famous Bengali writer Ashutosh Mukherjee. In this film, he played the role of a sensitive writer and poet suffering from a mental disorder who is cured by the love of the eponymous nurse of the story, played by Waheeda Rehman. Again, *Khamoshi* was a heroine-oriented film, but Rajesh Khanna eschewed his trademark mannerisms to give a solid, intense performance.

Khamoshi did average business, but the superstar's effort of doing a different film was lauded. The high point of the film was Gulzar's beautiful dialogues and poetic lyrics, especially *'Woh shaam kuch ajeeb thi, tum pukaar lo'* and *'Humne dekhi hain in aankhon ki mehekti khushboo'*, put to haunting music by Hemant Kumar.

As if to balance out the seriousness of *Khamoshi* came Manmohan Desai's entertaining thriller *Sachaa Jhutha*, which had the superstar in a double role. This became Rajesh Khanna's trump card. He played the roles of a village bumpkin Bhola and the suave city criminal Ranjeet. In strange circumstances their lives get swapped. Mumtaz was once again the heroine. This was the only action film of Rajesh Khanna in those times. In fact, he looked awkward in the action sequences but this was expertly compensated for in the romantic scenes and songs. Like the movie itself, the film's music was a hit. A wedding song 'Meri Pyari Behaniya' from the film still remains without a substitute when it comes to wedding celebrations in north India.

Sachaa Jhutha was Rajesh Khanna's third giant success in less than a year. Herds of fans were flocking to theatres everywhere. Rajesh Khanna enjoyed the degree of adulation associated with rock stars in the West. Every single film and trade magazine was talking about him. His stardom had eclipsed all the other stars in those years. He received his first Filmfare Award for best actor for *Sachaa Jhutha*, though many believed he had given a much better performance in *Khamoshi*.

Another strong performance came in his film *Safar* that same year. Rajesh Khanna played the role of an artist Avinash who is diagnosed with cancer. The film had many memorable scenes. In one such scene, Avinash asks his doctor how many days of his life remained. The doctor (Ashok Kumar) doesn't answer, but just inverts the hourglass on his table. In the slowly falling sand Avinash finds his answer.

In *Aradhana* the previous year, now *Safar* and later *Anand*, the characters portrayed by Rajesh Khanna die. Generally, the Bollywood film formula steered clear of tragic endings. The idea was that traditional Indian audiences liked happy endings, where they can leave the cinema halls feeling upbeat about the fate of their hero. But Rajesh Khanna changed this trend. His death scenes created a strong impact on his fans. Before Rajesh, the only other actor who had left such an impact with his death scenes was the Tragedy King Dilip Kumar himself. His on-screen deaths in films like *Devdas*, *Deedar* and *Mela* were applauded and created millions of fans.

Rajesh Khanna, in his own style, resurrected the character who smiles in the face of death, who actually finds the courage to laugh at death. Sadness did not overshadow his characters' penchant for living. The Marathi poet Dilip Chitre wrote about Khanna's peculiar talent vis-à-vis his death scenes: 'Rajesh's screen deaths have some novelty—he is a warm, ebullient, vivacious, blithe young man. Even if he is destined to die, it seems unfair and too early. One has seen teenaged girls sob, witnessing him die.'[1]

This also started a new obsession in Rajesh's career. He started believing that if his character dies in the film, his fans will sympathize with the character even more and this would hence boost the film's chances of success. One of his co-stars told me that Rajesh was fixated with dying on screen. Rajesh saw himself as a combination of Guru Dutt and Devdas, and his roles repeatedly reflected this obsession.

But his Chaaiji was most upset by his on-screen deaths. According to Rajesh, after a trial show of *Safar*, his mother was taken seriously ill and had to be hospitalized the same day. After this, it is said that he did not permit her to see any film in which he suffered or died. But there were other things that made Leelawati distraught, and these were because of the many rumours and scurrilous gossip in the media that accompanied his instant fame. He later said, 'What hurt her most, and what she couldn't come to terms with, were the constant nasty rumours about my accident and ill health.' His mother would say, '*Mere bete ko duniya ki nazar lag gayi.'* [My son has been plagued by the evil eye.] So, eventually, to pacify her, a big havan was organized at their home.[2]

***

Rajesh Khanna was on a roll. He monopolized almost all theatres throughout 1970 with a succession of hit films. This was turning out to be a grand year for him. His roles in *Kati Patang, The Train* and *Aan Milo Sajna* were greatly loved by his fans. His movies were not only commercial successes but also musical blockbusters. With *Kati Patang*, the trio of Rajesh Khanna, R.D. Burman and Kishore Kumar became an iconic partnership. Songs like 'Yeh Shaam Mastani', 'Pyaar Deewana Hota Hai' and 'Yeh Jo Mohabbat Hai' are signature Rajesh Khanna numbers. Yet again, he was able to outshine Asha Parekh in the heroine-centric *Kati Patang*. He was the golden goose. His charm seemed to be affecting more and more people with every passing day. And the queue of producers lining up to sign him on only grew longer. One of the films he signed in this phase was Hrishikesh Mukherjee's *Anand*.

Hrishikesh Mukherjee had talked to some other actors for the lead role in *Anand*, but ultimately he zeroed in on Rajesh Khanna. Being the disciplined film-maker that he was, Hrishikesh wanted to finish *Anand* very quickly. But Rajesh had no time even to read the script. He was working day and night like a machine. He was overworked and growing increasingly restless during shoots. He recounts in an interview later, 'Nobody knows this, but *Anand* was shot during the busiest phase of my career. I was turning hysterical with work pressure. I got a sore throat telling everyone I couldn't sign more new films, but nobody cared and nobody listened . . . Now I had films by kilos and no dates. I was being criticized for being overworked, for being disorganized, for being greedy. I wasn't any of these. My problem was that I didn't know how to say "no" . . . The more fan letters I received the more confused I became. It's strange, but the true struggle of an actor begins only after success. Because the expectations became too many.'[3]

Under pressure, Rajesh resorted to having friends over every evening to join him for drinks. This helped him to relax and unwind after a hard day's work. As the drinks flowed, the conversations and laughter deepened. They would take him back to his theatre days where many new ideas and plans had materialized in such sessions. He invited the best from the industry every evening and offered them the best of food and drinks. Even on outdoor shoots, these *mehfils* continued, with him being the magnanimous host. Senior journalist Bharathi S. Pradhan recalled that if you were his guest, you were served the best. At his parties Rajesh personally ensured that every plate was filled with piping hot food. According to Pradhan, 'Once, while having dinner at his hotel suite, I was so busy talking that I didn't notice that every time a fresh hot roti was brought in, Rajesh Khanna would quietly take the cold one from my plate and put it on his own, making sure that the garam rotis came to me. Honestly, I don't know of any other superstar or even minor celebrity who could play host as wonderfully as Rajesh Khanna did.'[4]

But these sessions were soon growing into an unhealthy habit. Rajesh started depending on them to counter his maddening work schedule. He was in constant need of companionship as his stardom increasingly kept him from living a regular life. These evening drinking sessions would go on generally till late in the night. Rajesh would compensate for them by sleeping till late the next morning and, therefore, he would reach his sets late. This, in turn, would mean working till late in the evening. And so this cycle would continue. One day Hrishikesh Mukherjee caught

him in a reflective mood on his sets and asked, 'When was it last
that you saw the sun rise, Kaka?'[5]

Rajesh replied that he didn't remember.

Mukherjee again asked, 'And when was it last that you saw
the sun set?'

Rajesh could only smile as the answer was evident.

Rajesh Khanna loved Hrishikesh Mukherjee's straight talk
and profound wisdom. Mukherjee was one of the few directors
who could get away with reprimanding Rajesh over his starry
tantrums. When Mukherjee finally narrated the script of *Anand*
to Rajesh, he loved it so much that he signed *Anand* at a lower
market price, just to work with Mukherjee.

A very important role in the story was that of Dr Bhaskar
Banerjee. Amitabh Bachchan, a new, tall and lanky actor
who had debuted last year, was signed for this role. Amitabh
Bachchan in later interviews said that his celebrity status really
started when he signed *Anand* with the superstar. He later
recalled, 'I was being cast opposite him in *Anand*. This was like
a miracle, God's own blessing and one that gave me "reverse
respect". The moment that anyone came to know that I was
working with THE Rajesh Khanna, my importance grew. And
I gloated in its wake.'[6]

Describing Rajesh Khanna and his phenomenal popularity
Bachchan wrote, 'He was simple and quiet. The frenzy and
the following he garnered was a sight to behold. In the 1970s
era his fans came from Spain to meet him—a most unheard-of
occurrence then.'[7]

Most of the shooting of *Anand* was done at Mohan Studio in
Bombay. Hrishikesh Mukherjee actually shot the film in just a
month's time. Rajesh Khanna was so busy shooting for so many
films that he didn't have much of a clue as to what was happening
on the sets of *Anand*. Actress Seema Deo, who played an important
role in the film, recalled, 'He couldn't remember the lyrics of any

song, so there would be a prompter sitting on the sets to tell him the lyrics; he would listen to each line and then lip-sync it, but no one realized this.'[8]

It is difficult to believe that he was working round the clock, running from one shooting to another, while enacting his most memorable character Anand on screen. During the shoot Hrishikesh Mukherjee would get angry at Rajesh's habitual late arrivals, but he would wait for the shoot to be over to express his anger. Actor Ramesh Deo recalls that Hrishi-da didn't want the scene to be affected: 'Rajesh used to enact the scene so well, that after the scene, Hrishi-da used to say, *"Tumne itna aacha kam kiya hai, tumhe sau gunah maaf."'* [You have done such good work that all your sins are forgiven.][9]

***

By the end of 1970 Rajesh Khanna's stature had become even bigger. It is said that Dharmendra was the only star who was not majorly affected by the storm of Khanna's success. Apart from him, most of the established stars like Rajendra Kumar, Manoj Kumar and Shammi Kapoor were almost out of the race. The Dilip–Dev–Raj trio were still around, but they were doing selective work and had their loyal fans from the previous generation backing them.

The authors of the book *R.D. Burman: The Man, the Music*, Aniruddha Bhattacharjee and Balaji Vittal, explain that Rajesh Khanna had hit upon a style that worked and did a sensible thing by continuing with the formula. It helped that he was working with the crème de la crème of the industry, be it directors like Hrishikesh Mukherjee, Raj Khosla and Shakti Samanta, or writers like Gulzar and Salim–Javed, or a clutch of composers who were at their creative best at that time. In fact, what stands out about Rajesh Khanna' reign at the top was the quality of music his films had. Some of Hindi cinema's most enduring songs have featured Rajesh Khanna. And almost all belong to this phase beginning with *Aradhana*.[10]

Veteran scriptwriter Javed Akhtar, who worked closely with Rajesh Khanna in the initial years, said in an interview, 'In 1969–72 there was just one horse in the race and that was Rajesh Khanna.'[11]

Recalling Khanna's extraordinary success, Javed's one-time scriptwriting partner (of the Salim–Javed duo), Salim Khan, told me, 'He was the biggest star ever. Salman Khan, Shah Rukh Khan and many stars came after him, but his phase from 1969 to 1972 was different. The heights that he reached remain unparalleled. For example, the point on the river overflow measuring rod, which shows the highest breach point of the river water at the time of flood, becomes a scale to measure the intensity of floods. Rajesh Khanna's popularity breach point is a similar scale for stardom . . . and that point has not been touched by anyone before or after him.'

As a measure of the incredible and astonishing success that Rajesh achieved in such a short span of time, the media started using a new term to describe him: 'The Phenomenon'.

CHAPTER 13

Bandra is a popular suburb in west Mumbai. Today, the Bandra Bandstand and adjoining Carter Road area of Mumbai is a landmark location. Many film stars and businessmen reside in this posh sea-facing locality. It is a much-sought-after neighbourhood among Mumbai's elite. Now it has started looking overcrowded due to a number of high-rises dotting the area. But in the midst of all these grand houses and posh apartments, one can still see dilapidated houses and old bungalows that date back to many decades ago. These old bungalows enclose a history within them.

During the 1950s, Carter Road had a number of bungalows mainly belonging to the east Indian and Parsi communities. In the 1960s, a very well-known sea-facing bungalow was Ashiyana, belonging to the ace music composer Naushad. And located near Ashiyana, also on Carter Road, was another bungalow—a two-storeyed one, in a decrepit and dilapidated state. Veteran film journalist Ali Peter John wrote in one of his articles, 'People in the locality called it a haunted house, aka *bhoot bangla*. There were no takers for it, and it stood there without anyone willing to buy it even when it was offered at dirt-cheap prices.'[1]

According to Ali Peter John, when actor Rajendra Kumar got to know about the bungalow, he decided to buy it. He rushed to the well-known film-maker B.R. Chopra and told him he was not only willing to do *Kanoon* (a song-less film) but also two other films, if he were paid his fees in advance. B.R. Chopra paid him Rs 90,000 in cash. Rajendra sealed the deal for the 'haunted house' for Rs 60,000. Rajendra then consulted his best friend, actor Manoj Kumar. Manoj advised him to perform a puja to ward off any traces of evil. Rajendra did as suggested and finally shifted there. He named the house Dimple after his daughter.

It is said that the house changed Rajendra Kumar's fortunes. During the time he lived there, he saw the best phase of his career. Most of the films he starred in became 'jubilees', meaning they ran successfully for more than twenty-five weeks and thus became 'silver jubilee films'. This earned him the popular nickname Jubilee Kumar. Later, he decided to shift to a new bungalow in Pali Hill.

By the early 1970s, the supposedly haunted bungalow that changed Rajendra Kumar's fortune was waiting for a new owner. History was waiting to be repeated.

***

Rajesh Khanna loved the ocean. It was his dream to own a sea-facing house. This bungalow came very close to his idea of a dream house. He decided to buy this bungalow from Rajendra Kumar, but needed a large amount of money to own it.

Around the same time, a producer named M.M.A. Chinnappa Devar came to Bombay from Madras. He wanted to make a Hindi film. With his idea for a story, he managed to meet the superstar. The story was about a man and his pet elephants. A film had already been made in Tamil on the same subject. Devar offered Rajesh Khanna a huge sum of money for the film. Thinking about his dream house, this was an offer Rajesh Khanna felt he couldn't refuse.

Actor Dheeraj Kumar—who at the time was shooting for a film *Tyaag* with Rajesh Khanna at Famous Studios in Mahalakshmi—told me, 'Those days, everyone in the film industry was talking about the signing amount of Rs 5 lakh that Kaka had received. This was huge money. I hadn't ever seen 5 lakh in cash myself. One day, while shooting at Famous Studios, Kaka called me to his room. He told me to open a suitcase lying there. I opened it and was stunned. It was filled with new currency notes. I had an astonished look on my face and Kaka was smiling his famous smile while looking at me. It was not just me to whom he showed the suitcase with 5 lakh in cash. For days, he walked around with that suitcase and showed its contents to many people.' Rajesh Khanna was a true-blue Punjabi. In his mind, this was a great achievement, and he perhaps could not resist the urge to show off.

But when M.M.A. Chinnappa Devar sent him the script a few days later, Rajesh Khanna was both shocked and disappointed. The script was not of Rajesh's choice, nor did the role suit his image. He felt a film on this script could never work. It was then that he remembered the maverick scriptwriting duo Salim–Javed, who had also written a special and very popular role for him in G.P. Sippy's *Andaz*.

While recalling that day, Salim Khan smiled and told me, 'He took a lot of money when he signed the film. When he read the script later and got to know about Devar's Tamil films, he got scared. He called me and said, "This is a terrible script. I could have rejected it outright, but I have taken a huge amount." I think he needed money to buy a house and a new car. So he took more than his market price. I think it was 9 lakh, which was

4 lakh more than his market price at that time. And 5 lakh was the signing amount.'

Javed Akhtar said that the condition to rewrite the script was that they (Salim–Javed) should be given a free hand to make changes. Rajesh replied, 'Do what you want, but save me.'

The film was named *Haathi Mere Saathi*. Salim–Javed reworked the script and dialogues entirely, keeping in mind Rajesh Khanna's popular image. They only retained the four elephants from the original story. In fact, such was the extent of their revisions that many years later, a Tamil film was made based on this almost different Hindi version. Rajesh Khanna was really happy with the new script. The Salim–Javed duo had outdone themselves, and he found a new level of respect for his new writers.

***

In just one year of superstardom, Rajesh Khanna had achieved one of his most cherished dreams—owning a sea-facing house. He asked his father, Chunnilal Khanna, to rename the bungalow. His parents were ecstatic about his success, but his mother was often apprehensive and used to worry about others' jealousy and the wrath of the evil eye.

Sachin Pilgaonkar, a veteran actor and film-maker in the Hindi and Marathi film industries, later worked with Rajesh Khanna in his mega hit *Avtaar*. He told me that Khanna's bungalow was named Aashirwad (blessing) by his father. The logic behind this was that Rajesh would constantly live under a blessing. Even if anyone were to send hate mail or write an abusive letter to him, the address would be written as 'Rajesh Khanna, Aashirwad', thereby neutralizing any kind of evil intent. Thus, he would be blessed by every letter, every message coming to his house.

With a puja and havan, Rajesh Khanna shifted to Aashirwad. His family and close friends from the film industry were in attendance. He got very emotional and told a producer-director who was very close to him, 'I have finally come home today. My home. This is the result of Chaaiji's prayers.'

***

It was said that in those times only Devyani Chaubal had direct access to Aashirwad, which was fortified from the rest of the world behind an enclosure of high walls. The inside gossip of Rajesh Khanna's life was often leaked by Devyani who had become his friend and confidante. Film critic Suparna Sharma tells me, 'In those days you could directly approach the star, unlike today, when you have to go through the PR machinery. Those were definitely better times as far as film journalism was concerned. Devyani claimed that she had single-handedly marketed the phenomenal image of Rajesh Khanna.'

According to Namita Gokhale, who published the famous *Super* magazine, 'Every week, her column would revolve around The Khanna: what he said, what he did, and all of this would be flavoured with meaningful innuendos about the "special" relationship between The Superstar and her.'[2] In fact, the whole industry was abuzz with questions on their relationship. Some called her his self-styled lover, some a crazy fan, and many more labelled her as just a pawn in Khanna's fiefdom.

An interesting incident throws light on the special relationship between Rajesh and Devyani. Once, when Rajesh was shooting near Lonavla, Devyani and Sudhir Gadgil went to visit him for an on-location interview. Throughout the journey, Devyani continuously talked about the superstar, so Sudhir asked her the obvious question, 'Are you having an affair with Rajesh Khanna?'

Sudhir says that Devyani looked at him and laughed. She then said that their real relationship was more than that of a mere lover or wife. 'I am everything to him . . . *Woh mera bachcha hai!* [He's my child] I am like is mother.'

Sudhir gave her a puzzled smile, not fully understanding what she meant. Later that day, they had lunch with the film crew at the shooting location: yellow dal, rice and some vegetables. Rajesh Khanna was having dal–rice using his bare hands. Post lunch there was some dal sticking to his hands. Sudhir told me, 'I saw this myself: he came near Devyani, who was sitting next to him, and like a child he wiped his hands and mouth with the *pallu* of her saree. Devyani immediately looked at me and said, "*Dekha na tuney . . . ye rishta hai hamara.*" [Saw that, didn't you? This is our relationship.]'

Gadgil narrated what he noticed during some of his visits to Aashirwad with Devyani. Gadgil observed that the star would often be found standing on his terrace, staring at the sea in contemplation. He had a profound love for the sea, and was drawn to the sound of its crashing waves. At such times, it seemed that he was oblivious to the clamour of journalists and producers waiting downstairs for an audience with him. They would count the trophies lining his wall, waiting restlessly for the superstar to make an appearance, but would never dare to venture out on to the terrace to disturb him. Meanwhile, his fans would keep vigil outside his gates. It really seemed as though he was the king, and the people of Tinseltown were his subjects.

According to Gadgil, Rajesh Khanna would sometimes stand there for hours, lost in thought as he gazed at the undulating waves. However, it makes one ponder more deeply about these solitary moments of Rajesh Khanna. Was it just the simple matter of a star seeking respite from the constant media attention? Or perhaps this was a way to assert his star power, knowing that people were waiting eagerly for him? But one wonders if there was something more to it. It seemed as though, despite all the adulation he received, something was weighing down on him.

If so, what was it that troubled him so? After all, he was a king with the world at his feet . . .

CHAPTER 14

Salim Khan, who was a prime witness to the era, philosophizes, 'It is a very different kind of intoxication that comes from the wine made of success. It is different, and it is very many notches higher. The climb up the rungs of stardom in the film industry is accompanied by a rise in wealth—a double intoxication. Hordes of fans fight for a single glimpse and producers line up with ready cash. This is akin to mixing and drinking two different spirits. This creates a strong cocktail. Any man can stagger and fall under this heady mix.' Both those spirits were in sudden abundance in Rajesh's life.

Every film magazine and newspaper published pictures of the superstar's new abode. Aashirwad became as famous as the superstar himself. It became one of the unofficial tourist spots of the Bombay tourism department. Fans would send letters with just 'Aashirwad, Bombay' written in the address line. Thousands of letters from his fans reached the residence on a daily basis. Among these were passionate letters from girls declaring their love for him, many were marriage proposals, and then there were those letters written in blood about which a lot has been already said and discussed.

Prashant Kumar Roy—who had known Rajesh from his theatre days, and later became his office secretary—tells me, 'There were heaps of fan mail daily. I was responsible for reading them and selecting the very best among them. Often Kakaji would come and ask me: Which is the best one today? He would then read the letter out aloud and then shine a brilliant smile at us. He was amazed at the number of mails and would say in his mother tongue, Punjabi: *"Hunn ki karaan? Idhar se log, udhar se log, khoon de letter . . . Mai kya karoon? Ai ki ho gaya?"* [People from here . . . people from there . . . letters in blood . . . what should I do? How did this happen?] I have seen at least two–three letters written in blood come in every day. In response to all the letters, I used to send an autographed picture of Kakaji.'

A witness to his female-fan following, journalist Nina Arora compared the spread of Rajesh hysteria with a prairie fire. It razed to the ground the puny star–fan relationships of earlier generations. Rajesh was often discussed late into the nights and was a constant at 'women's kitty parties, old women's kirtans and in adolescent dreams'.[1] Rajesh cut across the fantasies of all classes and mindsets.

***

Across the country, millions of girls were ready to do anything to win Rajesh Khanna's heart. But the superstar's girlfriend was Anju Mahendroo. She had taken upon herself the duty to decorate Aashirwad and spent most of her time there. She was almost like a live-in girlfriend, a concept that was considered quite bold for that era.

The entire staff of Rajesh Khanna used to call her 'memsaab'. Prashant Roy recalls, 'Anju memsaab used to look after the entire bungalow. If there was any party or function, it used to be under her supervision. Although Chaaiji wasn't overtly fond of her. She was very modern . . . All of us at Aashirwad thought that sooner or later Kakaji would marry her and she would be our boss.'

Their personalities were as different as chalk and cheese. Rajesh was a shy person from a Punjabi family. Anju, on the other hand, was a New Age girl belonging to a modern family where women had an equal say in all the important decisions. In her family, women could pursue their dreams without any restrictions. But when people are falling in love, such matters are rarely discussed or given a second thought.

As Rajesh's success became more and more bewildering with each passing film, perhaps Anju was unhappy with the way her career was shaping up. But Rajesh Khanna never wanted his girlfriend to pursue a career in films. In his Punjabi family, the men would work and the women were essentially homemakers. He had similar expectations from his future life partner. He now believed that being a superstar he had everything, and therefore Anju need not work. Possibly, he could never understand that it was Anju's dream too to make a successful career in films. This topic became a bone of contention between them. Rajesh being the big star he was could have easily facilitated Anju's career as an actress. But this never happened. Instead, with regular disagreements on this issue, perhaps Rajesh Khanna began to fear that Anju wouldn't abide by his wishes.

These kinds of disagreements happened even before Khanna's phenomenal success. A famous anecdote goes that during one such fight with Khanna, Anju happened to meet the famous cricket player Gary Sobers. Those were times when the West Indies was the best cricket team in the world and Gary its star cricketer. Gary and Anju started making public appearances at parties and cricket stadiums together.

Anju was still grappling with her new feelings for Gary when something unexpected happened. Gary Sobers proposed to Anju with an engagement ring at a party in Calcutta. When the news reached Rajesh Khanna, he became hysterical. Anju returned to Bombay, and a loud argument broke out between the two. Anju remembers, 'To tell you the truth, at that time I was in a relationship with Kaka. We had a fight over something and then I had an affair with Gary. But it doesn't mean that I disliked Gary. I don't know what would have happened if Rajesh Khanna hadn't come back in my life. I called up Gary from Kaka's home and broke off the engagement.'[2]

After this incident matters between Rajesh and Anju did improve, but Rajesh became excessively possessive of her. He wanted Anju to be around him always. When she was away, he wanted to know exactly where she was, what she was doing, who she was with. After the onset of his superstardom, the situation escalated. This frantic behaviour of Rajesh Khanna exerted even more pressure on their relationship and he started to keep a tab on her every movement. Even if Anju wanted to spend an evening with her friends, Rajesh would not like it. Anju reminisces, 'He became so suspicious that he would ring up my house and keep track of my whereabouts . . . All he wanted me to do was wait, wait, wait for him.'[3]

Rajesh Khanna's close friends agree that in matters of the heart as well as friendship, he was not balanced and mature. He was extremely emotional and abnormally possessive. He was too young to handle his tremendous fame. His insecurity mixed with his outstanding success was getting too difficult too handle. It was as though he never understood how to separate his career from his personal relationships. After becoming the superstar, he found that there was nothing private left about his personal life. Every little thing was under scrutiny from the media and his fans.

This was also the time when his evening drinking sessions were becoming more regular. He would have get-togethers at his bungalow every evening, the famous 'Khanna Durbar'. At these sessions, the costliest of imported liquors were served to his friends and acquaintances from the industry. And as his fame soared, his genuine well-wishers gradually came to be replaced with sycophants. In these sittings, Khanna played God while all the others present where like his followers. These cronies would agree with all his whims and fancies. Continually surrounded by these yes-men Rajesh Khanna never realized how far away he was being carried from reality. His admirers soon became his closest friends, and he started believing their grandiose flattery.

But his actual well-wishers, especially Anju, could see through the facade. She was only a superstar's girlfriend, reaping no benefits of his name in her career. With Rajesh continually surrounded by admirers, Anju preoccupied herself with friends and parties. Talking about those days, Anju said, 'He accused me of always having my friends around. He said there was never any privacy for us. What about his yes-men who were always hanging around when I went to meet him? So often I pleaded with him that I didn't like his chamchas, that at least when I went over to him, he could have the courtesy to keep them away. But, no, they were always there. He needed them . . .'[4]

Perhaps it was the case that unconditional praise had become a constant in Rajesh Khanna's life. He received it from his fans and expected it from his loved ones. A character actor who worked with Rajesh Khanna offers an interesting line of thought. He says that the reasons for this behaviour of Rajesh Khanna might be rooted in his past.

While growing up, Rajesh got everything in his house: a prosperous family, nice school, good lifestyle and friends. But is it possible that he was always haunted by an absence of a sense of acceptance? Was there an event in his past where his trust had been betrayed? Was he on a lifelong quest for trust and acceptance at different places, by different people?

If this was so, then his magnificent superstardom brought him a great deal of unconditional acceptance from his fans. But his relationship with his fans was only one-sided. Fans never questioned him; they could not advise him or scold him for his mistakes. He seemed to love the fact that his fans embraced everything he did. Perhaps he had come to expect the same from the people he was closest to in life.

A senior journalist who extensively covered Rajesh Khanna in the 1970s told me, 'Everyone knew that their [Anju and Rajesh's] relationship was going through a bad phase and every month there was news regarding their break-up. But then, as if to prove everyone wrong, they used to appear together hand in hand, to a party or premier. They appeared so lovey-dovey that we used to be surprised about what to believe!' Another senior actor adds, 'Kaka really loved Anju. He was magnanimous; he gave her a bungalow as a gift. All of us believed that despite the tiffs, they would end up together.'

Rajesh Khanna and Anju Mahendroo's relationship continued to be the subject of much speculation and gossip, but it essentially seemed to all that they were going strong and would overcome the minor hurdles.

***

On a rainy morning in Bombay, according to a report that appeared much time later in *Super*, 'an eleven-year-old Gujarati girl from St Joseph's Convent' bunked her classes to watch Rajesh Khanna's latest release. She knew every dialogue of the film by heart because she had already watched the film twice. Like most of the girls from her school, she was also a huge Rajesh Khanna fan.

By the time the movie ended, the rain had stopped. Lost in her dreams of Rajesh Khanna, she started walking towards Aashirwad. Reaching the gate of the bungalow, she told the guard that she is a big fan of Rajesh Khanna and wanted to meet him. The old guard smiled at her. By now he was used to seeing all types of fans cluster around the gate for just a glimpse of his employer. He told the girl curtly, 'He is not in the house. Don't know when he will be back.'

The girl was young and naive. She didn't leave and instead went to stand at the side of the gate. In a few minutes, a white Fiat car rushed past her through the gates and into the bungalow, splashing muddy water on to her socks and shoes. Once the car stopped, Anju Mahendroo stepped out of it and went inside the house. The schoolgirl, looking at her soiled shoes, shed tears of indignity. 'The girl returned home, sobbing,' claims the report.

Her name was Dimple Kapadia.[5]

CHAPTER 15

It was a Friday in January 1971. A college in Bombay saw a very low turnout of students that day. Puzzled by the overall low attendance, the teachers in the staffroom wondered what had happened. It was not a national holiday, festival nor a religiously auspicious day. Where were all the students? It was the canteen boy, entering with tea, who revealed the reason behind this mass absence: Rajesh Khanna's film *Anand* had released that day!

In that respect, it was indeed a festival.

This was not the case with only one college. Students, especially girls, from many colleges in Bombay bunked their classes for a meeting with their favourite star. Accompanying them were boys dressed like Rajesh Khanna—clad in 'guru kurtas' and trousers, and with sunglasses half-perched on their noses, hoping that this might impress the Khanna-smitten girls. Everyone flocked to the theatres in the hope of another romantic journey with Rajesh Khanna.

But with Hrishikesh Mukherjee's *Anand*, the journey was not the usual romantic offering. Mukherjee weaved laughter and tears into a fable of human emotions with such magic that, by the time

the film ended, there was hardly an eye that was not moist. Till
now Rajesh Khanna had charmed his fans with romance, but
with *Anand* he awed them. He breathed life into the character of
Anand Saigal who became larger than life. The audiences came
out of the theatre inspired by this character and repeated the new
'Anand Mantra': *'Zindagi badi honi chahiye Babu Moshaye, lambi
nahi!'* [Life should be magnanimous, sir, not just long!]

The film revolved around the happy-go-lucky hero, Anand,
who is diagnosed with cancer, in its last stages. With steely resolve
Anand continues to laugh at the very concept of death and makes
fun of it. Instead of lying down helpless, Anand goes about helping
others make a better life and in the process, he teaches everyone
an important lesson about happiness. While Anand kept smiling
and laughing throughout the film, the audiences responded with
soulful tears. Illustrious film director Frank Capra said that tragedy
is not when the actor cries, but when the audience cries. And how
the audiences cried for Anand!

The sensitivity and intensity of emotions that Rajesh Khanna
showed in *Khamoshi* and *Safar* reached their zenith in *Anand*.
While recalling one of the film's memorable scenes that featured
her with Rajesh Khanna, actress Seema Deo still gets tears in her
eyes: 'In the film, there is my wedding anniversary scene where
Rajesh Khanna comes to give me his blessing, and says, *"Main
kya tujhe aashirwad doon, behen, yeh bhi toh nahin keh sakta ki
meri umar tujhe lag jaye."* [What blessing should I bestow upon
you, my dear sister. I cannot even wish my remaining life to be
yours.] He did that scene so well that I went out of the shooting
field and started crying.'

In an era when Rajesh Khanna had eclipsed every other
performer in a shared frame, Amitabh Bachchan—in the role of
Dr Bhaskar Banerjee, whom the ailing Anand affectionately calls
'Babu Moshaye'—made everyone take notice of his intensity.

It will not be an exaggeration to call the climax of *Anand* the watershed moment of Rajesh Khanna's career. This was an epic climax, without which no discussion on Rajesh Khanna is ever complete, even today. Towards the last scene of the film all prayers and medicines have been exhausted to save Anand. The end is near. Anand, writhing in pain, finally shows signs of fear. In a moment of extreme helplessness, Dr Banerjee rushes out to buy some homeopathic medicine that he has heard about. By the time he comes back with the medicine in hand, Anand has passed away. Filled with extreme frustration and remorse, Dr Banerjee starts shouting at the dead body, 'Talk to me!' At that precise moment, a recorded message by Anand starts playing, 'Babu Moshaye . . . life and death are in the hands of God . . . we are all theatrical puppets in his hand . . . when and who will die, this no one can foretell . . .' The message ends with both the on-screen actors and off-screen audience in uncontrollable tears. Amitabh Bachchan, in his impeccable baritone, speaks the immortal line summarizing the character, *'Anand mara nahi . . . Anand marte nahi.'* [Anand did not die . . . a thought like Anand doesn't die.] And so, by the end, Anand did not remain a character any more. Anand was now a philosophy of life.

In the past, director Hrishikesh Mukherjee had been an ace editor, editing films of the likes of Bimal Roy. *Anand* is a classic example of great editing mastered over time. The way he used the pre-recorded dialogue in the climax ensured the film and Rajesh Khanna's inclusion into Hindi cinema's roll of honour. The memorable dialogues were written by Gulzar; the elegiac poem 'Maut Tu Ek Kavita Hai . . .', narrated so poignantly by Amitabh Bachchan to explain the spirit of Anand, also deserves a special mention.

Recalling the days of shooting this film, Amitabh Bachchan wrote about how he was most worried about shooting the iconic last scene, when his character breaks down after Anand's death. It was an emotionally draining scene and he wanted to get it right. 'Not being able to find a method in my own very limited acting experience, I sought the help of Mehmoodbhai, in whose house I was living with his brother, Anwar Ali. And I still remember what he told me—he said, 'Just think, Amitabh, R-a-j-e-s-h K-h-a-n-n-a is dead! And you will get everything right.' Bachchan further explains, 'It was not so much a tutorial in acting that he expounded; it was an exalted acknowledgement of Rajesh Khanna's presence and position in the psyche of the nation, that he was drawing my attention to.'[1]

Each song of *Anand* is a gem and is considered a classic. The important thing was that none of the songs were sung by Kishore Kumar, who usually sang Rajesh Khanna's numbers. Composer Salil Chowdhury felt that Mukesh's voice would better suit the spirit and pathos of the character of Anand. His confidence proved bang on, with Mukesh breathing life into 'Maine Tere Liye Hi Saat Rang ke Sapne Chuney' and 'Kahin Door Jab Din Dhal Jaaye'. Manna Dey sang just one song, but it proved to be par excellence. The song 'Zindagi Kaisi Hai Paheli Haaye . . .' created a stir of its own while sublimely talking about life. There was a magical originality in the way the song was picturized: Manna Dey's lilting voice accompanied shots of Rajesh Khanna as he walked barefoot on a beach, symbolically releasing colourful balloons of resilient spirit into the sky.

It was inevitable that such a classic would sweep the Filmfare Awards that year. Besides Rajesh Khanna, who bagged the Best Actor award, *Anand* also won the Best Picture and Best Story awards, as well as the National Award for the best Hindi film.

Beginning with *Aradhana*, Rajesh Khanna was clearly still a 'not-out' batsman at the box office, delivering one hit film after another. Gauging the unceasing hunger of his fans to see him on the big screen, he signed too many films. In 1971 alone, in addition to *Anand*, Rajesh Khanna's main films were *Andaz*,

Haathi Mere Saathi, Maryada, Dushman, Mehboob ki Mehndi
and *Chhoti Bahu*.

***

Sudhir Gadgil recalls an interesting episode he was witness to.
Rajesh Khanna was very excited about *Anand*. He wanted to show
the film to the press and get good reviews.

A special show of *Anand* was organized in the Excelsior
theatre near VT in Bombay, for the media. After the film got
over Devyani Chaubal came running to Sudhir and asked
him to skip the food and go to the car parked outside. When
Sudhir reached downstairs, he realized it was Rajesh Khanna's
car. A few minutes later Devyani sneaked out of the theatre
with Rajesh Khanna and came straight to the car. Once inside,
Rajesh Khanna inquired if she liked the film. Devyani looked
at him for few moments and said, 'Don't ever work with that
lambu [tall fellow] again. *Woh teri chutti kar dega* [He will finish
your career].'

It was clear that 'lambu' was a reference to Amitabh Bachchan.
Rajesh Khanna was surprised at her reaction. He laughed and
casually asked, *'Kya hua, us lambu mei aisa kya hain?'* [What
happened? What is so special about that tall guy?]

To this, Devyani answered, 'Have you noticed his eyes?
Did you hear his voice? I am telling you, do not work with
him again.'

Apparently, Rajesh laughed and did not take her seriously,
although Devyani tried her best to persuade him.

***

Veteran film-maker G.P. Sippy, who gave Rajesh his first
break, was making his new film *Andaz.* His young son, Ramesh

Sippy, was directing the film, his debut as a director, which had Shammi Kapoor and Hema Malini as the main leads. Shammi Kapoor, by this time, was a fading star. His last few films hadn't worked well at the box office. To increase the box-office stakes, G.P. Sippy decided to include a special role for superstar Rajesh Khanna in the film. Out of respect for G.P. Sippy, Rajesh said yes to the role.

Together Salim–Javed wrote a special role for Rajesh Khanna in *Andaz*. In the film, he appears for a very short time, but the impact of his small role completely overshadows every other element of the film. This role became one of the most famous guest appearances of all time in Hindi cinema. The entry song picturized on Rajesh Khanna and Hema Malini, 'Zindagi Ek Safar Hai Suhana', became the song of the youth and achieved a cult status at the time of its release. Salim Khan recollects, 'We wrote a guest role for him in *Andaz*. I have been a witness to those times. To tell the truth, in those times it wasn't the film that would be a success . . . it was only Rajesh Khanna who was a success.' Across the country, people flocked to the theatres just to watch Rajesh Khanna riding a bike with stylish sunglasses, lip-syncing to Kishore Kumar's full-throttle crooning and yodelling.

Echoing the lyrics of *Andaz*'s cult song, at this point, life indeed was a beautiful journey for Rajesh Khanna.

***

Haathi Mere Saathi was an unusual film in the way that here the focus was not on the love story of the lead actors . . . It was in fact a love story about the protagonist and his four pet elephants. It might sound comical in today's scenario, but in *Haathi Mere Saathi* the unconditional love of animals was compared to the distorted and selfish motives in human relationships.

Rajesh Khanna carried the burden of the entire film on his shoulders. He played the happy-go-lucky hero with style—now his trademark. This was not path-breaking cinema nor was a path-breaking performance given, but people lapped it up. *Haathi Mere Saathi* was a roaring success. Salim Khan told me, 'This was the film that scared Rajesh Khanna the most. But this film eventually went on to become the biggest success of his career.'

It is said that the Rajesh Khanna craze had reached its zenith with this film. There was no one who could escape his powerful charisma. According to Dinesh Raheja, editor of the Bollywood News Service, Rajesh Khanna went on to sign a large number of films. Due to this, there came a time when almost all the big or small theatres of Bombay were running at least one of his films. Most of these films used to run from twenty-five to fifty weeks. Such was his charm that even average films like *Bandhan, Doli, Aan Milo Sajna* completed silver jubilees. This was a strange madness—or hysteria, as it was called in those days. Recalling that era Mahesh Bhatt has said in an interview that for those few years Rajesh Khanna was God and all fans and film producers were his loyal followers.

Film journalist Monojit Lahiri, who witnessed the mass hysteria surrounding Rajesh Khanna first-hand, wrote in one of his articles on the 1970s: 'I can only say that one had to experience the Rajesh wave to fully understand its impact. It was truly unbelievable. No Dilip, Raj, Dev, Shammi, Rajendra—or later Big B or the Khans—can ever hope to match it for the sheer passion and intensity that powered it. It was mass hysteria on a continuous overdrive, associated normally with rock stars of the iconic stature of Elvis, the Beatles, the Rolling Stones and Michael Jackson.'

The fans would never leave him. They were everywhere: running behind his car, standing outside the gates, waiting endlessly for days, pouring their hearts into letters written in blood, queuing up to watch his film shoots, and often making it almost impossible for him to go outdoors.

Sometimes, this mass hysteria could pose a hazard for the star as well. Bhupesh Raseen, who was close to Rajesh Khanna in later years, told me about one such unsettling incident. It was during a shoot in Pune for the film *Dushman*, some time in 1970. Rajesh Khanna was shooting a scene with Mumtaz. Hundreds of villagers had jostled to witness their screen god in person. As if surrounding him wasn't enough, they spread out, standing atop their mud houses or climbing the nearby trees. At 2 a.m. the shooting wrapped up. Rajesh was preparing to leave when he felt a hundred eyes on him. A hundred voices were chanting his screen names. The crew panicked as the army of villagers grew uncontrollable at the sight of the superstar. They closed in on him, pushing him, pulling him. They wanted him. A hundred hands reached out for him, but could only manage to grab on to his clothes. Rajesh was scared and shouting out for help, but he couldn't be heard above the voices of the clamouring villagers. The crew was worried too, concerned that the star was going to be literally crushed under his own stardom.

At this moment, Mumtaz emerged, fighting with the crowds. She reached him and pulled him out of the melee in one brave, quick move. She knew that the crazed fans just wanted to touch him, feel him, see if he was real. In a twisted way, their destructive act was born out of extreme love. This love bewildered Rajesh, and he was left quite stunned and shaken by this incident. He was yet to fully comprehend the dizzying heights of his own popularity.

In the context of Rajesh Khanna's stardom, a very interesting analogy was being used in the film industry: '*Upar Aaka, neeche Kaka.*' [God above, Kaka below.] Such words had never been spoken for any other star before Rajesh Khanna, and haven't yet for anyone after him. In fact, a beggar positioned outside his shooting at Mithibai College in Vile Parle, Bombay, had been known to beg for alms in the name of his new God—Rajesh Khanna! Perhaps this was a reflection of the fact that Rajesh's transition from man to God was metaphorically complete.

What more could he become now?

PART III

1971–72

Chingari koi bhadke, to saawan use bujhaye
Saawan jo agan lagaaye, use kaun bujhaye
Patjhad jo baagh ujaade, wo baagh bahaar khilaye
Jo bagh bahaar mein ujde, use kaun khilaye

(Song from *Amar Prem*, 1972)

Question: Whom would you like to throw a rotten egg at?

RK: The one who ditches me.

CHAPTER 16

In the 1970s, Hindi music lovers would tune in every week to listen to *Binaca Geetmala*, a popular countdown show of Hindi film songs. Sponsored by popular toothpaste brand Binaca, this weekly show was hosted by the legendary Ameen Sayani on Radio Ceylon. People would avidly wait to hear their favourite film songs on their Murphy Mini-Boy radios. Such was the boom of Rajesh Khanna's songs that the show had invariably one or more of his chartbusters in the top five. In 1970, 'Bindiya Chamkegi' from *Do Raaste*, and 'Zindagi Ek Safar Hai Suhana' from *Andaz* in 1971 were the numero uno songs of the year. *Ji haan, behenon aur bhaiyon, pehle aur doosre dono paaydaan par superstar Rajesh Khanna ke hi geet hain . . .* [Ladies and gentlemen, occupying the top two slots are the songs of superstar Rajesh Khanna] was how regular listeners remembered Ameen Sayani's frequent refrain from those days.

The show ensured Rajesh's songs enjoyed cross-border popularity as well. Indian films had been banned in Pakistan in 1965, what with the two countries going to war. The second Indo-Pak War took place in 1971, further deteriorating relations between the two countries. Indira Gandhi, the then prime minister of India, had come to power a second time and had led the country to war, resulting in an Indian victory and the creation of Bangladesh. This victory increased India's influence in South Asia and cast Indira Gandhi as a game-changing politician of international stature. Because of her iron-fisted approach, her global popularity soared in the early 1970s—a fact acknowledged by even Richard Nixon and Henry Kissinger.

The Marathi poet Dilip Chitre, in 1971, wrote, 'If there is one person in India today who surpasses the prime minister's charisma, it is Rajesh Khanna.'[1] This definitive essay put the two giants of India in 1971 on the same pedestal. In his essay, 'The Charisma of Rajesh Khanna', Chitre further described the superstar, 'Millions of Indians queue up for long hours to see him break into his smile, get drunk, become furious, whisper love-words or burst forth into a husky, vibrant played-back song.' This essay went on to be later prescribed in the University of Bombay curriculum.

The same year, the organizers of the state lottery in Bangalore decided to capitalize on the Rajesh Khanna wave for their promotions. He was invited to announce the lucky winning lottery number. Scriptwriter Javed Akhtar was travelling with Rajesh Khanna to discuss some scripts. The moment they reached the venue, an unexpected spectacle unfolded before them. A spectacle that spoke volumes about Khanna's unprecedented popularity. Remembering the Bangalore event, Javed Akhtar recalled in an interview, 'I don't know if I will experience that again, the sound of 50,000 people gasping [when they saw him]. He was like Caesar. It was unbelievable.'[2]

Needless to say, the lottery was an astounding success. Bangalore was a city with empty streets that day, because a 50,000-strong crowd had gathered together for one man at one place. All had gone to pay homage to their king. All that one could see were heads bobbing down the whole road, which was almost ten miles long. It was a spectacular display of superstardom. Recalling the day, Rajesh Khanna said, 'I felt next to God! I still remember the exact moment when, for the first time, I became aware of how mind-blowing success can be. It psyches you totally . . . You know, it was like a stadium from the time of the Romans. I wept like a baby.'³

It was at this Bangalore event when his colossal stardom dawned on Rajesh Khanna. He realized his crowd-drawing power, his massive popularity and the almost religious fervour with which his name was chanted. That day Rajesh Khanna became a superstar in his own mind. This enormous size of his own fame reduced him to tears . . . a defining moment when he felt the power of being God to so many people.

Today there are PR machineries that transform actors into stars and then strategically navigate the course of this stardom. They manage everything, from 'renting' fans to 'paid' media coverage. But Rajesh Khanna was the original superstar. And it is this star power that PR agencies today try to duplicate. 'It was an innocent age,' says journalist and author Sidharth Bhatia. 'Stardom today is stage-managed. This was organic and spontaneous with no artificial support. He began the cult of fandom.'⁴ The women who slashed their wrists for him or wrote him letters in their own blood were not staging stunts for breaking-news headlines but were simply part of a phenomenon akin to mass hypnosis.

Navin Nischol, a star in his own right in the 1970s and 1980s, had a first-hand experience of the frenzy: 'Believe me, the kind of mass hysteria he aroused in his day, I don't think even Amitabh has seen. And I was a witness to it. I had gone for a wedding reception at the Taj. Kaka was coming out of the hall while I was going in. We crossed each other on the way, and—this is the incredible part—the whole damn hall walked out behind that guy! It was such a stunning sight—that whole sea of humanity simply following him as he made his way out. It was unforgettable . . . Look, I'm getting goose pimples just talking about it!'⁵

This storm of success was blowing Rajesh Khanna along with it. He had little time to check his footing or hold on to a strong rein. In an interview he gave during that time, Rajesh Khanna himself accepted that he was scared of his stupendous success, 'Ten cars with ten stars would come for the premiere of a movie, but when my car would arrive there was mass hysteria. I got scared of my own superstardom.' It was increasingly becoming difficult to not drown in the sea of hysterical stardom. After all, how is it possible for anyone to remain immune to such adulation and worship?

Reflecting upon the changes that affected Rajesh Khanna, Salim Khan told me, 'Your entire life has changed. The attitude of others towards you has also changed. Just for one glimpse of you there are crowds running behind. Fans are even tearing your clothes in sheer hysteria. How is it possible that you do not change? Many people become humble after experiencing such success, but some people are just unable to handle such success. Change could either be good or bad, but change is inevitable.'

Rajesh was also undergoing a transformation within. After overcoming the initial fear and shock, he started realizing the power of his stature. And once he started wielding this power, there came the next stage: the stage of enacting that self-image in daily life. Malavika Sangghvi says, 'It was heady success that bred arrogance in the saintliest of saints.'[6] With the kind of magical success Rajesh achieved, his attitude kept on becoming more and more melodramatic and filmy in his public persona. He saw himself in the eyes of crazed fans and read about himself in film magazines. He was too young, the success too quick and unprecedented. And so his stardom started consuming his existence. It was as if he was donning the role of Superstar Rajesh Khanna in real life as well.

Javed Akhtar remembered, 'I can't say if he behaved like one [a superstar] because there was no one like him before. He was an original. He was huge and crazy. You can't blame him.'[7]

We cannot see God. But perhaps if God were to descend on earth, 'huge and crazy' would be how he would be defined too.

***

Salim Khan told me about a curious incident. Once, a film magazine did a cover story about Sanjeev Kumar, who was a rival of Rajesh Khanna. The magazine considered Sanjeev Kumar to be a 'serious' actor with a wide repertoire of performances. Among the several film personalities who were interviewed, Salim Khan too was quoted praising Kumar's acting abilities. When Rajesh got hold of the magazine, he sent his driver to pick up Salim Khan.

When Salim Khan arrived, he found Rajesh 'stylishly sitting on the bonnet of his imported car, reading the same magazine'. Rajesh looked at Salim Khan in his inimitable style and asked, 'You said this?'

Salim Khan replied in the affirmative.

'So you think Sanjeev Kumar is a very good actor?'

Salim Khan again nodded in agreement.

'And me? . . . What do you think about me?'

Salim Khan seemed shocked at the turn the conversation was taking. The story was about Sanjeev Kumar. Khanna had not even been discussed in the magazine interview. Then what was this interrogation about?

Still awaiting a reply, Rajesh continued to stare at Salim Khan. Then he asked again, 'What do you think?. . . Am I a good actor or not?'

Salim Khan replied, 'You are a good actor too. If they ask me about you then I shall say the same about you too.'

Rajesh looked at Salim and then at the magazine and then shifted his gaze back to Salim. He seemed to be weighing Salim Khan's words in his head. Then, just as suddenly, he got up and walked away with a smile on his face, without even acknowledging goodbye.

A puzzled Salim Khan was left looking after the retreating figure of the superstar for a while, and then himself went back. 'I used to live nearby and we used to meet almost daily . . . But after that incident he didn't contact me for nearly six months.'

He was a god who demanded absolute reverence lest you change your religion.

CHAPTER 17

'Six or sixty, he is the hangover of his roles in *Anand, Aradhana* and *Haathi Mere Saathi*. . . When you are with him, he is most of the time sixty—a grandpa abounding in worldly wisdom, preaching, scoffing and trying to correct you when you falter; or he is six—a child pouting, getting hurt, giving away the scoop story to your rival journalist just because you fail to turn up at the appointed hour. Then he sits back and enjoys your disappointment with the delight of a child who gives away your share of chocolate to another,'[1] wrote Devyani Chaubal, elucidating the superstar's almost dual nature.

For Rajesh Khanna, his life and his films became an extension of each other and he started taking it to absurd limits. Like all stars, he was quite jealous of the praise his contemporaries received. However, he also wanted absolute loyalty from his friends and colleagues. As each and every film of his at this point was a success, he started expecting the people around him to show him the same undivided devotion he was shown by his fans. In line with this showcasing of devotion, people were expected to mark their attendance every evening at Aashirwad at the 'Khanna

Durbar'. It became mandatory for any film-maker who wanted
to work with him to pay his respects at the Durbar at least a few
times. These parties used to go on till 2–3 a.m. every day. Until
Rajesh Khanna himself did not go to sleep, the others could not
be expected to leave.

Prashant Kumar Roy recalls, 'Kakaji would note who all
had attended the durbar regularly and who all were missing.
If an important person was missing for many days he used to
remark sarcastically, "He hasn't come for many days . . . so busy
he is . . . isn't it?" According to Rajesh, "busy" meant that, for
that person, something or someone else has taken priority over
Rajesh Khanna. This would immediately place the person in
Khanna's bad books.

According to Prashant, during the initial years at Aashirwad,
the Khanna Durbars were the initiating points of very creative
conversations, which resulted in great story ideas, songs
and music. The people in attendance used to be artistic and
resourceful. Prashant tells me, 'Initially Kakaji was surrounded by
brilliant people, most of them were from the Bengal group like
Shaktida [Shakti Samanta], Hrishida [Hrishikesh Mukherjee],
Panchamda [R.D. Burman], Salilda [Salil Chowdhury], Kishore
Kumar, Salim Khan—even Yash Chopra used to come. But slowly
the frequency of these people kept on decreasing. Kakaji wanted
daily *baithak*s [sittings], so these creative people were replaced
by small-time producers and some parasitic character actors and
cronies. Earlier there used to be *tehzeeb* [refined sophistication]
and discipline, but later on the quality of the attendees kept on
declining. After drinking free liquor, these cronies only praised
Rajesh Khanna, sometimes even without reason. Kakaji was falling
into a trap. All of us working at Aashirwad used to see this, but
we couldn't do anything.'

Film director Saawan Kumar Tak, who later made a successful
film *Souten* with Rajesh Khanna, told me from his experience

that Rajesh Khanna loved his chamchas: 'Some of them were third-rate unsuccessful people from the industry. I remember a small-time writer who used to be with him all the time. He used to give him all kinds of wrong advice career-wise. The worse part was that Rajesh Khanna, despite his experience and stardom, used to trust people like him blindly.'

In his life and career, Rajesh Khanna was intensely possessive. He wanted the film-makers with whom he had made successful films to only work with him. This kind of set-up wasn't entirely possible. Also it was very impractical and difficult for these professional people to attend his late-night durbar on a daily basis. This was the main reason why many important people stopped going to his durbars and gradually even stopped working with him.

A person who regularly attended his *baithak*s in the 1970s tells me with bitterness, 'His possessiveness was still bearable . . . But with time he couldn't handle his success. I had seen him changing. His attitude had become demeaning to other people. He had created a camp. Anyone working outside this camp would be insulted. He used to abuse them—such swear words! Initially, he was the ultimate superstar and there was a huge amount of money riding on him, so people actually tolerated this behaviour. But gradually the ideal option was to have some self-respect and leave him.'

Explaining this behaviour, Salim Khan said to me, 'His cronies used to instigate him in such matters. We [Javed and I] told him, "You are doing ten films with different producers and expect that we work only with you. How is that possible?" But he did not have the maturity to understand that we would work with him as well as other stars. He was a very possessive person by nature.'

The persona of the on-screen actor morphed into the everyday personality of Rajesh Khanna. He grew difficult and demanding. He increasingly believed that he deserved every ounce of the adulation he was getting and there was no room for criticism. And only the useless chamchas could supply this. A popular character actress who has worked with him in some films recalled to me, 'He lived in a bubble, totally cut off from reality. The situation required him to be level-headed, but he reacted in an extreme manner. He trusted the wrong people. In fact, if you got into his bad books, he would turn vindictive towards you.'

Speaking on the subject, senior film journalist Rauf Ahmed said to me, 'There had been many stars in the film industry who had started behaving really badly after a successful Friday. Rajesh Khanna is the perfect example I can think of.'

In a reflective mood, Salim Khan remarked to me, 'A Hollywood film-maker once said that success has destroyed more people than failure will ever do. In failure, we look back to try to see what went wrong and analyse it. But in success there is no looking back and no analysis, because whatever we are doing is liked by people. We are doing everything right. I will give you an example from my career. Our [Javed and I] film *Immaan-Dharam* flopped miserably. I watched it eleven times to understand what went wrong with the script. But I watched *Sholay* just once.'

Success was about to destroy yet another icon.

CHAPTER 18

Loving the screen icon Rajesh Khanna was easy, but being in love with off-screen Rajesh Khanna was another matter altogether. As more and more of Rajesh Khanna's celebrity persona took over, the further the old Jatin inched away from Anju. While Rajesh's career was unstoppable, Anju's was going nowhere. Any amount of time spent together was becoming a luxury that Rajesh, at least, was not in a position to afford. The relationship was starting to take a back seat. Gradually, cracks in their romance became more evident.

Rumours of affairs between Rajesh and his co-stars Mumtaz and Sharmila Tagore added fuel to the fire. In his interview with Bunny Reuben, Rajesh defended himself by saying, 'People think that I have had affairs with all my co-stars, or that I have bedded every desirable female fan who wanted to go to bed with me. This is far from true. I cannot have sex with any woman without a finer tuning-in of the emotions. I'm no stud bull. You have to be a good stud bull or a good actor. God is never so generous as to give both qualities to the same man.'[1]

But the incessant rumours had made Anju very insecure. Despite keeping a constant tab on her whereabouts, Rajesh didn't want her on his film sets. She abided by this rule and did not interfere in his professional life. But her friends fed her with spicy on-set stories of Rajesh being overtly friendly with Mumtaz. He addressed her as 'Mumu', and they were said to be inseparable. Also, with the audience loving their on-screen chemistry, Rajesh had every reason to work with her repeatedly. Mumtaz said, *'Shaadi mein jaise sitaare milaaye jaate hain, hum donon ki jodi ke sitaare milte the . . .'* [As the stars are aligned in horoscopes for marriages . . . similarly the stars were aligned for our pairing (on-screen).] 'Our rapport was very good. We'd rehearse in advance for hours because tapes carrying the film's track would be sent over to our homes.' Moreover, they were neighbours, and their camaraderie and closeness on outdoor shoots fed gossip columns in film magazines. While many other heroes refused to work with Mumtaz, her jodi with Khanna made her the highest-paid actress of that time.

Anju later said that she never wanted to believe the scurrilous rumours. 'I told Rajesh that the day I caught him red-handed with another woman, it would be THE END.'[2] According to Rajesh Khanna, he tried to explain to Anju that it was all gossip, but she allegedly continued to behave rudely with Sharmila and Mumtaz. That used to put him in an uncomfortable and embarrassing position while shooting with them.

After these incessant lovers' tiffs, they would always end up back together again. But their relationship was constantly on a media trial. And in most of the stories, Rajesh was blamed for the failings in their relationship. Rajesh Khanna's friend—and, incidentally, the runner-up in the same Filmfare–United producers' talent hunt—Dheeraj Kumar remembers an entirely different facet of Rajesh Khanna's personality. Dheeraj told me that in that era, despite his phenomenal stardom, there were only negative stories circulating about him. According to Dheeraj, Rajesh was a magnanimous Punjabi, ready to do anything for his friends. Dheeraj is surprised that even now no one talks about this superb and humane aspect of his personality. He says, 'Maybe the media loved his arrogant and crazy self more as it made for more juicy stories in the gossip magazines. Their magazines sold a million copies every month in the name of Rajesh Khanna. But the stories were unbalanced and tilted only towards negative.'

Whatever Dheeraj said was endorsed by many film-makers and co-stars who worked with Rajesh Khanna in his heyday. After becoming the superstar, Rajesh gifted Anju Mahendroo a plush bungalow in which she still lives. Not only this, Anju herself admits that whenever they fought, it was always Rajesh who used to sort it out or say sorry. Maybe he too couldn't adapt to the changes that plagued their relationship after he achieved his grand stardom. He started comparing the actions of his fans and cronies with Anju's behaviour. Those fans and cronies liked and praised everything he did. But his relationship with Anju was equal. When she used to raise objections to Rajesh's decisions, he found it intolerable. He was the king, and he couldn't seem to understand why Anju didn't see it that way too.

As their relationship underwent more strain, the differences in their backgrounds came to stand out in starker contrast. Perhaps the biggest issue in their relationship was Anju's determined ambition of becoming an actress. Anju wanted to pursue acting even after marriage. This was unacceptable to Rajesh, and he even laid down a condition to this effect. It was possible that this controlling nature of Rajesh stemmed from his insecurity. In fact, after he became aware of his newfound power and godlike stature, the sense of control and power he exercised over his fans started seeping into his relationships with friends, even with Anju. Salim Khan told me, 'If someone disagreed with him over something, he used to think that the person was against him. If someone even suggested something that was not of his choice, he would take it as opposition. He never took to disagreements kindly. Then he used to act in a manner as if the person, even a close one, was his enemy.'

***

Reportedly, even his girlfriend, Anju Mahendroo, couldn't escape the brunt of his ego. It was often reported in the media that Rajesh Khanna tried to stall the release of films featuring Mahendroo. Film historian Gautam Kaul recounts a similar episode. While he was the film expert on board the official committee of the excise department in the Delhi administration, a film featuring Anju Mahendroo came to him for tax exemption and was issued the same. But according to Gautam Kaul the film met with a similar fate. According to him, Rajesh Khanna was behind it. He even went so far as to declare that he would allegedly pay double the cost incurred to all film-makers to buy the rights of the films that featured Anju Mahendroo.[3]

In May 1973, Anju herself went to the extent of accusing Rajesh of sabotaging her career. They had a big row over her role in the film *Dastak*. 'He canned my film *Uski Kahani*,' she claimed. 'The film till today is with him and his partner Shakti Samanta. He wanted me to quit acting so he made me get out of a film with Sanjeev Kumar for which I had already completed a week's [worth of] shooting.'[4]

This issue was a matter of great speculation in the film industry. Rajesh retorted, 'Yes, I didn't want her working in films. I've always said that I wanted a non-working wife. But what career did she sacrifice for me? Those two-bit roles like [in] *Jewel Thief*? Where would have those stray roles taken her?'[5]

Inscribed in the dark ink of ego, stubbornness and possessiveness, this was a major aspect of the superstar's real-life romantic relationship—and it was starkly different from his romantic image worshipped on the cinematic screen.

CHAPTER 19

1972 began with the hit film *Dushman* in which Rajesh Khanna played a truck driver with elan, singing 'Vada Tera Vada' in his trademark style. This was followed by *Amar Prem* in March, when he delivered a performance that reached a poetic intensity that was heartbreaking, intense and sweetly painful. This was Rajesh Khanna's *Devdas* moment—one that gave him a chance to go down majestically in Hindi cinema history with an *Amar* performance.

Amar Prem was based on a story by Bibhutibhushan Bandyopadhyay; Bengali film *Nishi Padma*, based on the same plot, had been made the year before. Shakti Samanta bought the rights for the film's remake in Hindi. Once the script was ready Samanta approached Sharmila Tagore for the female lead character, Pushpa. Sharmila had been on a hiatus since the birth of her first child. She instantly agreed to the script as it was a pivotal role and gave her another chance to prove herself as a serious actor. *Amar Prem* was thus one of the first films she signed on after the birth of her son, Saif Ali Khan. For the role of the male lead character, Ananta, actor Raaj Kumar was Samanta's first choice, as he believed that Superstar Rajesh Khanna wouldn't be interested in doing a film which had a stronger female character. However, when Rajesh Khanna heard of this he convinced Samanta that he could do justice to the role.

It is said that for his character research, Rajesh Khanna went to Uttam Kumar's Moira Street residence in Calcutta. Uttam Kumar had played the role of Ananta in the Bengali original. At the *Amar Prem* premiere at Paradise theatre in Calcutta, Rajesh confessed that he had watched *Nishi Padma* some sixteen times and that he would consider himself lucky if he could do at least 50 per cent of what Uttam Kumar had done in the Bengali version. For luck, Rajesh Khanna had character's name changed from Ananta to Anand, thereby drawing a connection to his character in the critically acclaimed *Anand*.

Amar Prem did not follow the conventional storyline of romance that was usual in the Hindi film industry at the time. It was about the selfless love between three strangers—a man, a woman and a child—who form a nameless bond that transcends conventional societal ties.

The story is a poignant one: Pushpa (Sharmila Tagore), under dire conditions, ends up as a prostitute in Calcutta, where she meets the dhoti-clad Anand Babu (Rajesh Khanna). A reluctant Anand is drawn to her melodious singing and ends up being her regular and eventually exclusive client. Gradually Anand helps Pushpa come to terms with the reality of her life. In the scene when Anand meets Pushpa for the first time as she sings the song 'Raina Beeti Jaye', there is a definite foreboding of the intense love to follow. Rajesh's dialogue, *'Aap ruk kyun gaye, gaaiyye na.'* [Why did you stop? Please sing on.] is delivered with a deep aching pain. According to Sharmila Tagore, 'He delivered the dialogue with so much emotion and sensitivity that it left me spellbound. In the last scene when he bids goodbye . . . saying, "Pushpa", he mingled his smile with his tears like no other actor of that period could.'

Senior film journalist and editor of Bollywood News Service, Dinesh Raheja, wrote about the confident swagger that Khanna acquired for this role. He made the most of his 'wry grin, pained eyes and softly delivered acerbic lines' to let the 'the inner turmoil peek through the surface calm'.

The subtle romantic melancholy of Anand Babu as he says, 'PUSHPA, I HATE TEARS,' although a mere part of a dialogue, became an iconic line delivered in Rajesh Khanna's trademark style. This is picked up till date by mimicry artists.

Crazed fans had made it impossible to shoot any Rajesh Khanna movies in the daytime at outdoor locations. Film-makers usually resorted to constructing sets for late-night shoots of Rajesh's scenes. Confirming this statement film-maker Shakti Samanta narrates a bitter experience that he underwent during the song sequence 'Chingari Koi Bhadke'. Samanta said, 'As luck would have it, the news leaked out that Rajesh Khanna is coming to Calcutta, and to my horror, at the airport, I witnessed a sea of people anxiously waiting for their beloved superstar! After battling Khanna fans, we somehow managed to reach our hotel. Outside the hotel too, a mammoth crowd gathered to have a dekko of their heart-throb. Looking at the mob, I pictured them coming to the actual shoot. It sent a chill down my spine and I immediately decided to cancel the shoot and packed my bags to return to Bombay. Later, in the comfort of the Mehboob Studio, I recreated the Howrah Bridge set and got the song picturized.'

The songs by Anand Bakshi and R.D. Burman (sung by Kishore Kumar and Lata Mangeshkar) are some of the most richly melodious, haunting Indian songs ever composed. Gems like 'Kuch Toh Log Kahenge', 'Chingari Koi Bhadke', 'Yeh Kya Hua', and 'Raina Beeti Jaye' are timeless classics. Pancham, as R.D. Burman was widely called, said in an interview: '*Amar Prem* has been my most inspired film. It was a challenge in more ways than one. The film was a hit in Bengali. So I had to make it even better with the Hindi version. I hit the bullseye with this film. Of course, there was a combination of several factors. Rajesh Khanna was magic in those days. He looked so good singing those songs; perhaps if Amitabh Bachchan had to sing all those songs then, they may not have been appreciated. His image was different. Those songs fitted Rajesh Khanna like a glove. Its songs were super-hits and they remain my personal favourites.'[1]

The movie became a huge hit and enhanced Rajesh Khanna's popularity, particularly in Bengal, where the men copied his 'style' every time they wore their spotless white kurtas and dhotis. The actor Biswajit taught him how to wear a Bengali-style dhoti in *Amar Prem*.

The politician Amar Singh, who used to live in Calcutta in those days, told me that he had never seen such passionate fans as he had witnessed in those days. 'I was in Calcutta and I still remember the theatres in which I watched his films. *Sachaa Jhutha* in Majestic, *Do Raaste* in Orient, *Dushman* in Moonlight and *Ittefaq* in Roxy. *Amar Prem* was a story based in Bengal, so the craze was even bigger. I'm not exaggerating—before going to watch Rajesh Khanna's films, the girls got ready, in beauty parlours, as if they are not just going to watch a film, but going on a date with him. Believe me, this really happened.'

Today, it is very difficult to imagine films like *Anand* and *Amar Prem* generating such levels of mass hysteria. While most of his films touched upon prevalent social themes, his acting was refreshingly personal. Social commentator Santosh Desai explains the secret of Khanna's success with women: 'He brought women closer to the imagined ideal of what cultural psychologist Sudhir Kakar calls a "two-person" universe that exists between a man and a woman . . . His romantic style was based on thoughtful attention communicated through gaze rather than touch'.[2] He promised a deeper understanding, attractiveness and vulnerability. Desai insightfully says that Rajesh Khanna

exhibited the more poetic side of masculinity—an actor who
poetically deals with the issues and emotions of life. Perhaps this
was the reason Rajesh Khanna stood out in his performances
when it came to the song sequences.

***

While *Amar Prem* was Rajesh Khanna's favourite film, his favourite
director remained Hrishikesh Mukherjee, who always challenged
him to push his acting boundaries. The shooting of their second
film, *Bawarchi*, was in its last stages. Rajesh Khanna was working
with Jaya Bhaduri in the film, though she was not paired with him.
Film journalist Ali Peter John narrates an interesting incident[3]
that took place during the *Bawarchi* shoot, 'Jaya was madly in love
with a then struggling actor Amitabh Bachchan. Rajesh Khanna
would openly tell her not to roam around with Amitabh. He said
to Jaya, *"Kyun tum is aadmi ke saath ghumti ho? Tumhara kuch
nahi hoga."'* [Why are you going out with this man? He is not
going to amount to much.]

According to Ali, when Amitabh Bachchan came to meet Jaya
during the shooting of *Bawarchi* at the Ranjit Studio, Rajesh
Khanna did not even acknowledge Amitabh's presence. 'Jaya was
very upset about this and one day she told him, *"Ek din dekhna
yeh kahan hoga aur tum kahan hoge."'* [One day you shall see
where he will be and where you will be.] History proved these
words to be prophetic.

Bawarchi was a triumph of Rajesh Khanna's acting abilities.
For the first time in his career, he attempted comedy and came out
with flying colours. Based on a story by Tapan Sinha, *Bawarchi*
was a story of a dissatisfied family headed by the old and stern
patriarch Shivnath Sharma (Harindranath Chattopadhyay).
Each member of his family had a set of problems. Then, like an
angel, enters the multitalented Raghu (Rajesh Khanna) who sets

everything right in the family. He cooks, he sings, he dances, he advises on relationship issues—in short, he wins everybody's hearts and restores order in the chaotic family, with an interesting twist in the climax.

Senior journalist and author Suresh Kohli writes about what Rajesh Khanna told him about *Bawarchi*: 'In *Bawarchi* I did exactly the opposite of what Hrishida had made me do in *Anand*. He allowed me to interpret the role and perform it my way. I had done enough intense roles, and *Bawarchi* gave me the opportunity to interpret and perform the role the way I wanted. So I let myself go.'

In fact, this low-budget simplistic film actually proved something that was contrary to what critics have always said about Rajesh Khanna—that his success was due to his romantic-hero roles, jodis and chartbuster songs. *Bawarchi* was not a love story; it had no romantic songs and the music had some classical tunes by Madan Mohan, with lyrics by Kaifi Azmi—rather than the sort of chartbusters associated with Rajesh Khanna's image.

After *Bawarchi*, Jaya Bhaduri spoke about her intentions of 'never working with that man who thinks he is Jawaharlal Nehru'.[4]

Interestingly, for his next film *Namak Haraam*, Hrishikesh Mukherjee again wanted to cast his *Anand* stars Rajesh Khanna and Amitabh Bachchan together.

***

Meanwhile, the actor-film-maker Raj Kapoor was in financial doldrums after the failure of his magnum opus, *Mera Naam Joker*. Post that, he decided to direct a teenage love story where he was launching his son Rishi Kapoor as a lead actor. The film was named *Bobby*. For the title role, he selected a fifteen-year-old girl, Dimple Kapadia. Dimple was the daughter of the Gujarati entrepreneur

Chunnibhai Kapadia, who was based out of Bombay. Kapadia was an acquaintance of Rajesh Khanna, and would often mention his daughter Dimple, a true Khanna fan, to the superstar.

During the shooting for *Bobby*, rumours of an affair between the Kapoor scion Rishi and the new-girl-on-the-block Dimple Kapadia came to the fore. As the shooting of the film progressed, it was reported that Dimple and Rishi got so serious about their relationship that Dimple was spotted wearing a ring given to her by Rishi. In gossip circles, she was already touted as the Kapoor *khandan*'s next bahu.

CHAPTER 20

Film journalist Rauf Ahmed once told me[1] of an incident that occurred during the shooting of B.R. Chopra's *Karm* in 1976. An outdoor schedule had been planned in the beautiful locales of Srinagar for shooting a song sequence. The film crew and its director, B.R. Chopra, had reached ahead of the stars to prepare for the shoot. For the lead actor, Chopra had signed on the superstar Rajesh Khanna, and was pleased to be working with him again after *Ittefaq*.

The crew judiciously set to work to prepare for the shoot. On the appointed day of the arrival of the superstar, the crew grew ecstatic with anticipation. A man was dispatched to receive the actor at the airport. The word had spread in the valley of the impending arrival of the superstar and the locals were also making inquiries. The sets were abuzz with expectancy. Then the news came in—the superstar was missing!

B.R. Chopra sent a message to him in Bombay inquiring after his reasons for not showing up. Three days passed. There was no answer. The entire unit was waiting for their hero to arrive, but he was still in Bombay. Chopra continuously sent many messages asking about the reasons for his delay but to no avail. Was he not receiving the calls? Were the messages not being relayed to him? Where was he?

Finally, to the surprise of the director, Gopal, the superstar's cook arrived in Srinagar—on the business-class ticket of the actor. The cook had come with a message: 'Master is unwell, and so he cannot come for the shoot'.

The master and his whims were synonymous with each other, it seemed. 'He became emblematic of all the excesses that come tagged with stardom,' said film journalist Rauf Ahmed to me.

But the beginnings of Rajesh Khanna's full-blown excesses had become evident years earlier.

Salim Khan explains the atypical superstar behaviour with an illustrative analogy, 'This happens with all actors normally. There is an old saying in Sanskrit which gives the example of a bullock cart travelling between two villages. A dog keeps pace with the cart and travels alongside it. The cart protects the dog from the intense sun and provides shade throughout the long journey. The dog starts doing this time and again. It travels alongside the cart every time. After a few years the dog gets used to this set-up and starts to think that the cart is moving because of him. Similarly, when films start becoming successful, one after another, an actor starts to believe it's only because of him.'

This could just as well be applicable to Rajesh Khanna. Narcissism and self-obsession had taken over him—evident from his octagonal sea-facing bedroom that had large blow-ups of himself adorning the walls. But the mass hysteria he evoked perhaps warranted this thinking. Rauf Ahmed says that, by way of justifying his high-handedness, Rajesh Khanna once said, 'People come to see my films to see ME.' According to Ahmed, this was the undeniable truth: 'With a dozen consecutive hits to his credit at the time, you couldn't argue with him.' Starry tantrums were starting to become Rajesh Khanna's prominent quality. He was often blamed for staging illnesses as excuses for no-shows which, in turn, kept his directors waiting at length cluelessly—like during the shooting of *Karm*.

His biggest champion in the media at that time, Devyani Chaubal, later said that Rajesh was a much nicer person to know before his superstardom. Elaborating on the way in which Rajesh had changed over the years Devyani said that he had become so self-involved and self-centred that he had nothing to offer to those around him any more:[2] 'I knew him really well. He is so insecure . . . so complex.'

One excess led to another. To say that he was fond of drinking would be an understatement. Like a true-blooded Punjabi, everything under the sun was an excuse for drinking. A film-maker who had attended many durbar sessions at Aashirwad recalls, 'His favourite was Red Label scotch. The first peg used to be a large one which would go down very quickly. He never used to stop at one or two pegs . . . and continued till the wee hours of the morning. Also, he never used to eat anything, food or snacks, while drinking. It was just alcohol.'

He was never an early riser. Now with these late-night parties, his mornings usually started late in the day. Ali Peter John, who had known Khanna from his theatre days, said, 'There were early morning shoots, but for him the day used to begin at 3 p.m. But he was a very good actor. You give him dialogues and he would finish his whole day's work in a few hours. So they couldn't complain though they were losing money.'

The question is: Isn't such behaviour associated with every big actor? Why single out only Rajesh Khanna? Senior journalist and film-maker Khalid Mohamed does not agree that Khanna's behaviour was abnormal. Khalid said in one of his interviews,

'One has heard that success went to his head, he developed an attitude problem, which I am sure every superstar would have. But he just made it more obvious. While Raj Kapoor and Dev Anand kept to themselves, Khanna's coterie damaged him. But that was not unusual.' Veteran film-maker J. Omprakash who made many films with Rajesh Khanna agrees, adding, 'Kaka's problem was that he was not an extrovert. He used to talk less but was very suspicious of others around him.'

***

As his films continued their succession of consecutive hits, Rajesh Khanna became the favourite subject of film journalists. The superstar's mere sneeze made headlines. As word spread of his time management and ego issues, the reports on Rajesh Khanna started taking a turn for the negative. Everyone loves running down the successful. And why should have it been any different with Rajesh Khanna—the first superstar and a man who showed India what success could mean?

Rajesh Khanna's vision of the world around him came either from the gossip columns of film magazines or from the cronies who continuously surrounded him. Their opinion became Rajesh's compass to base his judgements and decisions on. Apparently, if you didn't know the superstar directly, it became almost mandatory to go through his chamchas. Even his manager, Gurnam, and driver, Kabir, became famous and much sought after in the industry as men with 'high connections'.

But when I met J. Omprakash, he vehemently denied such stories related to Khanna's starry tantrums: 'I never had to attend his durbar to work with him. I always got his dates comfortably.' But he did accept that Rajesh Khanna came late for his shoots: 'He was always late and we used to call him "Mr Late". But then he used to do his homework on his characters and prepare his scenes well in advance. He was a brilliant actor.' This problem came about at the height of his stardom, when such admirers like J. Omprakash were too few and too many who spoke ill of him in the industry.

Arriving late for shoots was a persistent trademark of his that stuck with him throughout his career. It harmed his career more than he could ever understand. Gossip magazines thrived on stories related to his mood swings and the manner in which the shoots often had to be cancelled. They also wrote about the losses that producers had to face due to his behaviour. His image was battered with such allegations that the industry had started believing that he would never change. It was all a matter of tolerating him till the point his films were doing well.

As a result of the onslaught of negative stories, Rajesh Khanna started giving it back to the journalists. Those who were not in his good books, unlike Devyani Chaubal, had to face his wrath some time or the other. This was famously described as 'The Rajesh Khanna Treatment' among the film scribes of the era.

Former film journalist Ingrid Albuquerque was a huge Rajesh Khanna fan—to the extent that she came to Bombay from her native Ajmer with the express desire of meeting the superstar and marrying him. She said that she had fostered a bond with Rajesh—whom she called her 'heart-friend'—after watching *Baharon ke Sapne* when she was just fifteen years old. 'Only those who have been raised in small, uneventful towns know how important a heart-friend becomes. I would go each day on the terrace of my house and share everything with Rajesh (it was always Rajesh; I found "Kaka" a rather downmarket name)—problems, joys, quarrels with siblings, success in studies, even my desire to become a nun (which I felt he did not approve of).'[3]

As a result of this special bond, she watched *Aradhana* twenty-three times, *Aan Milo Sajna* twenty-one times, and *Kati Patang* four times. She finally decided that it was time to meet and marry her idol: 'I had no doubt he would look at me and immediately fall in love with me.'

After coming to Bombay, Ingrid completed a media course and kept on waiting for the day when she would come face to face with her heart-friend and talk her heart out. She joined a film magazine and finally got a chance to meet Rajesh Khanna and interview him. She went for the 'date' flushed with romantic anticipation. She wrote in an article: 'The first time I met Rajesh Khanna face to face was at Mehboob Studio when he was shooting for *Namak Haraam*, seated outside, under a large sun-umbrella . . . I introduced myself and said I wanted to interview him. "Okay, come," he said coolly, as he got up and walked into the studio. I followed him as he pushed open the door, went in and left it to shut in my face. Reality bites!'

***

Rounding up this phase of his career, film magazine *Star & Style* did a cover story later.[4] It carried the interviews of many famous personalities from the film industry along with the interview of the man himself. It threw some very interesting insights on how the people working with Rajesh perceived him. It was actually a story that showed the kind of person Rajesh Khanna had become. In this same story, talking about Rajesh Khanna, a famous actress remarked, 'All the actresses respect Manoj Kumar, fear Rajesh Khanna, love Randhir Kapoor and want to sleep with Dharmendra.'

Fear. This was the word people from the film industry had started to use to describe Khanna. In the same article, Randhir

Kapoor said, 'I am an open-minded person. I say things as they are. But my brother Chintu [Rishi Kapoor] hides everything inside himself. He doesn't let anyone know what he is thinking, or what he is planning next. I call him "Junior Rajesh Khanna".'[5] This seemingly incidental remark quite clearly indicates the way Rajesh's peers viewed him.

With such comments appearing about Khanna in print, he started becoming jittery and increasingly insecure. These negative reactions of people baffled him to no end. His cronies took advantage and fed him stories of conspiracy and camp formations. Ajit Ghosh, who handled the PR for Rajesh Khanna for many years, recalled to me, 'If he was told someone has criticized him, he would believe it and turn against that person without bothering to verify [the facts]. That was the reason he became isolated. He made more enemies than friends.'[6] Describing the storm raging inside him in those times, Rajesh Khanna himself accepted in an interview, 'Suddenly, too many enemies sprang up on the scene. They say success brings its own set of problems. I was facing my set of problems too.'

He tried to maintain his equanimity, but he had signed so many films that there was little time left to maintain the balance. He was of the opinion that his fans wanted to see him in more films, and hence he should work in as many movies as he could. Some senior film-makers close to him constantly advised him that this will soon lead to overexposure. But Rajesh Khanna never believed that his fans could ever get bored of him.

Though he was signing different films as far as the individual storylines were concerned, most of the movies belonged to the same romantic genre. As an actor, his USP was romantic roles. Senior film journalist and editor of the *Film Street Journal*, Bharathi S. Pradhan is among the few journalists who had interviewed Khanna many times. Describing his acting range she wrote, 'Khanna will be remembered for his charm and charisma, rather than his acting range. There was not much versatility there.'

Perhaps this was the reason that, despite many releases every year, his trademark mannerisms—of batting his eyes along with slight head-tilts and uttering his dialogues in the same sing-song manner—were consistent throughout. Although these gestures were starting to get repetitive, Khanna had so far adapted them well into the characters he was playing—whether it was the intense passion of *Amar Prem*, the happy-go-lucky *Anand*, the flamboyance in *Apna Desh*, the comic touch in *Bawarchi*, the suave criminal in *Sachaa Jhutha*, or the village bumpkin in *Bandhan*. But now the same charming trademark mannerisms had begun to overshadow his versatility as a serious actor.

***

In the middle of 1972 came the film *Dil Daulat Duniya*, which flopped miserably. This was Rajesh's first major flop after the superstardom that had started with *Aradhana* almost two years ago. But he regained some lost ground with a brilliant performance in Hrishikesh Mukherjee's *Bawarchi*. Though *Bawarchi* did average business at the box office, it received great reviews for Rajesh Khanna's comic talent.

But subsequent events were as dramatic as his magical rise. The fans who were all queuing up outside theatres all across the country to watch his films had suddenly decided to reject him. One after another, three of his films—*Shehzada, Joroo ka Ghulam* and *Mere Jeevan Saathi*—bit the dust. In fact, *Mere Jeevan Saathi*, with a brilliant soundtrack, seemed to hold extreme promise. Songs like 'O Mere Dil ke Chain', 'Chala Jaata Hoon',

'Deewana Leke Aaya Hai', etc. were huge chartbusters and had all the ingredients that had made Khanna the superstar that he was. But still, *Dil Daulat Duniya* crashed with a screenplay that was saturated with Rajesh Khanna.

Given his stature, these films were surprise disasters—something no one could comprehend at the time. Though it appeared sudden and abrupt, perhaps this was something that was waiting to happen. Fans were asking for something more from his performances, and when barraged with weak films and repetitive performances, their patience finally waned.

It was Ravikant Nagaich's *Mere Jeevan Saathi* that exposed the chinks in the superstar's armour. Khanna had been in a position where he could have been selective, but instead of choosing the right projects, he signed many films with weak plots and bad screenplays. He arrogantly believed that he could carry even a weak film on his own shoulders.

Rajesh Khanna himself never anticipated this. It was a rude shock that jolted him from his starry slumber. Destiny had suddenly decided to turn its back on him. Four flops in a row gave him a panic attack.

As for the media—which had already been contemplating and perhaps awaiting this fall—they sank their teeth into his plummeting string of flops. There were instant cover stories stating that the sun had set on the superstar's career. He was rejected outright as a two-year wonder whose luck had finally run out. While talking to the BBC reporter Jack Pizzey, Devyani Chaubal had said, 'He would tell the story of this one going down and that one going down, but he never thought of it happening to him.'[7]

Talking about the sudden string of flops, Rajesh Khanna said later in retrospect, 'My decline came about just as suddenly as my success. Out of the blue. And this was expected after the kind of insignificant films I had been signing left, right and centre. I was paying the price for not being able to refuse producers.'[8]

The last Rajesh Khanna film to be released in 1972 was *Maalik*. Vexed at the bad fate of his last four films, he assembled an entire team of publicists to create a marketing wave and salvage his stardom. Rajesh strongly believed that *Maalik* would stall the storm of failure, and so he put all his efforts into its publicity.

Maalik hit theatres during the festive season of Diwali at the end of 1972. It was an epic disaster.

CHAPTER 21

'My films might have flopped, I have not. I am still the Superstar.'

This was Rajesh Khanna's angry retort towards reports saying that his days of superstardom were over.

Not all respond the same way to acclaim. For some it's a birthright. Others withdraw into a carefully constructed shell. Very few actually introspect. Running from one day of success into another, there was little time for rumination for Rajesh Khanna—too little, perhaps, to recognize the thin line between a star's whims and a superstar's tantrums, and far too little to realize the overexposure he was subjecting his on-screen image to. As a cover story in *Star & Style* said, 'It is also true that hysteria, no matter how strong it is, or from where it originates . . . has a tendency to die down.'[1]

Film-maker Ramesh Talwar recalls that Khanna would get angry at such reports and always iterated that he was not a flop. He was vehement in his refusal. But, alas, everyone likes to see a great fall from the high chair of success. And after his many flops, the press was having a field day.

Such phases come about in every actor's life, but the superstar was just not ready to accept this. In reality, even those four flop films had not made a dent in his overall stardom and market value in the industry. They were simply bad films that had not worked. He was still the number-one star of Hindi cinema. But something of course had changed. The aura of being invincible, unbeatable was no longer there. The talisman of unceasing conquests was broken. He was like any other big star actor.

Rajesh Khanna was vulnerable, consumed all the time by the thought of his superstardom slipping away. Recalling those difficult days, Anju Mahendroo later said, 'Rajesh was becoming increasingly difficult to get along with. His flops had upset him mentally, and he was moody, temperamental, irritable. All the time he was so tense . . . almost a nervous wreck.'

He had never fully grasped his sudden success. And the sudden spate of flops was just as bewildering. The success had put him up on a pedestal. The flops lurked nearby with a sense of revenge—as if fate had been misguided for some time with his superstardom, and now the imbalance of his inordinate success was going to be rectified with failure. If this success was to be taken away, Rajesh stood to lose everything. Such situations can easily bring out the worst in a person. No wonder he was a 'nervous wreck'.

Anju recalled, 'Sometimes he was so petty-minded. In his insecurity, he often behaved like a baby . . . He made mountains out of molehills.' But these were different points of view. For Anju, what might have been molehills were bleak emotional mountains for Rajesh. He was looking for small gestures of love and support from Anju in these turbulent times. 'Did I need my woman just to make love to? Love is emotion, feeling, not just sex . . . I admit I was so shaken up by my flops that I wanted Anju by my side. I wanted her to understand me . . . to soothe me.

When I most needed her, she was never around,' Rajesh Khanna retorted in the same interview given to journalist Uma Rao in *Stardust* magazine.[2]

Anju said that she tried to console him. She tried to tell him that such ups and downs were a part of show business, but Rajesh Khanna was constantly frustrated. He was oversensitive to everything she said and did. 'The tension was too much for me,' she added. 'I too became edgy.'

Too many issues had wedged apart the growing gaps in Rajesh and Anju's relationship. Superstardom had granted Rajesh immeasurable power in the industry. With this great power he had acted with great irresponsibility. He had shown extreme arrogance in the treatment of everyone around him. He had never failed to impress upon everyone his superior position. Perhaps to protect herself from the same treatment—to ensure that the balance of power in their relationship wasn't swept away in the extreme wave of superstardom—Anju remained Rajesh's biggest critic. She maintained a relationship between equals. She saw him as the man she had always known him to be. She treaded where none dared. 'I was critical, because that's how I am. If he was bad I always said so. Why should I have praised him just to keep him happy? There were plenty around to boost his ego. He has always been sensitive to criticism and I've always been very frank.'

Perhaps the last thing Rajesh needed in such times was to be reprimanded for bad choices. He stubbornly refused to be criticized. When his father had passed away shortly after he achieved superstardom, Rajesh had few who could reprimand him. In fact, Anju bitterly recalled that Rajesh's mother was so scared of him that 'she didn't dare object to my presence in the house'.

And there were many things for Anju to be bitter about. Prashant Roy recalls, 'Chaaiji was traditional and used to complain that Anju doesn't take good care of her son.' On this issue Anju said she made an effort to get along. But his mother, being 'a typical, old-fashioned Punjabi woman', was very difficult to please. 'She didn't approve of me and I knew it,' Anju said. 'Do you know what it is to know that you are disliked?'

Anju had almost let Rajesh systematically destroy her chances of a film career. She found an alternative life as a socialite. She refused to be only a trophy girlfriend and 'wait, wait, wait for him'. She refused to shower him with praise or overtly express her love in public. But the more she didn't, the more Rajesh wanted it. He was hungry for her praise, her approval. He held her in high regard. Being a smart and independent woman, unlike those in traditional set-ups, Anju had made a strong impression on Rajesh's mind from the start. He once said, 'I've always run back to Anju whatever our differences. It was always me ringing up or going to her to apologize and patch up.' But now he had the world at his feet. Perhaps he wanted her there too. 'How good it would make me feel if once in a way Anju had come to my side on her own . . . instead of sitting with her mother, and watching and waiting for me to go to her.'

Yes, superstardom had not tilted the balance of power in this relationship at least.

He became obsessed with ensuring her complete obeisance. 'The world was after me and I was after her.' He kept track of her movements and wanted her beside him every day. Only absolute obeisance would do. As his films flopped this hunger for hero worship perhaps deepened. An unattainable Anju unsettled him. 'I was a bloody fool . . . I had stooped so low for my woman that I fell in my own eyes.'[3] Feelings of destroyed self-esteem arose. As a 'nervous wreck' he must have wanted to feel in control and powerful again. But as he had never been able to shift the balance of power in this relationship, he decided to take control—and end the relationship itself.

The interviews of Rajesh Khanna were mostly very dramatic, like the dialogues in his movies. He described his failing relationship with Anju like a theatrical scene. In his interview to Bunny Reuben, he said dramatically, 'A love affair always breaks inside the heart first. I trace the break between Anju and myself to one fateful night when I was down in the dumps. Things had been going badly for me. There was this party which she had promised we'd attend. Everyone had to bring one dish along. Anju had given instructions for *dal gosht* to be prepared.'[4] Rajesh had started drinking early that evening and didn't want to go to the party. He asked Anju to skip the party, but things didn't turn out well. 'She [Anju] cared two hoots about my need. Taking the food, she breezed off to the party. I saw her go out of my house intent on the fine time she was to have at that party. I think it was at that moment that my love walked out on her, too.'

***

Around the same time an organization from Gujarat called Chitralok Cine Circle organized a function to felicitate Hindi film artists in November 1972. The venue was in Ahmedabad. Rajesh Khanna was to receive an award. A chartered plane was hired from Bombay to Ahmedabad to ferry Rajesh Khanna and many personalities from the film industry. Dimple Kapadia, the heroine of the still-in-production *Bobby*, was also on the plane.

Rajesh said, 'I knew Dimple since she was a little kid, but I hadn't set eyes on her for years. Then one day at a party I saw this girl, tall and gawky, a teenager with an arresting beauty and grace. She was sitting among a bunch of women and as she got up her glance at me flashed fire in my heart. I did not consciously realize it then that all the love-chapters of the past closed tightly shut, never to reopen. A few moments later I learned that she was the same Kapadia kid I'd known years ago.'

On the return flight, the seat next to Dimple was vacant. Rajesh asked her, 'May I take the seat?'

Dimple answered with a shy smile, 'Sure, sir.'

Throughout the duration of the flight, both were immersed in a deep conversation—some words spoken, many others exchanged in glances. He found her company invigorating.

The biggest superstar of India, thousands of miles high up in the skies, was looking into Dimple's eyes, and he saw in them the adulation he hungered for so deeply. This was indeed a dream flight for the new girl in the industry.

On reaching Bombay, Dimple tried to reconnect with the superstar. But those days Rajesh Khanna was busy shooting for many films simultaneously. He returned home very late every day. In his absence it was Prashant Roy's responsibility at Aashirwad to attend to phone calls and write the details in a notebook. In the evening he used to report all the calls to Rajesh Khanna. Prashant vividly remembers, 'Kakaji's number used to be 531117, and every minute there was a phone call. One morning a girl called and asked about Kakaji. I asked her name. She said, "My name is Dimple." I told her Kakaji was on a shoot and would be back in the evening. For the next three to four days she kept on calling continuously. She used to talk to me with great respect, calling me Prashant Sahib. One evening I told Kakaji that a girl called Dimple calls up all the time asking about him. Kakaji smiled and said . . . "Yes, yes . . . She is *Bobby*'s heroine. Attend to her calls properly."'

A few days later Chunnibhai Kapadia visited Aashirwad, a girl in tow. Seeing Prashant he said, 'Prashant, meet my daughter Dimple.'

Looking at the men, Dimple started laughing and said, 'Prashant Sahib, do you recognize me? I've spoken with you so many times.'

Prashant smiled in returned and welcomed the guests inside. This was the first time Dimple entered Aashirwad.

***

The superstar and the new girl started meeting regularly. The news couldn't stay away from print too long and gossip magazines started writing about their possible affair. Rajesh and Anju had not yet broken up and were still holding on to their seven-year-old relationship. Old bonds are difficult to break. But distrust had crept in deep. A very thin thread was keeping this relationship from being torn apart. And that thread was about to snap soon.

It was on Rajesh Khanna's birthday in December 1972, when a party had been planned at Aashirwad. As usual, the affair had been organized under Anju's supervision. She had to send out the guest invitations too. According to an interview of Rajesh Khanna, Anju invited all the people they knew except Chunnibhai and his daughter.

When Rajesh realized this, he was very angry and immediately called up Chunnibhai to invite him and Dimple for the occasion. When Dimple reached Aashirwad, Anju was receiving the guests. Recalling that event in an interview later, Anju said, 'Dimple stood at the door and with exaggerated sarcasm, said to me, "Can I come in?" She was just trying to bug me. So I said simply, "If you've been invited, come in. If you haven't, then leave."'

Naturally, Anju was dreadfully resentful of Dimple due to the strong rumours of an alleged affair between her and Rajesh. She said, 'Dimple is a clever little girl. When Rajesh and I met her for the first time, then we were Rajesh "uncle" and Anju "aunty" to her. She was nice then. In recent times I noticed a change in her. She was always saying things which appeared innocent, but were very calculatedly catty and aimed at me.'[5]

By this time both Rajesh Khanna and Anju Mahendroo had finally realized that they could not be together in the long run. Their relationship had run its course. As put by the superstar, 'Can you put toothpaste back into the tube? Can you repair a broken eggshell? Or restore virginity to one who has known sex? No. Nor can you resurrect love when once it is dead.'[6]

The time had come to make a final decision.

CHAPTER 22

Rajesh Khanna took Dimple, her family and some of his close friends to Khandala. He told no one about this trip, not even Anju. Prashant tells me that Rajesh had actually planned a party with Dimple and he wanted to keep it very private. The subsequent events had all the ingredients of a Bollywood potboiler.

The events of that fateful day are still fresh in Prashant's mind. Recalling the incident, Prashant told me, 'Kakaji had organized the function in Khandala. In those days, there used to be a popular hotel called El-Taj—that was the planned venue. Dimple, Chunnibhai and some very close friends were to stay there for a day. But Anju got some inkling that this had been planned.'

Anju had become very suspicious. She reached Aashirwad with her mother and asked Prashant about Rajesh's whereabouts. Prashant replied that he had no clue. Suspecting that something was amiss, Anju quickly left. Right after that, Rajesh's uncle K.K. Talwar reached Aashirwad. Prashant immediately told him about Anju. Talwar started thinking. Prashant could feel the tension in the air around them. 'Then Anju memsaab called

again. She said, "Prashant, please keep the Capricorn car ready."
I asked the driver Kabir to do the needful. After some time Anju
memsaab came back and left for Khandala in a hurry.'

This new development made K.K. Talwar and Prashant
anxious. Talwar, who knew everything about Rajesh's plans,
worried that if Anju reached Khandala, she might create a scene.
He asked Prashant to somehow alert Kaka in Khandala. In those
days there were no mobile phones. So it took Prashant some time
to find the phone number for El-Taj. But fearing that some crazy
fan was calling, the manager refused to divulge Khanna's presence
at their hotel. Prashant had to eventually make up a story about
Rajesh's mother being terminally ill for the manager to seek out
Kaka and bring him to the phone. Finally, Rajesh came to the
phone and was told that Anju would be reaching Khandala in
an hour.

The preparations for the party were in full swing. But within
the next hour, everything was halted and hurriedly shifted to
another place. It is said that Anju could not find Rajesh Khanna
that evening. Prashant says, 'Everyone disappeared from that
hotel. Anju memsaab came back to Aashirwad very angry. She
asked me if I had informed Kaka. I said I didn't know what she
was talking about. Then she left. Late that evening, Kakaji came
back very happy . . . K.K. Talwar and I told him about Anjuji
and whatever transpired during the day. Looking at me, Kakaji
said, "Well done, Prashant!"'

Then Rajesh thought deeply for a minute before asking
his uncle a peculiar question. Prashant says that only he and
K.K. Talwar were present when Rajesh Khanna surprisingly said to
Talwar, *Hunn tussi decide karo . . . Dimple ya Anju? Main bathroom
jakar aata hoon.'* [Now you decide . . . Dimple or Anju? I will
just be back from the bathroom.] After he left the room, Talwar
and Prashant looked at each other in astonishment. 'Then, in a
moment, we said together . . . "Dimple!"' According to Prashant,

it was obvious that Rajesh Khanna had already made up his mind to marry Dimple.

Talking about his break-up with Anju, Rajesh Khanna later said that he intended to finish the relationship amicably. 'But when I was coming back from Khandala, I met my driver who told me that Memsaab had asked him to give me a message that I shouldn't ring her up and that if I stepped through her gates, she would ask the gurkha to throw me out! She had sent all my belongings back through him. Imagine, through my SERVANT! A servant had to tell me these things! It was the biggest insult to my dignity. I decided not to go to her . . . What was the point?'[1]

Years later, Khanna blamed his success for him having parted ways with Mahendroo. Distances grew both socially and emotionally between them. 'Looking back I feel it was nobody's fault. None of us had anticipated this kind of success to happen to me. Neither of us knew how to handle it. My success brought a lot of mixed emotions and, successively, a lot of changes. All this was very disturbing. Ideally, we should have sat down and sorted out our confusion. We didn't.'[2]

***

After breaking up with Anju, Rajesh did not wait much longer. At midnight, on a walk with Dimple near a beach in Juhu, he proposed to her. Perhaps even Dimple too had no idea that the superstar would propose so soon. Also, the rumours of Dimple's alleged affair with Rishi Kapoor were still very strong. It is said that he had even gifted her a ring. Senior film journalist Bharathi S. Pradhan says, 'During the making of *Bobby* Rishi Kapoor and Dimple were dating each other. Rajesh Khanna made a dramatic midnight proposal to her. He'd taken the fifteen-year-old star-struck Dimple for a walk by the Juhu sea and had flung

Rishi Kapoor's ring (yes, she wore his ring on her finger) into the moonlit waters.' The dream man of millions of girls wished to marry Dimple. With her feet hardly on the ground, she said yes.

Rajesh Khanna had to go out of town for a shoot, so it was decided that they would marry in the coming week. 'Everything happened in such hurry,' says Prashant, 'that there was no time to even send invitation cards to everyone. These kinds of marriages happen rarely. Initially, the guests were invited by telegrams. The message in the telegrams said: "Rajesh and Dimple getting married. Please do come." And the name of the venue was also written.'

***

The news of the superstar's marriage had shocked the film industry. This was so sudden that there was little time for a reaction. It was a hurried decision and a hurried marriage. As always, Rajesh Khanna personified his spontaneous streak. In kitty parties and colleges, on film sets and in film magazines, this was the only topic of discussion—with most people sympathizing with Rishi Kapoor, whom they thought was in love with the superstar's bride-to-be.

Remembering those days, senior film journalist Mohan Bawa wrote in one of his articles for the film magazine *Super*, 'I knew, of course, before everybody else, that Chintu Kapoor was madly in love with Dimple Kapadia. In fact, the first story I did on them for *JS* had Dimple Kapadia talking madly, ecstatically about Chintu, and Chintu talking madly, ecstatically about Dimple. If you read between the lines, of course, the answer was love-love-love.'[3]

Mohan Bawa further wrote that Rishi Kapoor seemed quite shaken by the news of the Kaka–Dimple engagement and impending wedding. 'I met him in the Oberoi-Sheraton a few days after the announcement. He dragged me down to the coffee shop for a cuppa. We talked about Dimple and you could see he was upset. But Chintu was trying to be very, very brave. When I asked him the inevitable question he said, "Oh, who cares. Kaka can have her if he wants."' Bawa was nevertheless compelled to add that 'there was a tear on the brim' of Rishi Kapoor's eyes as he spoke.[4]

CHAPTER 23

And so it came to pass that Rajesh Khanna and Dimple Kapadia tied the knot on the evening of 27 March 1973 in Bombay, amidst a star-studded gathering at the Kapadia residence, while a tremendous amount of whispered gossip was brewing all around them. The unexpected and spiteful twist to the superstar's wedding day—when he led his baraat past Anju Mahendroo's house—only fuelled the frenzy.

It seems that, as his films began to flop, his hunger to hold on to the hero worship had perhaps deepened. Flop films meant an unravelling of the superstar image. And to protect this image in his own mind, he perhaps married a young star-struck fan, someone who loved and validated his own screen image. The hurriedness and secrecy surrounding the engagement and subsequent marriage show that it was not just a simple case of a rebound. Rather, it was rooted in anger at Anju for having stood as a mirror to his real self. Perhaps he also wanted to teach Anju a lesson by 'clinching' a devoted naive girl who saw him only through rose-tinted glasses. He loved the importance that the media and fans showered on his wedding. It resurrected his 'loved by all' image that confirmed the idea that a few flopped films hadn't broken the superstar.

In fact, many people close to Rajesh were of the opinion that he took this step to exact revenge on Anju. However, if one endeavours to read between the lines, the superstar's wounded core is revealed. A streak of passion marked his stubbornness, much like his character in the film *Aap ki Kasam*. While he wanted to control and dictate his relationships, he ended up suffocating and smothering the people he was closest to. Throughout his life, he repeatedly tried to tie the loose fibres of his many close associations but all to no avail.

***

Raj Kapoor arrived at the wedding to bless his 'Bobby', who had decided to get married without even completing his film. Dilip Kumar was also present, as well as producer J. Omprakash, director Shakti Samanta and some friends from his theatre days.

After the wedding, a cocktail party had been organized for close friends, film stars and friends from the media. Rishi Kapoor also came to this party. Senior film journalist Mohan Bawa, who was also present, later wrote about that evening: 'And then a very ironical thing happened. On the wedding day, on the day when the whole world went mad, the three of us—Chintu, Dimple and I—met for a brief moment at the after-the-marriage cocktail party which was given exclusively for the stars. The looks that were exchanged, the smiles that were tossed, told a million words in a heartbreakingly untold story.'[1]

By all accounts, even Dimple's family wasn't completely prepared for the sudden marriage. Her father was happy that he was getting a superstar son-in-law, but her mother, Bitti Kapadia, was upset about the age difference between the bride and groom.

According to Bharathi S. Pradhan, 'At Dimple's wedding, her mother, Bitti Kapadia, wept that her daughter was marrying a man who was closer to her mom's age than to her own.'[2]

In the midst of such diverse reactions on her wedding day, Dimple entered Aashirwad as the Superstar's bride.

***

Film journalist Uma Rao of *Stardust* interviewed Rajesh and Anju a few days after the superstar's wedding.

Rajesh would have been fully aware that the gossip columns were calling his marriage a publicity stunt, while casting Anju as the victim of his starry tantrums. So he decided to clean up the whole mess about Nikki and gave Uma Rao his version of their relationship.

'I'm happy, very, very happy,' he said, smiling. 'All my tension's gone. I'm so totally relaxed . . . and at peace at last.' He had reason to be pleased. Dimple was a completely devoted wife. She made him a home.

In her article, 'What really happened between Rajesh and Anju', Uma Rao describes the post-wedding glow on Rajesh's face as well as the fact that Anju was putting up a brave front. Both the estranged souls indulge in rash mud-slinging and, like teenagers, cry foul at the other's actions. Anju admits that their relationship was on its last legs and the break-up wasn't a surprise, while Rajesh admits that his decision to marry Dimple was an overnight one. On this matter, Anju says that Rajesh should have had the decency to tell her that he wished to marry another girl, rather than leaving their seven-year-long relationship without closure.

But Anju wasn't the only relationship Rajesh left shockingly midway. While his marriage ended his relationship with Anju, this post-marriage *Stardust* interview supposedly soured another relationship—his friendship with Devyani Chaubal.

As mentioned in the story rerun in 'The Best of Stardust' collection, 'There was a stage when Rajesh feared the wrath of his favourite columnist-cum-keeper-of-his-secrets, more than the wrath of Anju, Dimple or God. As per her instructions, he dutifully refused all interviews and reserved his scoops for her and her alone.' According to Devyani, she was the first person to know about Rajesh's decision to marry Dimple. She said in a documentary by BBC reporter Jack Pizzey that a highly drunk Rajesh called her up at 3 a.m. to tell her he had proposed to Dimple—because he had promised to tell her first. She had even played the important role of tying his *safa* (headgear) at the wedding.

But 'in a rash moment' Rajesh gave *Stardust* his most coveted post-marriage interview and the complete story on the ending of his relationship with Anju. 'Not only had he lost face, but he'd also lost his lady columnist friend. She never did forgive him for cheating her out of a scoop and giving us a story,' said *Stardust*. Devyani, when asked about it, replied at the time, 'I no longer see him. He is too much a victim of his own image.'

Thus the two women who had stood by him through his rise and fall—Anju and Devyani—were sidelined in the wake of his sudden spate of flops and subsequent marriage.

Interestingly, when the *Stardust* interview came out, Devyani was not the only person who felt cheated. According to Uma Rao, Rajesh 'hit the ceiling' when he saw the interview. It took several hours for Rao to learn that Rajesh's '*real*' grouse' was the photo on the cover: it was of Anju. An article in *Stardust* captures Rajesh's stormy reaction: 'Dammit!' he hollered. 'It was MY story and you put HER on the cover!'

Even while talking about the past he sought to play the wronged hero—always a hero.

***

It has always been insinuated that by the end of 1972, the stardom of Rajesh Khanna had come to an end. This is completely false. For the first time after becoming the superstar, some of his films were unsuccessful. But this was not as big an issue as it was made out to be in the cover stories of the film media. The press, fearful of Rajesh for so long, had been waiting for him to stumble, and now seized the chance to lash out at him. Perhaps this can be explained as the tall poppy syndrome wherein he was now being criticized and attacked, particularly because his unprecedented success had elevated him to a much higher pedestal as compared to others.

The truth is that some of these flops actually did good business and recovered their costs. But when compared to his blockbusters, they were mere whimpers. J. Omprakash told me, 'Just a few films flopped. It doesn't mean he was out of the industry. In fact he signed many big banner films during the same phase. We in the film business know that destinies change every Friday. It was just a matter of time and we knew he would be back with a bang.'

Rajesh admitted that he lost perspective at the peak of his extraordinary success. His fans also wanted some freshness from their superstar. Perhaps this was the reason that his next release *Raja Rani* also bit the dust. He himself accepted later that he was repeating himself: 'Directors would insist *"Usi tarah aankhen jhapko jaise Aradhana mein kiya tha."* [Blink in exactly the same way as you did in Aradhana.] The overuse of my mannerisms have finally gone against me.'

About a month and a half after the news-making wedding, an important film hit the Indian theatres. In an era of romantic films, came an action-packed revenge drama. The film was called *Zanjeer*. Its hero was Amitabh Bachchan, who had played second fiddle to Rajesh in *Anand*, and the story was written by Salim–Javed, who were Rajesh's favourite scriptwriter duo.

The superstar Rajesh Khanna.
Photograph courtesy: Jagdish Aurangabadkar and the late Shyam Aurangabadkar.

Rajesh Khanna with Anju Mahendroo in *Bandhan*.
Photograph courtesy: Jagdish Aurangabadkar and the late Shyam Aurangabadkar.

From left to right: Hrishikesh Mukherjee, Rajesh Khanna
and Amitabh Bachchan during the making of *Namak Haraam*.
Photograph courtesy: Jagdish Aurangabadkar and the late Shyam Aurangabadkar.

Kaka, the emperor of Bollywood.
Photograph courtesy: Jagdish Aurangabadkar and the late Shyam Aurangabadkar.

Rajesh Khanna and Sharmila Tagore playing cards.
Photograph courtesy: Jagdish Aurangabadkar and the late Shyam Aurangabadkar.

Once upon a time: Anju Mahendroo feeds the birthday boy some cake, December 1971.
Photograph courtesy: Jagdish Aurangabadkar and the late Shyam Aurangabadkar.

Rajesh Khanna's birthday celebration at Aashirwad, December 1974.
Photograph courtesy: Jagdish Aurangabadkar and the late Shyam Aurangabadkar.

From left to right: Sharmila Tagore, Shakti Samanta
and Rajesh Khanna during the making of *Aradhana*.
Photograph courtesy: Jagdish Aurangabadkar and the late Shyam Aurangabadkar.

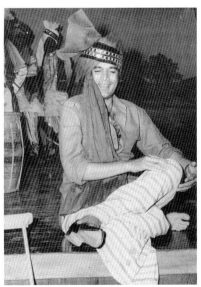

Rajesh Khanna on the sets of *Aakraman*.
Photograph courtesy: Jagdish Aurangabadkar and the late Shyam Aurangabadkar.

Dimple Kapadia weds Rajesh Khanna.
Photograph courtesy: Jagdish Aurangabadkar and the late Shyam Aurangabadkar.

From left to right: Dimple Kapadia, Rajesh Khanna, Raj Kapoor,
Dilip Kumar and Saira Banu at the superstar's wedding.
Photograph courtesy: Jagdish Aurangabadkar and the late Shyam Aurangabadkar.

The superstar signing autographs. Photograph courtesy: *Super*.

Scribe wars: Extract from an article about Salim Khan,
Javed Akhtar and Devyani Chaubal. Photograph courtesy: *Super*.

Anju Mahendroo. Photograph courtesy: *Super*.

Tina Munim.
Photograph courtesy: *Super*.

Dimple Kapadia.
Photograph courtesy: *Super*.

FILM MONTHLY SEPT. 78 Rs. 3.50

Super

THE NEW
DIMPLE

ZEENAT: IT
A CURSE TO
A SINGLE GI

MYSTERY BEHIN
OD'S DECISIC
TO QUIT FILM

Super
blow-up of
ANJU
MAHENDRI

Dimple Kapadia and young Twinkle Khanna on the cover of *Super*,
September 1978. Photograph courtesy: *Super*.

Dimple's parents, Chunnibhai and Bitti Kapadia.
Photograph courtesy: *Super*.

Tina Munim and Rajesh Khanna. Photograph courtesy: *Super*.

Rajesh Khanna's childhood home in Amritsar.

Rajesh Khanna's childhood home in Girgaum.

Aashirwad, Rajesh Khanna's Bombay home.

On the campaign trail: Rajesh Khanna addressing a rally in New Delhi.
Photograph courtesy: Press Trust of India.

From left to right: Rajesh Khanna with Harsh Raseen and
Akshay Kumar. Photograph courtesy: Bhupesh Raseen.

Rajesh Khanna at a family puja in Aashirwad with (from left to right) son-in-law Akshay
Kumar, grandson Aarav and Bhupesh Raseen. Photograph courtesy: Bhupesh Raseen.

From left to right: Bhupesh Raseen, Rajesh Khanna, Dimple Kapadia and Rinke Khanna holidaying in Goa on the superstar's birthday in December 2011—his last birthday. Photograph courtesy: Bhupesh Raseen.

Rajesh Khanna's final public appearance, with Akshay Kumar and Dimple Kapadia, from the balcony of Aashirwad. Photograph courtesy: Press Trust of India.

The superstar with his wall of trophies. Photograph courtesy: *Super*.

The film was an astounding success, and it gave India a new icon: the Angry Young Man. This character didn't take the youth on a rosy romantic journey, but fought back against the injustices in society. It broke away from convention and finally breathed freshness into the movies—something that the country had been calling out for.

CHAPTER 24

It is an unsaid rule in Hindi cinema that star actors should keep their marriages a secret to maintain their public appeal. It is often conjectured that a married actor offers less of a romantic fantasy to the eager fan than a young and 'available' actor. Perhaps this was the reason that many married actors in the 1960s were almost never photographed with their wives. In their interviews they would provide ample fodder for gossip through quotes on their co-stars and alleged affairs, but the wives were kept at a distance. Big stars like Ashok Kumar, Dev Anand, Raj Kapoor, Dharmendra and Rajendra Kumar are a few examples of actors who maintained this unsaid rule and reigned. With time, this trend has changed, and today's top actors talk openly about their marriages and relationships. But in the 1960s and 1970s, it was felt that the private lives of stars warranted a certain amount of secrecy.

Rajesh Khanna's marriage brought a lot of anxiety to the film industry, especially to those who had their money riding on him. Firstly, Rajesh Khanna's films were already going through a lean phase and now his sudden marriage to a nubile teenager had upset his female fans across the country. In just five months, Dimple had succeeded—where no one could—in bringing Rajesh to the marriage altar. Dimple became the target of the collective jealousy of all of Rajesh Khanna's fans. Hrishikesh Mukherjee used to laughingly narrate this anecdote to describe this anger. According to him, a female fan got so enraged by the marriage that she got herself a puppy and named her Dimple. She used to beat the dog every day. When it became unbearable for the neighbours to tolerate the howling and crying of the dog, action had to be taken and the dog was rescued.

Everyone believed that the marriage had cracked Rajesh's romantic image and would further exacerbate the bad business his films were doing. Film distributors feared the fate of his next release, *Daag*.

Daag was the first film under the now-legendary Yash Raj Films banner. It was founded by Yash Chopra, who had directed Rajesh in his first successful film, *Ittefaq*. Yash had been working with his elder brother and film-maker B.R. Chopra for his prestigious banner B.R. Films. But now, as Yash Chopra set up his own company, he found it really hard to meet the fund requirements. Yash met Rajesh and offered him the lead role in his first film—without the signing amount. Film-maker Ramesh Talwar, who had worked with Yash Chopra as his chief assistant director, told me that not only did Rajesh Khanna instantly agree to do his film, but he even offered to take his payment only when Yash Chopra acquired a financer for his movie. It was implied in film magazines that Yash Chopra was so indebted to Rajesh for his friendship and largesse at this crucial point that he named his company Yash Raj Films: named after Yash and Raj(esh). However, no such official statement has ever surfaced from either side.

Ramesh recalls that Rajesh Khanna cooperated completely during the making of *Daag*, and eventually a financer came in to

back the film which had the superstar in the lead role. And so the
first movie of Yash Raj Films was ready for release.

Daag was inspired by an English film *Sunflower* that itself
was based on Thomas Hardy's novel *The Mayor of Casterbridge*.
But to adapt the story to Indian sensibilities Yash Chopra got
the famous writer Gulshan Nanda to script the film. This was
a brave film that challenged societal norms and its view of love
and relationships. The theme was deftly handled by director
Yash Chopra. Rajesh Khanna gave a restrained performance
aptly suited for his character in the film. The film had a slow
start, but in a week Rajesh Khanna fans were back, thronging
the theatres.

The film was a success.

The depth of love, its confusion and the societal pressures on
relationships were all captured beautifully in the very popular
songs written by the lyricist-poet Sahir Ludhianvi. *Daag* had very
popular songs like 'Mere Dil Mei Aaj Kya Hai', 'Hum aur Tum'
and 'Jab Bhi Ji Chahe Nai Duniya Basa Lete Hain Log', along
with the experimental 'Ni Mai Yaar Manana' that was a rebellious
announcement of love defying the rules of society, sung from a
female perspective.

It was Sahir's speciality that he expressed deep philosophical
thoughts within the confines of mainstream Hindi film lyrics.
Sahir also wrote poetry for a crucial scene of *Daag* that was
picturized on Rajesh Khanna: 'Yeh Bhi Ek Daur Hai, Wo Bhi Ek
Daur Tha . . .' [This is one era, and that was another . . .]

***

But love wasn't only blossoming in the movies. Dimple had
brought love back into Rajesh's life and possibly also success and
happiness. Marriage and subsequently a much-needed hit film
brought back the golden days in Aashirwad.

Sixteen-year-old Dimple was not the usual teenager—she was the King's wife. Her childlike vivaciousness and exuberance made the days in Aashirwad fun-filled for all living there. Recalling those days Prashant told me, 'Kakaji was extremely busy shooting in those days. Dimpleji was very naughty and childlike. She would play and gossip with all of us. There was no ego in Chunnibhai's daughter. Looking at her you could never gauge that she was the Superstar's wife or the heroine of Raj Kapoor's film.' Even Chaaiji used to like Dimple a lot. Dimple's devotion to Kaka made Chaaiji feel that she takes good care of her son.'

Prashant remembers, 'We were all very happy. Once Rajesh Khanna gifted me a Lambretta scooter. When he left for shooting, Dimple came smiling and said in jest, "Teach me how to drive a scooter otherwise I will complain to Kakaji that you don't listen to me." Then she made me ride pillion as she rode out of Aashirwad on to the main road. Those were glorious days in Aashirwad.' The memories bring tears to the eyes of the now ageing Prashant.

***

Dimple rejected all film offers that were coming her way and concentrated on quickly finishing the already halfway-completed *Bobby*. She also put all her energies into playing the dutiful wife to the superstar. They often used to appear at filmy parties, where they invariably became the cynosure of all eyes. They were the hottest couple in showbiz. In the afterglow of a news-making marriage, a successful film and with the return of clamouring fans, producers and the media, Rajesh Khanna looked every bit the charismatic superstar. Dimple, on the other hand, too naive and young, used to look like someone adapting to her new surroundings. A journalist of those times told me, 'When she used to smile, it appeared as if an instant weight of name and stature has come on her shoulders. But gradually she became confident and it was clear that she was adapting to her new life very well.'

Every little bit of news related to the most popular couple of the film industry inevitably found its way to the gossip columns of the film and lifestyle magazines. Film magazine *Stardust*'s column 'Neeta's Natter', *Star & Style*'s 'Frankly Speaking' or *Super* magazine's 'Grapewine'—all talked about the star couple. In less than a year Anju had been completely replaced. People talked about the older, wiser woman being displaced by a much younger and naive child. But, Anju in her *Stardust* interview gave an interesting quote: 'People call him [Rajesh] a cradle-snatcher for having married a kid. But I think she [Dimple] is the cradle-snatcher who's bagged a baby! Dimple is much more mature than Rajesh . . .'

Was this prophetic of the times to come?

PART IV

1973–90

Aaj main hoon jahaan kal koi aur tha
Yeh bhi ek daur hai, woh bhi ek daur tha

(Song from *Daag*, 1973)

Question: What are you frightened of?
RK: Of being Amitabh Bachchan.

CHAPTER 25

In 1973, while north India was rocked by angry demonstrations protesting against high inflation, Bombay was undergoing rapid urbanization—large areas of land were being used to build flats and residential cooperatives for the rapidly expanding middle class. As more and more people headed for metropolitan cities, problems concerning labour acquired immense magnitude. This led to the passage of the MRTP Act, 1969, and the Contract Labour (Regulation and Abolition) Act, 1970. Into this simmering background—of large-scale uprisings, lockouts and strikes declared by various trade unions and political outfits all over the country—came Hrishikesh Mukherjee's *Namak Haraam* towards the end of 1973.

Namak Haraam was an adaptation of the 1964 Hollywood classic *Becket*. Concept-wise the film had a strong theme depicting how the tussle between capitalism and socialism cruelly destroys human relationships and morality. This issue was brilliantly packaged within the format of mainstream Hindi cinema and deeply resonated with the prevailing societal issues seen in India at that time.

Becket had heavyweight actors like Richard Burton and Peter O'Toole. For the same roles in *Namak Haraam* director Hrishikesh Mukherjee brought back his *Anand* actors Rajesh Khanna and Amitabh Bachchan. Amitabh had received great reviews for his intense role in *Anand*, and with some forthcoming important films in his kitty the industry heavyweights were taking keen notice of him. All this only intensified the rivalry that had begun at a time when Rajesh Khanna was a much bigger star than Amitabh Bachchan. And everyone was keen to see how this development would now play out.

The film was a story of two close friends: the soft, inhibited, poor Somu (Rajesh Khanna) and the loud, gregarious, super-rich heir of an industrialist Vikram or Vicky (Amitabh Bachchan). After a confrontation with the trade union leader of his mill, Vicky is made to apologize. He takes this as an insult to his big ego. To avenge the insult of his close friend, Somu joins the mill as a common worker. But Somu undergoes a change of conscience after seeing the lives of the mill workers at close quarters. Vikram's father exposes him as a management stooge and Somu is killed. In a surprise twist to the climax, Vikram takes the blame for Somu's death and is jailed.

This time the two actors had their roles switched, temperament-wise. 'I cast Rajesh Khanna and Amitabh again, but this time in reversed roles. I wanted Amitabh to play the extrovert, while Kaka an introvert,' said Hrishikesh Mukherjee.

News related to the climax of *Namak Haraam* appeared in almost every film magazine of that time. Hrishikesh Mukherjee revealed in an interview that during the entire shooting of *Namak Haraam* both the actors had no clue about the climax. If anyone knew about the climax, it was the film's co-writer and dialogue writer, Gulzar. Hrishikesh wanted to keep the climax a secret for both the actors. According to the original climax of the film, as a departure from the *Becket* storyline, Amitabh's character had to die. When Rajesh Khanna got to know about this he was not happy. Everyone knew about the Rajesh Khanna's obsession with dying characters. He believed that his most memorable films are indeed those where he dies at the end of the story. In *Namak Haraam* too he wanted the death scene at any cost.

Rajesh Khanna became adamant and told Hrishikesh that being the bigger star, he should get the death scene. In fact, it was widely reported that to convince Hrishikesh Mukherjee he even went to the extent of putting a garland of flowers on his own picture. This was the final signal for Hrishikesh Mukherjee that the death scene would go to the hero of the film, Rajesh Khanna. Talking about *Namak Haraam* Gulzar said, 'In *Namak Haraam* we had to change the end because Hrishida had promised Rajesh Khanna the death scene.'[1]

Amitabh Bachchan was extremely upset with this decision. The script was changed on the insistence of Rajesh Khanna and this was hidden from Amitabh till the day of the shooting. He was terribly disappointed at the 'betrayal' of the director. Hrishikesh Mukherjee said in an interview, 'In Hindi films, the one who dies is considered a hero, so both were keen on being heroic. It was only on the day of the shooting that Amitabh finally learnt the truth. He was crestfallen! He was so hurt that he didn't speak to me for several days. He felt I had betrayed him.'

The issue apparently created such a rift between Amitabh and Rajesh Khanna that they never worked together again after this film. As a witness to a number of parties in Aashirwad for many years, Prashant Roy recalls a different version of the story. Prashant told me, 'Those days Kakaji used be very angry with Amitabh Bachchan. He used to tell his close friends that

Hrishikesh Mukherjee is his favourite director, but Amitabh has filled his ears. Kakaji used to say that during the entire shooting of *Namak Haraam*, Amitabh played dirty politics with him. During my twenty years working with Kakaji, I never saw Amitabh coming to Aashirwad. Earlier Hrishikesh Mukherjee used to come quite often, but after *Namak Haraam*, even his visits were rare.'

This issue was highlighted even by Susmita Dasgupta, who did her doctorate on Amitabh Bachchan. She happened to meet Rajesh Khanna in Delhi. On the basis of their conversation, Susmita wrote, 'Rajesh Khanna used to believe that Amitabh Bachchan played dirty politics against him, especially by antagonizing Hrishikesh Mukherjee against him.'[2] However, it must be said that Amitabh Bachchan has never ever said a word against Rajesh Khanna on record either about *Namak Haraam* or any other problem. Even after Rajesh Khanna's death, whatever he said to the media or wrote on his blog was in absolute praise of Rajesh Khanna and his incredible superstardom.

***

Namak Haraam released towards the end of November 1973. The reviews of the film lauded Rajesh Khanna's controlled performance, praising him for not using his much-used mannerisms in this serious role. He was absolutely brilliant as a man undergoing a rapid change in conscience while being torn between his love for his friend and duty towards his fellow mill-workers. But the surprise element of the film was Amitabh Bachchan. The anger and intensity that he showed in *Zanjeer* was now impressively taken a few notches higher in *Namak Haraam*. The film reveals a glimpse of the mega-star that Bachchan was to become in later years.

Both the actors were brilliant in their individual performances and even to the keener eye it was difficult to tell who was better. But as the loud and gregarious Vicky, Amitabh's character, had a more lasting impression on audiences. According to film journalist and author Rauf Ahmed, 'The first time I watched *Namak Haraam*, I was more impressed with Bachchan, because he had an author-backed roles with dialogues, the whole taking-the-law-into-his-own-hands persona. But when I watched it the second time I realized that Rajesh Khanna was brilliant. He underplayed his role, a very difficult one, throughout the film. To me it was one of his finest performances . . .'

Eventually, the death scene that Rajesh Khanna had fought so hard for became his undoing. His character Somu dies too early in the build-up to the climax. There was no 'death scene' as such to call his own, unlike in the case of his memorable blockbusters *Aradhana* or *Anand*. He just suddenly gets run over by a truck and dies on the spot. Before the audiences even have a moment to absorb this and consider the magnitude of this scene, the screen is eclipsed by the giant Amitabh—and perhaps the film too. In the climax, after an intense father–son confrontation, an angry and distraught Amitabh Bachchan 'avenges' his friend's death by serving a life imprisonment for murder as punishment for his unscrupulous capitalist father. This won the sympathy of the audiences and so the climax entirely went to Amitabh Bachchan. While Rajesh died a lame death, it was Amitabh who heroically took centre stage by selflessly honouring his friendship. And so he is the hero who remains in the audiences' minds long after the movie ends.

Veteran sound recordist Mangesh Desai watched the film some time after its release. He called up Amitabh immediately and said that he was brilliant in the film. Amitabh, who was upset with Hrishikesh Mukherjee over the film, was surprised to hear this. Later Hrishikesh Mukherjee said in one of his interviews, 'Next Jaya and Gulzar saw the trial and were vastly impressed. Again he was unconvinced. He felt he had screamed too much in the last scene. But then that's Amit. Overcritical and a perfectionist.'[3]

Amitabh had no clue that it was his loud anger that had the audiences spellbound. Especially the scene when the mill workers beat up his close friend, Somu. He goes to their *basti* and shouts in anger, *'Hai kisi maa ke laal mei himmat jo mere saamne aaye?'* [Is there courage in any mother's son to face me?] Actor and film-maker Sachin Pilgaonkar, who has seen the many changing faces of the film industry, says, 'I was in a theatre watching *Namak Haraam*. The moment that scene came where Amitabh Bachchan challenges and shouts in anger, the entire theatre echoed with applause. Every single person was clapping. This was strange. The hero of the film was Rajesh Khanna, but people were cheering for Amitabh Bachchan. It meant only one thing: that the times were changing.'

Audiences being fed on mostly romantic stuff hadn't witnessed this kind of simmering fury and intensity for many years. For this role Amitabh won the Best Supporting Actor Filmfare Award. He had even been nominated in the Best Actor category for his film *Zanjeer*. But the award went to Rishi Kapoor for his debut in *Bobby*. Rajesh Khanna did not win any awards that year.

Namak Haraam was actually the first film that saw a shift in the balance of power within the film industry in favour of Amitabh Bachchan. Even Rajesh Khanna had predicted the same after watching the trial show of the film. Years later he said in an interview, 'When I saw *Namak Haraam* at a trial at Liberty Cinema, I knew my time was up. I told Hrishida, "Here is the superstar of tomorrow."'[4]

***

When the shooting for *Namak Haraam* had begun, Rajesh Khanna was the superstar and Amitabh was considered a flop actor. Since the producers couldn't get Rajesh's dates easily, they decided to go ahead with Amitabh's scenes as he was freely available. So most of Amitabh's scenes were shot first. These rushes were shown to a group of distributors. The distributors got the impression that Amitabh was the real hero of the film and that Rajesh Khanna was doing a guest appearance. They were uncertain about the project and reluctant to buy the film of this flop actor.

Since Hrishikesh Mukherjee was a senior film-maker with a fantastic track record, the distributors were wary of rejecting the film outright. Nevertheless, many of them voiced their concerns about Amitabh by finding fault with his performance. Finally, some distributors targeted his 'hairstyle that covered his ears' and said, 'Your hero looks like an ape. Do tell him to have a good haircut so that we can see whether he has ears or not!' Everyone in the group laughed at this comment.

A few months after this event, Prakash Mehra's *Zanjeer* was released and Amitabh created history, emerging as the new hero of the youth. This was also the time when Rajesh Khanna's career was going through a lean phase, with five of his big films not working their magic. At this stage, *Namak Haraam* was still being shot.

Success changes everything. Post the success of *Zanjeer*, the same distributors called to say that Amitabh's role should be increased and some angry scenes should be added to the film. They even demanded that Amitabh should be given equal footage in the posters and publicity of the film. During the planning of *Namak Haraam*, Amitabh was just a co-actor. But by the time the film released, Amitabh was on almost equal footing.

Furthermore, Amitabh's 'hairstyle that covered his ears' became a rage. It was a fashion statement now followed by millions across the country. While a lot has been said and written about this shift in the balance of stardom, the most significant marker of this change came from the establishments of Bombay's barbers. Across the city, their boards now reflected a new entry that marked the changing winds of time:[5]

Rajesh Khanna Haircut----Rs 2/-
Amitabh Bachchan Haircut----Rs 3.50/-

CHAPTER 26

Amitabh's stature was slowly increasing in the industry. He was an antithesis of the attitude that film-makers attached with Rajesh Khanna's name. Rajesh Khanna was notorious for coming late to shoots, even cancelling the shoot sometimes. On the other hand, Amitabh was discipline's other name. To reach before call-time was his forte. On sets he surrendered himself to the director, not interfering much in the script. In addition there was a prominent anti-Rajesh wave in the media. They had started calling Amitabh the new superstar. The media, which had given him the title of 'The Phenomenon', had now started referring to him as 'Ex-Phenomenon'. The magical phase of Rajesh Khanna was now a thing of the past.

Yash Chopra had started his banner Yash Raj Films a year before with *Daag*. The film with Rajesh Khanna had firmly established the banner. Now Yash Chopra had got a wonderful script written by Salim–Javed, and Gulshan Rai has come on board as producer. As director of the film, after much deliberation, Yash Chopra decided to cast Amitabh Bachchan as the hero of his new film *Deewar*—though Rajesh Khanna has said in an interview that Yash

Chopra first offered *Deewar* to him. But scriptwriter Salim Khan told me that there were no talks with Rajesh Khanna for the lead role of *Deewar*. 'We wrote that role for Amitabh Bachchan. He fitted into the role completely. They were not exchangeable roles.'

It was around this time that Yash Chopra started planning the next film *Kabhi Kabhie* under the banner he'd set up. While *Deewar* was an action film, *Kabhi Kabhie* was an ambitious multi-starrer romance spanning two generations of people. The lead character in *Kabhi Kabhie* was a romantic poet—which suited Rajesh Khanna's soft romantic image. But Rajesh Khanna was not considered for the role. The angry young man Amitabh Bachchan was selected to play the poet. The roles of Shashi Kapoor and Rishi Kapoor were also romantic. Yash Chopra was often asked why he didn't sign Rajesh Khanna for these films. He said in an interview, 'Once you work with a man, you develop an understanding and rapport and you go on working with him. It just happened with me also. It is like this: After *Daag* I felt Amitabh was more perfectly suited for *Deewar*, as it consisted of an emotional as well as the "tough man" type of role and then in *Trishul* also the same type of role was there.'[1]

Yash Chopra justified signing Amitabh for his action films, but when he was asked about his romantic films *Kabhi Kabhie* and *Silsila*, he repeated the answer of 'better tuning' as the main reason: 'You see, because of such habitual team spirit, I never tried to come out of the shell. As far as my relations with Kaka are concerned, they were never strained and are still very good.'[2]

But the writer of his films *Kabhi Kabhie* and *Silsila*, Sagar Sarhadi, who also knew Rajesh Khanna from his theatre days, told me a different story. He remembers once asking Yash Chopra about why he didn't sign Rajesh again after making a successful film like *Daag*. Yash Chopra answered, 'Yaar, working with him is very difficult . . . He calls his producers to his home and indulges in drinking till late [in the] night. Till the time he doesn't want to sleep himself, producers have to show their presence there. Then if he is going to Madras for shooting, the producers are to drop him to the airport and receive him when he comes back. I can't do this. I can't handle these superstar tantrums on a regular basis.'

The editor of the *Film Street Journal*, Bharathi S. Pradhan, has a different view on the issue: 'Yash Chopra also did all these things till the point he needed Rajesh Khanna. Then he got an alternative in Amitabh Bachchan. Otherwise he would have continued doing whatever Rajesh Khanna asked of him. They are all the same. The moment a star's market is down, they start thinking: why should I be his chamcha?'

Yash Chopra had made the crucial decision of leaving Rajesh Khanna and casting Amitabh Bachchan in his films—a decision Rajesh Khanna didn't like one bit. In any case, after *Namak Haraam*, he had become too insecure of Amitabh. Sagar Sarhadi told me, 'Once I went to Khandala to write a script. I met Rajesh Khanna there. I asked him, "Yaar, why are you not doing films with Yash Chopra?" He replied irritatedly, "Yash is not a good director. He makes me work hard from morning till evening. I can't work so hard." I started laughing at his answer.'

It is to be noted that in those years while film-makers like Yash Chopra did not work with Rajesh, there were directors like Hrishikesh Mukherjee, J. Omprakash and Shakti Samanta who made many films with Rajesh Khanna. J. Omprakash told me that working with Rajesh was the easiest and most memorable experience of his life. According to him, it all depends on how you handle your artists. Rajesh never troubled him and he never had to show his attendance at the Khanna Durbar to get dates.

A senior technician from the industry told me that since Shakti Samanta had given Rajesh a crucial break and due to the immense respect he had for Hrishikesh Mukherjee, he generally refrained from throwing as many tantrums in front of them and used to remain in control. J. Omprakash has his version on this: 'In his personal life Kaka was an introvert. So he didn't used to speak much with everyone. Many human beings have more failings of personality and are generally known by their action–reactions. His reaction and general behaviour was not liked by people. I know this for sure.'

People close to Rajesh have said that he was very possessive and wanted absolute loyalty from his friends and colleagues. He wanted the people working with him to continue working with him exclusively. However, the reality is that film-making is a business and such associations are not always possible. When his films started failing, people started leaving him.

The chance taken by Yash Chopra on Amitabh Bachchan proved to hit the jackpot. *Deewar*, released in 1975, changed the landscape of Hindi cinema for ever and consolidated the action-packed persona of Bachchan. Amitabh was in top gear. *Chupke Chupke*, *Mili* and *Zameer* were released and introduced new shades of Amitabh. It is noteworthy to point out that *Chupke Chupke* and *Mili* were directed by Hrishikesh Mukherjee, and *Zameer* was produced by B.R. Chopra—film-makers who had made successful movies with Rajesh Khanna not long ago.

In the same year—1975—itself, a huge cracker of a film was released: *Sholay*. This action-packed dacoit saga went on to become the most successful Hindi film of all time. *Sholay* effectively was the game-changer, in the way it heralded an era of action films in Hindi cinema. People suddenly moved towards action, leaving romantic films in a lurch. *Sholay* was directed by Ramesh Sippy—whose directorial debut *Andaz* had been a huge success a few years ago just because Rajesh Khanna had done a guest appearance in it. But despite that triumph, he never worked with Rajesh again. Also, the writers of *Sholay* were Salim–Javed, one-time favourites of Rajesh Khanna.

It is said that Rajesh had major disagreements with the scriptwriter duo Salim–Javed, once considered close to him. He had to pay a heavy price for this altercation, the repercussions of which he did not realize initially. There were two ill effects: firstly, the two were in-form writers because of which Rajesh Khanna lost out on some good scripts; and secondly, Amitabh Bachchan got all those scripts and together they weaved a new screenplay for success in Hindi cinema.

In that era, stories of a fight between Javed Akhtar and Rajesh Khanna appeared regularly in film magazines. Different reasons were cited for their clash. But both of them never went on record on the issue. When I asked Salim Khan about it, he said, 'There was a film *Bhola Bhala* based on a Marathi film. Rajesh wanted to remake it in Hindi. He asked us to do the screenplay. He was adamant that he would play a double role in it. Creatively, we didn't agree to it.'

According to Salim Khan, Rajesh supported them during *Haathi Mere Saathi*, but that was not the first break for the writer duo. They were already working with Sippy Films when Rajesh was signed for their film *Andaz*. 'But in his mind he always thought that "I have given Salim–Javed their first break, I have supported them and now they are disagreeing with me." He couldn't handle a disagreement. Then *Zanjeer* came and Amitabh became a star. Then we wrote *Deewar* and *Trishul* for him—so naturally Rajesh must have thought that these people were with me and now they left me for Amitabh.'

It is often said and written that Salim–Javed deliberately tried to bring about Rajesh Khanna's downfall, that they wrote wonderful scripts and roles for Amitabh Bachchan, helping him to topple Rajesh from the throne of superstardom. But is it really true? Salim Khan refutes these rumours, saying that there was no question of them deliberately sabotaging anybody else's career. He says, 'There was a line . . . We simply drew a bigger line without touching the previous line . . . You cannot duplicate success. When Amitabh came, eleven to twelve of his films flopped initially, and he was going back. If *Zanjeer* was not successful he would have gone back . . . Salim–Javed were not God to bring about the downfall of Rajesh Khanna [by replacing him] with a new actor. In those times no one could think that there could be a bigger star than Rajesh Khanna.'

Film-making is all about teamwork and at that time Salim–Javed and Amitabh Bachchan were in great form. They made a strong team with directors like Yash Chopra and Ramesh Sippy, amongst others. Salim Khan says, 'It is very ridiculous that people said we planned his downfall. Just think—we didn't have a secure future ourselves. Sometimes our film was a success and sometimes a failure. When Rajesh Khanna became the superstar, he also overtook many stars like Rajendra Kumar and Sunil Dutt—was that someone's planning or conspiracy? Believe me, in that era everyone felt that no one could beat Rajesh Khanna. When his films finally started flopping, he didn't introspect on what went wrong. Instead, he started blaming others, saying that everyone was scheming against him.'

Obviously, such conspiracy theories made good copy in the gossip magazines, but, logically, the reasons of his downfall were varied. Talking about Rajesh Khanna, a loyal fan told me dejectedly, 'Nothing's wrong with him now. It's just that all his fans have grown up. A whole new generation has come into being. He took his fans for granted. You can't do that. Because they are not the same people. Every five years there is a distinct change in tastes. The old kids have grown up and gotten married. The new kids want something else.'

Was this the beginning of the end of the superstardom? In the eyes of his fans and film journalists, his magical era had already passed. There was a consensus in the film industry that he was no more the number-one star. At the end of 1973, in the annual issue of *Stardust*, film journalist Monojit Lahiri's article openly declared the downfall of the superstar, 'Today Rajesh Khanna is sadder (but hopefully a wiser mortal). "The Phenomenon" is no more. It is a matter of great pity that the crown and the sceptre have suddenly slipped away. It is unlikely that he will regain the symbols of power. Nobody does. Not in showbiz. When a giant falls—he falls. It doesn't matter if he rises again because to the world he has fallen.'

To recover from this great fall, Rajesh had realized that he needs to shed his overused mannerisms and work with good scripts and directors who can tap his potential. So, trying a little to push his starry tantrums to the backseat, Rajesh attempted to hold on to the few people who were still willing to work with him. Film journalist Bharathi S. Pradhan narrated an interesting incident in this vein. Rajesh Khanna was doing a film called *Aavishkar* with Basu Bhattacharya. He went to Madras for the shoot. The film was a low-budget one, so instead of a Mercedes, a normal taxi reached the airport to pick him up. Being the quintessential superstar, it had been years since Rajesh had boarded a taxi. He was amused but then got into the taxi and reached the set without any tantrums.

His trilogy on marital relationships and its complexities started with *Daag* in 1973, followed by Basu Bhattacharya's *Aavishkar* and J. Omprakash's *Aap ki Kasam* in 1974. His role in *Aavishkar* was completely non-glamorous and, unlike the famous Rajesh Khanna image, had little scope for his typical mannerisms. The role earned him his third Filmfare Best Actor Award. But despite his hard work and experimentation, the film didn't work. *Aap ki Kasam* was also an experiment of sorts. Here, in a departure from traditional Hindi-film hero roles, he played a character who loses everything in life.

J. Omprakash told me, 'When I started this bold film based on a Malayalam film, Rajesh was going through his worst phase. So he actually requested me to consider someone else to play the hero as he does not want me to bear the brunt of his bad phase. He was actually thinking about my losses. But I told him I will make the film only with him.'

The film was a success. Its blockbuster music is still remembered as one of Pancham's better albums. The songs comprise the energetic 'Jai Jai Shiv Shankar', the soothingly romantic 'Karvatein Badaltey Rahe' and the very profound 'Zindagi ke Safar Mein Guzar Jaatey Hain Jo Maqaam'.

But despite this success, perhaps Rajesh hadn't learnt from the lean patch he had faced earlier. He was still overexposing himself as an actor, with starring roles in seven films releasing in 1974, of which only three were notable successes. As a star he still seemed to believe that his success could be measured by the number of films he had successfully acted in. Not surprisingly, this proved to be the wrong strategy, as it reduced the average of his successful films with every new release.

Emphasizing on the same point *Stardust* did a famous cover story on him which said that no matter how fabulous you are, how popular or how handsome, too much of anything is bad. 'The audiences tend to throw up. Overexposure is poison.'[3] This poison was eating into his superstardom and hollowing it out.

Around this time, Rajesh Khanna's memorable film *Anand* was rereleased at some theatres across the country. But, ironically, this time Amitabh Bachchan dominated the film posters, while the original hero Rajesh Khanna was demoted to a 'supporting' status.

Indeed, the crown and the sceptre had been passed on.

CHAPTER 27

'The life and happiness in our house came to an end the day I and Rajesh got married,' remarked Dimple in an interview given to *India Today* many years later.[1] The five-month courtship period had not given the couple a chance to get to know each other. They knew each other more from gossip columns and on-screen images than in person. The initial days passed so quickly that there was little time to feel and understand anything. As soon as the honeymoon phase in the marriage waned, reality reared its head. Along with the differences in their ages and maturity levels, the differences in their personalities were coming to the fore as the marriage progressed.

In November 1973, almost eight months after the wedding, Dimple's first film, *Bobby*, was released. Since Dimple got married during the shooting of *Bobby*, the mehndi on her hands can be seen in the famous song 'Mujhe Kuch Kehna Hai'. In fact, she was pregnant with her first child even before the shooting for *Bobby* was completed. When she attended the premiere for *Bobby* she looked heavily pregnant. Raj Kapoor's eldest son, actor Randhir

Kapoor, said in one of his interviews, 'What was *Bobby*? It was a series of compromises . . . We had to hurry filming up because Dimple went and got married and then got pregnant, and she was becoming huger and huger—I mean, she was eight months pregnant and it showed. So we introduced Prem Chopra to do all kinds of things to cover up the fact that Dimple was pregnant. We have no control over stars, and who expected Dimple to run away and marry Rajesh and get banged into motherhood—all in one take? For a man of the world, Rajesh showed total ignorance of the famous red triangle.'[2]

Bobby became the biggest blockbuster of the year. The bumper success of the film brought back Raj Kapoor's confidence, which had been shattered after the debacle of his magnum opus, *Mera Naam Joker*. In a way it saved the iconic R.K. Studios. Post *Bobby* Rishi Kapoor and Dimple became youth icons. The story was based on the classic tale of Romeo and Juliet, with a twist in the climax that made it a happy ending.

Riding on Laxmikant–Pyarelal chartbusters, bold picturizations and fresh lead actors, *Bobby* gave a new style and language to Hindi cinema. The film was a trendsetter in more ways than one. Like Shah Rukh Khan has reportedly said in one of his interviews, 'Before *Bobby*, Indian cinema was about men and women, but after *Bobby*, it became about boys and girls.' Though Raj Kapoor made this film to launch his son Rishi Kapoor, a Dimple craze emerged after its release. There were reports in film magazines that Rajesh Khanna was unhappy over the bold scenes and dresses that Dimple wore and told Raj Kapoor the same when he saw the rushes before the release. As *Bobby,* Dimple became the heart-throb of the nation's youth. Her bold attitude and glamorous dresses with her knotted polka-dotted blouse and earphone hairstyle were copied by millions across the country.

For young men Dimple was a dazzling fantasy. Producers and directors were predicting a glittery future for her. Stardom was pulling her towards itself like a magnet. Despite all this, Dimple said no to a brighter future and became a housewife. To play the real role of the Superstar's wife she said no to all the other roles coming her way—exactly as her husband had wished—and this made for a proud husband in Rajesh. Years later Dimple's father, Chunnibhai Kapadia, said in an interview, 'At that time Dimple was getting five lakh for a film. There was no other heroine in her competition, but she gave up everything in a hurry [to get married].'[3]

According to Bhawana Somaaya, the marriage was wrong from the very beginning. It is interesting to note that Dimple's complaints against Rajesh were very similar to Rajesh's complaints against Anju Mahendroo. 'Everywhere I went, I was told that I was the most gorgeous woman in the world. But I never got a word of praise from him. It was as if he hadn't noticed me,'[4] said Dimple to Bhawana Somaaya.

What was Dimple to Rajesh? The younger girl who had replaced Anju or the to-be Kapoor daughter-in-law that he had stolen? Or the amalgamation of all his fans, on-screen image and power? Though Dimple was the talk of the town post *Bobby*, Rajesh Khanna never gave any interview praising her performance or *Bobby*'s success.

Dimple said in the interview that she was always waiting for a reaction which never came. All her energy was spent in doing what he wanted, and anticipating his approval: 'It was like climbing a ladder. No matter how fast I climbed, he was still many rungs ahead.'[5] She was so in awe of her superstar husband that she totally eroded her own self-esteem. Perhaps the difference in star power and age helped subjugate her and robbed her of confidence. She wore what Rajesh liked and mixed with the people he approved of.

Dimple gave birth to their first child, a lovely daughter, incidentally, on Rajesh's birthday. Prashant recalls, 'Kakaji had nicknamed Twinkle as Tina. She used to be very unwell as a kid. Kakaji used to take her to Dr Mahendra himself. He used to dote on her.' Dimple's focus had now completely shifted to their little one. It would have been good had their private life remained private. But every little personal detail of their family life was transplanted as gossip into the pages of film magazines.

There were constant rumours that many film-makers were regularly attempting to sign the blockbuster heroine of *Bobby* for their films. Such stories always had quotes from 'reliable sources' saying that Dimple herself wants to rejoin films. It was insinuated that Dimple was trying to convince Rajesh to let her work in films. Rajesh Khanna always refuted such stories. According to him Dimple had herself chosen to be a housewife. Just after their marriage, he said in an interview given to *Stardust*, 'Look at Dimple. Hers is a real sacrifice! She had signed umpteen films as the HEROINE, with all the topmost banners and stars. I didn't even have to "ask" her to give up films. She did it of her own accord, out of her love for me. Because she wanted to be my wife and nothing else.'[6]

Who made the decision was perhaps known to the entire film industry. Was this just another example of Rajesh Khanna's possessiveness for the people around him? His expectation of complete loyalty from everyone had manifested into a situation where he did not allow his producers and directors to work with anyone but him, and in his personal life he had Dimple focusing all her energies on his house and the family. But by the end of the third year of their marriage, Dimple was totally disillusioned and dissatisfied, not knowing what to do with her life. Before she could find her bearings, she got pregnant again with their second child. Prashant Roy recalls, 'There were expectations that the second kid should be a son.'

But instead another daughter was born on 27 July 1977. Film journalist Ingrid Albuquerque reported in one of her articles,

'Rajesh (who'd wanted a son) did not look at the second daughter for months, and the family forgot to give the poor child a name.'[7] Later the second child was named Rinke.

Prashant confirms that Rajesh was initially upset that his second child was not a son. His disappointment was perhaps exacerbated by the fact that his career was going through a very lean phase. But later on, little Rinke was able to win him over as well as the rest of the household.

***

The 'lean phase' in his career kept Rajesh busy in his efforts to save his diminishing superstardom. In the meanwhile, Dimple had nothing to do, except wait for him. Sometimes this wait also extended into many hours deep in the night. Rajesh Khanna was always working to belt out the large number of films he had signed. Journalist Nina Arora, while describing Dimple from those days, wrote in a famous cover story, 'Her eyes had taken on a yearning quality . . . her present life has turned into a peculiar, fantastic arc in slow motion . . . her pet obsession remains that she can never have more time spent with Rajesh Khanna.'[8]

Based on a sensational interview that was the cover story of *Super* magazine in September 1978, she further describes Dimple's days in Aashirwad: 'On evenings when he does return home, they sit side by side on the terrace outside the master bedroom, in a tight bond of silence. Kaka smokes cigarette after cigarette, relaxed yet pensive, while his young wife bubbles with an expectance which all too soon turns into disappointment when he doesn't speak at all.' This account explains the story of their relationship aptly.

After the fairy-tale wedding, Dimple had become Rajesh's wife, but she was yet to become an equal partner in the marriage. She would spend hours waiting for Rajesh to come home and then spend hours waiting for him to unwind. She waited around, brimming with the hope that maybe Kaka would speak up and ask about her . . . about how she spent her day . . . or share with her the worries plaguing his mind and career. What was bothering him day and night? But he seemed lost in his own world. In those melancholic moments the only relationship between them was that of silence . . . a deep, piercing silence.

At last, Rajesh would extinguish his cigarette in the ashtray and turn towards Dimple, as though acknowledging her presence for the very first time. Dimple would eagerly await his next words, filled with a hope that finally her husband was ready to share his thoughts. But Rajesh would simply ask, 'How have the children been today?'

***

Rajesh and Dimple's marriage crumbled under the weight of the superstar's fading career. With no solution in sight, arguments and fights become a regular feature. Most of this reached film magazines through 'reliable sources'. It was once insinuated that Rajesh had hit Dimple and, eventually, that Dimple had left Aashirwad and gone to her father's house. Dimple said, 'I didn't even stop to think that it was the last place I should have run to at a time when there was already a lot of misunderstanding between him [Chunnibhai] and Kaka. I took Twinkle with me and refused to talk things over with Kaka, even going so far as to obtain divorce papers.'[9]

This episode was widely splashed in the media. It was also reported that Dimple wanted to rejoin films and this was the main issue of contention between them. With Dimple at her father's house, Rajesh also left for a month-long outdoor shoot in Kashmir. With ample time to rethink, Dimple introspected and analysed the situation from all perspectives. Sometime the loneliness made her cry and sometimes she repented leaving her husband's house: 'I simmered and boiled with resentment for a month and then one day, as if by magic, Kaka appeared on my doorstep. It was my moment of truth. I realized that he was the only man I have ever loved or am capable of loving.'[10]

On the arms of her charming husband, Dimple came back to Aashirwad. But while distance did make their hearts grow fonder, it did little to change their relationship. Dimple decided to compromise on her situation, not knowing that their differences were too difficult to mend. She rued with a sadness in her voice, 'What fans do I have any more, anyway? If you ask me, people have forgotten all about me by now. It's [been] five years since the release of *Bobby*. If it hadn't been for the magazines, I'd be left in peace like any other normal wife and mother.'[11]

Communication was the key to save this relationship, but that was never Rajesh's strong point. Trouble in his personal life coincided with his poor professional run. His films were flopping, the media was writing him off and even taking potshots at his marriage. Years later, talking about his relationship Rajesh Khanna accepted his mistakes. He said that at that time he had built walls around him. He never shared his concerns with Dimple, never talked his heart out. This behaviour hurt his relationship the most. In an interview he said, 'Had I surrendered to her, she would have coped better than she did. But I withdrew. For fourteen months, I built a wall around me, stopped trusting people, stopped signing new films. Every day, my self-esteem was eroding a little more. Those days I was forever preoccupied . . . forever suicidal.'[12]

Journalist Bhawana Somaaya best summarized Rajesh's relationships when she wrote, 'Rajesh Khanna became more rigid and withdrew into his shell. If Anju couldn't cope with his success, Dimple couldn't cope with his failure.'[13] Dimple agreed in her later interviews and called their marriage 'a farce', but it took her a number of years to accept this. She said, 'Kaka should have married Mumtaz. She was the right sort of mate for him . . .'[14]

CHAPTER 28

'*Maha Chor* Hai Mahabore' [*Maha Chor* Is a Mega Bore] was the header for a film review of the 1976 Rajesh Khanna starrer *Maha Chor*. The film was a big flop. So was his next *Bundalbaaz*. A director who had worked with Rajesh Khanna tells me that as he hit his lean phase, Rajesh was advised by many to sign multi-starrer action films, which was the done thing in the late 1970s.

The trend started in 1974 with Manoj Kumar, Amitabh Bachchan, Shashi Kapoor and Zeenat Aman in *Roti Kapada aur Makaan*. Following this, a short spate of multi-starrers was seen. Films like *Yaadon ki Baaraat* and *Amar Akbar Anthony* gave the audiences a high dose of action-packed drama as well as oodles of romantic side-stories. Audiences loved the concept of watching multiple stars on a single ticket.

But this resulted in the actors signing on multiple films simultaneously because of which obtaining shoot dates became impossible. The films would often get delayed or else the shooting schedules would overlap. Also the rising star prices sent production costs soaring. In the latter half of the 1970s, twelve leading producers came together and formed a code which allowed actors to work only in six films simultaneously. To address this issue they even published a list of stars who had more than six films on hand at the time. Given his signing spree, even in his 'lean' phase, the list was headed by Rajesh Khanna, who had about 20 film shoots underway. It was a vicious cycle, because it not only oversaturated his star appeal but, in turn, overburdened him with work.

It was but natural for the audiences to be attracted to the New Age multi-starrer films. But Rajesh Khanna was uncomfortable with action films. As far as multi-starrer films went, Rajesh wasn't cut out for them. He believed he could carry the entire burden of a film on his shoulders alone. He was still only interested in solo-hero roles.

Now all hope rested on his three-time-successful director: Shakti Samanta's *Mehbooba*. It was the last ray of hope for a setting sun.

After the historic success of action-drama *Sholay*, Rajesh Khanna believed romance films would make a comeback. So he put every remaining ounce of his energy, power and influence into *Mehbooba*. It was a big-budget film with excellent music by R.D. Burman, who produced a haunting number 'Mere Naina Saawan Bhadon', still regarded among his top-notch works. It was reported in the film magazines that Rajesh used all his remaining goodwill and influence in the industry to garner good reviews from trade pundits and critics. The bar was raised and this hugely anticipated film had immense expectations to meet. Rajesh Khanna's stature was at stake.

***

Mid-year, in July 1976, the phenomenal debacle *Mehbooba* was released. The slate had been wiped clean. A desperate superstar's hopes as well as *Mehbooba* sunk without a trace, with a lot of money riding on it. The time was up. The era called Rajesh Khanna had ended. This was not all—his next five films tanked badly too.

All that now remained behind was a man with the name 'Rajesh Khanna', a name that had once enjoyed godlike stature. Now the God had fallen from grace; what was to become of the mortal? How far would this man be able to go now, carrying the burden of his once-famous name? Which road will he choose? Will Rajesh Khanna be just another Jatin Khanna again?

***

'Success has many godfathers, but failure is an orphan,' says politician Amar Singh, who was a close observer of those times. 'I will give the example of Amitabh Bachchan. He climbed whichever ladder of opportunity presented itself, used it and then broke away to go even further. He was a practical man and successfully reinvented himself. He was not an emotional fool . . . unlike Rajesh Khanna.'

When a man's stature is destroyed, the respect he commands from the people around him goes away. Rajesh Khanna said in an interview, 'An actor can continue being the same kind of person and still appear to have changed in the eyes of other people. If your films are successful, your every utterance is a pearl of wisdom. If your films flop, you are always talking through your backside. If your films are doing well, you are so easy to get along with. If they are not, you are the most insufferable human being. If your films are hits, [it is] because you are such a good actor. If the films are flops, it's because your style of acting is outdated.'[1] Rajesh Khanna had been abandoned by his fans and the critics were not just loud but so loud that the din had started engulfing everything around.

Hanif Zaveri, author of Mehmood's biography, told me that the late actor and comedian Mehmood used to address Rajesh Khanna as Kathor (translating to 'heartless' in English) in a friendly way. He signed Rajesh for a home production *Janta Hawaldar*, a major portion of which was to be shot at his own farmhouse. The entire production unit along with Rajesh was staying at Mehmood's farmhouse. Problems started when one of Mehmood's sons greeted Rajesh with a friendly hello. Rajesh took the boy's casual attitude as an insult, because he felt it did not contain the respect he thought he deserved. He showed his displeasure and his starry tantrums took a turn for the worse. It would take Mehmood, a respected senior actor, hours to get Rajesh to come out for a shot. Perhaps throwing his weight around in this manner was Rajesh's way of trying to command the respect he felt he was losing. One day, as the tantrums got out of hand, Mehmood's patience dried up completely. He lost his temper and gave Rajesh a tight slap. Rajesh was stunned. Zaveri says, 'I have this statement from Mehmood. He gave Rajesh Khanna one tight slap for his tantrums and said, "You might be a superstar of your own house. I have paid you and you will finish my film." After that the film shoot was completed without difficulties.'

It can be questioned whether this incident points towards the increasing loss of respect for Rajesh Khanna in the industry. Had his starry tantrums overstayed their welcome? Did he script his own downfall by alienating people who could have helped him? According to Hanif Zaveri, 'Rajesh Khanna didn't know how to maintain interpersonal relationships. Now look at Jeetendra, he wasn't a very good actor, but he knew how to keep good relations, and see how far he went. Jeetendrasaab told me once that he doesn't know how to cry. If a scene demands crying, then he hides his face with his hands and cries.' But Rajesh Khanna knew how to cry. He knew how to die, how to love, how to sing, how to emote, how to laugh and how to be angry . . . on screen. What he did not know perhaps was how to communicate well off-screen.

This lack of communication affected all his personal relationships, especially the one he shared with Dimple, his wife of nine years. Not only had the film industry started speaking against Rajesh, but so had his in-laws. The Kapadia family always believed that eventually Rajesh would relent and allow Dimple to get back to films. But when it became evident that this might not be the case, the Kapadias began to rant against their son-in-law. Towards the latter half of the 1970s Chunnibhai Kapadia became the prime source of stories against Rajesh's behaviour towards Dimple. This led to the gossip columnists coining the term CIB: Chunnibhai Information Bureau. He gave ample fodder to keep the gossip columns aflow with titbits from the personal life of Rajesh and Dimple. This was not to the liking of the ex-superstar. Journalist Ingrid Albuquerque wrote about this cold war in a piece called 'Rajesh vs. the Caucus of Four'—the 'four' being Dimple, her parents and her sister, Simple.

Time and again Dimple would walk out, threaten divorce and emotionally blackmail Rajesh, but she would always come back to him with the kids. Gossip magazines wrote about how every second month Dimple would leave Aashirwad only to come back in some time, suggesting that it all was a publicity stunt. 'Fear drove Dimple back to Kaka, not love. My daughter lacks the guts of a Raakhee to stand up for herself,' stated an agitated Chunnibhai Kapadia.[2]

Khanna maintained a calculated silence on all this. When Bhawana Somaaya directly asked him about his marriage being the biggest joke in town, Rajesh Khanna in his veritable filmy style answered, 'When everyone casts stones, the temptation to come out with the truth in all its gory detail is great. But ultimately, it serves no purpose, because your greatest pain becomes a source of ridicule. So I would rather be crucified than speak.'[3]

With both his in-laws and the media taking potshots at his tempestuous marriage and declining career, Rajesh's self-confidence deteriorated every day. Lots of new and younger men had come into the industry after him and were now standing at par with him or had overtaken him altogether. One can imagine his battered state of mind—he was alone, irritated, frustrated, and fighting a losing battle with a slowly expanding inferiority complex. Every day he tried to drown the inner turmoil of loss with alcohol, but it would just fuel the fire. Even alcohol couldn't take away the sting of his now-absolute downfall.

And then one fateful night, the incident occurred that shook the very foundation of his being. Years later he recalled, 'I remember once at three in the morning, I was pretty high on spirits and, suddenly it was too much for me to stomach, because it was my first taste of failure. One after another, seven films had flopped in a row. It was raining, pitch dark and up there alone on my terrace, I lost control. I yelled out, *"Parvardigar hum gareebon ka itna sakht imtihaan na le ki hum tere vajood ko inkar dein."'* [Don't test my patience to such an extent that I question your very existence.]⁴

Hearing his screams his wife Dimple and the house staff came running to the terrace. He was crying terribly. He couldn't forget this night for the rest of his life. One can imagine the drama and pathos of that night. It must have been a deadly cocktail: alcohol, depression and the crushing humiliation of failure. Perhaps he also felt betrayed by his fans who had written him off. Perhaps the pain he felt stirred other anguished memories from his past. Perhaps the fact that he had been pushed this far truly frightened him. One wonders if Rajesh was struck by the bizarre realization that he had recreated scenes just like this in his movies so many times before. He was a protagonist then. He was the protagonist now. Reel to real. It all played out like notes of the same melody, as though he was destined to live his roles. The actor who showed luminous dreams to millions of fans was faced with life's brutal realities that night. But he was struggling to comprehend and accept this reality. Perhaps he did not wish to learn how.

Later he admitted that in his lean phase he had even gone to the extent of thinking of suicide under depression. He said, 'Once, I even attempted walking into the sea, but at the last minute pulled myself out of the depression. "I will not die a failure," I promised myself. I don't want people to say Rajesh Khanna was a coward.'[5]

He must have been the most lonely man around. Not only had he failed to communicate to the people closest to him, but he had also pushed away well-wishers like Anju and Devyani. He said, 'I sat all by myself brooding, thinking. The truth was I could not come to terms with my failure. Had somebody intelligent and experienced talked to me, made me understand the games of filmdom, I could have been consoled. But there was no such consolation.'[6]

CHAPTER 29

'My diary is empty now, come whenever you want,' said a melancholic voice on the phone early one morning.

Producer-director Saawan Kumar Tak recalls, 'It took me a few moments to realize that it was Rajesh Khanna on the other side.' Saawan was a self-confessed Rajesh Khanna fan and had been trying to make a film with him for the last nine years. But Rajesh Khanna had always given him the standard reply, 'My date diary is full right now.' This had led Saawan to believe that perhaps Rajesh Khanna didn't wish to work with him, but then the phone call changed everything.

Faced with the reality of the industry giving up on him, Rajesh had now started turning to the people whom he had turned down for many years. Earlier, it would have been unimaginable for the superstar to be calling up a producer on his own accord. After his famous breakdown on the Aashirwad terrace, some of his films like *Amar Deep* and *Thodisi Bewafaii* were both moderate successes, providing much-needed relief. But in no way were they close to the success he had achieved in his heyday.

When Saawan Kumar reached Aashirwad that day, Khanna humbly offered him the date diary and asked Saawan to fill in any dates that he wished. A story idea was narrated by Saawan to which Khanna immediately said: 'Done.' The film was *Souten*.

***

Initially, for the two female leads in the film, Padmini Kolhapure and Parveen Babi were considered. But a few days before the shoot, Parveen opted out of the film. Zeenat Aman was considered next, but she didn't have the bulk dates to go for the long outdoor shoot schedule in Mauritius. Finally, Saawan Kumar zeroed down on the young, pretty and vivacious Tina Munim, who had been launched by Dev Anand in his film *Des Pardes* a few years back. She was already doing a film *Fiffty Fiffty* with Rajesh Khanna. They were friends and reportedly Rajesh had even attended a dinner at Tina's house along with Dimple.

When Saawan told Rajesh about signing Tina for the second female lead role, he instantly agreed. The music for *Souten* was composed by Usha Khanna. Saawan Kumar recalls an evening when he shared the lyrics of the most famous song of *Souten*, 'It was late evening, Kakaji was on his second round of drinks. I had written the opening of the song and I sang it for him: *"Shayad meri shaadi ka khayal dil mei aaya hai, isiliye mummy ne meri tujhe chai pe bulaya hai . . ."* [Probably my mother is thinking about my marriage, that is why she has invited you for tea]. On hearing the lyrics, he was shy and flashed the same famous smile while saying, "Yaar, what will people say if I sing this song at my age? I am a father of two kids . . ." To this, I replied, "Kakaji, just remember my words: this song will be a superhit."' Khanna took Saawan's word in good faith and agreed to do the song.

Film magazine *Star & Style* planned a cover picture of Rajesh and Tina. Film journalist Bharathi S. Pradhan spoke with both and they agreed. A Sunday was allotted for the photo session at Aashirwad. Bharathi tells me, 'The concept of that photo session was a very interesting one. Rajesh Khanna used to famously wear silk lungi-kurtas at home. We suggested that we take a set of the lungi-kurta and Rajesh would wear only the lungi part and Tina will wear only the kurta . . . In fact, Dimple really helped Tina during this shoot. It was the first time Tina had been to Aashirwad.' The bare-chested Rajesh in a silk lungi with a demure Tina in a red kurta had sizzling chemistry that garnered lots of eyeballs. Rajesh Khanna was in the news again. So far, so good.

Saawan had never met a star actor who agreed to all his decisions so easily and wondered why the industry had labelled Khanna as a difficult man to work with.

He was soon about to find out.

***

Saawan Kumar told me that *Souten* was the first Hindi film to be shot in the beautiful locales of Mauritius. The director and his crew reached before the cast for the pre-shoot groundwork. Finally, two days before the shoot Rajesh Khanna, Dimple, Tina Munim, Pran and Prem Chopra reached Mauritius. Saawan was surprised at the professionalism and easy-going nature of Rajesh Khanna.

The two days before the shoot were for the cast to relax and acclimatize themselves with their new surroundings. Saawan says, 'There was one chamcha of Rajesh Khanna: Vijay. Vijay was a writer, but very close to Kakaji. He came with Kakaji to Mauritius. That evening Kakaji started drinking with him and the session went on till four in the morning.' According to Saawan, Rajesh asked the driver who had been appointed for him to take them to some restaurant for dinner in those early hours of the morning. The driver politely informed them that in Mauritius everything is closed from midnight till 6 a.m. 'Those drivers were actually sub-inspectors. Since we were official guests, they were driving the cars themselves.' Saawan told me that Rajesh started shouting at them . . . 'What do you think of yourself?' They also answered back and an argument started. Rajesh was very drunk. He went to the hotel reception and started abusing Saawan Kumar, calling him names all the way up to his room. He kept shouting, 'What does Saawan Kumar think of himself? He has done terrible arrangements.' He created a huge scene.

Saawan Kumar tried to intervene and called up Rajesh in his room. The moment he heard Saawan's voice, Rajesh became hysterical and started throwing a volley of abuses. Saawan was stunned for a few seconds. He could not believe that this was the same Rajesh Khanna who had become so friendly with him in the last few weeks. He tried to pacify Khanna, but when he continued ranting, Saawan retaliated. He challenged Rajesh to come down and decide the matter once and for all. But Rajesh Khanna did not make an appearance. Instead, veteran actor Pran came downstairs and pacified a distraught Saawan Kumar, who was still wondering why he had become a victim of a disagreement between Rajesh and the drivers.

The very next morning Rajesh Khanna met Saawan Kumar as if nothing had happened the previous night. Saawan and the entire crew were puzzled. Around two or three days later, in the middle of a shoot, Rajesh hugged him and said, *'Yaar tum toh naraaz ho jaate ho.'* [Pal, you get angry so easily!] Saawan breathed a sigh of relief and the rest of the shoot was wrapped up in peace.

***

The team had worked very hard on Rajesh Khanna's styling and clothes. The lead actress, Tina Munim, had been a fan of Rajesh for many years. Rajesh realized this and gave his extra best to maintain his image. The camaraderie between them was obvious in the romantic scenes and songs of the film. Saawan Kumar was extremely happy with the chemistry of his lead pair. 'If someone didn't like their chemistry, it was Rajesh's wife, Dimple, who had also come to Mauritius. I could sense there was lot of tension between them on this issue,' Saawan told me.

According to Saawan Kumar, Rajesh and Tina's affair started during the shooting of *Souten*. Dimple was a witness to their increasing closeness. Then one day when Rajesh came back to his hotel room after a shoot, Dimple was not to be found there. Saawan Kumar recalls, 'He was calling out for her, "Dimpi . . . Dimpi . . ." but Dimple was nowhere to be seen. Then he called me into his room out of concern.' While deliberating on Dimple's whereabouts, Saawan looked around the room and saw something. 'Kakaji, you haven't noticed something. He looked at me. I pointed out the dressing-table mirror. There was something written on the glass with lipstick. I don't remember the exact words, but it went something like . . . "I LOVE YOU, BUT . . ." with a "Goodbye" in the corner of the mirror. Kakaji did not understand the hidden meaning in this message. I thought she had gone back to India.' According to Saawan, this was the incident that triggered Dimple's exit not only from Rajesh's room, but perhaps from his life too. Saawan told me that even before his film started, there were too many rumours of their marriage not working. 'I felt bad that this incident happened on the sets of my film. Afterwards, Dimple didn't come back to Aashirwad.' Saawan suggests that Tina Munim shifted to Aashirwad after this. However, there has been no evidence of her actually moving into Aashirwad to live with Rajesh Khanna.

After spending nine long years together, Rajesh and Dimple separated. Dramatic separations had been a regular feature of their marriage, with Dimple quite often moving into her parents' place. But she had always returned in the past. Now, however, the incident during *Souten* had proved to be the tipping point that made Dimple walk out, never to return.

***

Khanna's control over Anju's career had resulted in an acrimonious relationship between the two. Similarly, his control over Dimple's career stifled her. He once told Bharathi S. Pradhan, 'I was shaving in the morning when Dimpi started following me, trying to say something. I could see that she was hesitant, unsure of how to break it to me. And then it burst out from her that Manoj Kumar had offered her a film.' But Rajesh was determined that his wife would not work as an actress as long as she lived with him. Pradhan narrated how Rajesh Khanna brooded over the film offer made to his wife, and one night, after downing many pegs of his favourite whisky, he went to Manoj Kumar's bungalow, stood outside and hollered at the film-maker, charging him with trying to break up his marriage. Later, they called a truce, with Manoj Kumar dropping Dimple from his film.

For a while, it had become clear that both Rajesh and Dimple had entered into their nuptials with different expectations from the relationship. While Dimple had obeyed Khanna for almost a decade, the issue of Dimple's comeback into films might have remained the main bone of contention and the direct cause of the eventual fallout between the two. According to film journalist Bhawana Somaaya, 'The truth was that the two married each other for all the wrong reasons. They failed each other in every way. And separation was the only way out.'[1]

Dimple was still young and had many offers lined up for her return to films. Rajesh was facing an uncertain future. Perhaps with his new love interest around the corner, Dimple had decided to make a silent exit.

***

The shooting schedule for *Souten* got over and Rajesh came back to Bombay. The film industry was abuzz with the news of Rajesh and Dimple's break-up. He immediately left for the Vaishno Devi shrine in Jammu to shoot for Mohan Kumar's *Avtaar*. It was reported that he had appeared disoriented during the shoot in Jammu.

What was perhaps troubling him was the consequential displacement of his two daughters. After every fight with Dimple, one of the main reasons for patching up had always been the kids. He had grown utterly fond of his daughters. Staying away from them was very painful for him. After their separation, when asked whether he hated Dimple, Rajesh replied, 'No. Even on the day she left, I told her, *"Rishta toda hai, dosti na todna."* [We've ended the relationship; let's not end the friendship.] She is the mother of my two kids and we have shared so many beautiful moments. If, despite this, she desires a career, something must be missing somewhere. It means I have failed. The fault is mine.'[2]

CHAPTER 30

The release of *Souten* was near. Overseas prints had already been delivered. The delivery of the prints in India was to be done after two days. About a week before the release, a trial show had been organized on a Saturday. Meanwhile, the news had been seeping in that another Khanna starrer *Avtaar* had just been released and had become a surprise super-hit. Rajesh Khanna's performance as the ageing father had become the talk of the town, with audiences and critics praising it equivocally. Rajesh was overjoyed.

He specially invited veteran film-makers Shakti Samanta and Ramanand Sagar for the trial show of *Souten*. After the show he discussed the film with them. He was desperate to bank upon the sudden and unexpected success of *Avtaar*. He had almost given up. It was his last chance to rejuvenate his ailing star image. Saawan Kumar told me, 'After about twenty minutes of conversation [with Samanta and Sagar], he [Rajesh] came and said "Saawan, let's go home and have a drink." I asked, "What happened, Kakaji? Please tell me." He said, "Nothing . . . Let's go home."'

At Aashirwad Rajesh Khanna offered him drinks and after much insistence said, 'Saawanji, Shaktida and Ramanand Sagar have told me something . . . You will have to make changes in the film.' At this a confused Saawan asked him what changes the star wanted. Rajesh replied, 'Look . . . I am RAJESH KHANNA . . . I am the bigger star than the two heroines. But what am I doing in the climax?' Saawan was taken aback. Rajesh had seen the film before and hadn't felt the need for any changes. Now, as they stood a week from its release, the star suddenly wanted revisions in the film? With a lump in his throat, fearing the worst, a bewildered Saawan Kumar asked, 'What do you want to do now?' To this Rajesh non-committally replied, 'You should do something; think about it and tell me.' Rajesh wanted the climax of the film to change a week before its release—and didn't have an idea as to what that change should be! Saawan Kumar could only stare back in complete bewilderment.

Finally he told Rajesh nothing could be done now. The prints were ready for delivery. Saawan tried to reason with him, but Rajesh Khanna was fuming in anger and remained adamant. Saawan Kumar got up to leave and on his way out inquired if Rajesh Khanna was at least coming for the film premiere in Delhi four days later. Rajesh stared at Saawan Kumar in pure unforgivable anger for a few moments and then curtly replied, 'NO!'

Vijay Kaul walked Saawan to the gates and asked him not to speak to Kaka at that moment as he was in a foul mood. In an attempt to soothe Saawan Kumar, Vijay told him, 'Kaka is a good man, but he loses his mind for a minute sometimes.'

To this an irritated Saawan answered, 'I know that . . . but that one minute undoes all his goodness. This one minute has already harmed his career a lot and will continue to do so in the future.'

For the next three days Rajesh Khanna and Saawan Kumar didn't speak. On Wednesday morning, Vijay Kaul came to Saawan

Kumar's office and asked Saawan to call up Rajesh Khanna. 'I called up Kaka and he immediately said, "Where are you, yaar? Where do you keep disappearing off?" He spoke as if nothing had happened. I was surprised, but had seen this aspect of Kaka before, so I started laughing. He said that he will come tomorrow for the premiere in Delhi.'

***

On reaching for the premiere in New Delhi, Rajesh Khanna called up the distributor himself to ask about the report of the film. The distributor told him about the heavy advance booking for the weekend. Rajesh Khanna was beaming. He then asked, 'What about at Sheela?' The Sheela was one of the most popular cinema halls of that time in Delhi.

The distributor answered, 'You cannot enter Sheela theatre, sir . . . it's a full house there!' Rajesh started giggling with pleasure. Saawan Kumar proposed the idea of going to Sheela and Kaka readily agreed. So Kaka, Tina Munim and Saawan Kumar went there in the midst of a crowd of 3000 people. During the interval they came on to the makeshift stage near the screen. Kaka asked who wanted to go on the mic first. To this Saawan Kumar said, 'Of course, you will go. You are the face of the film . . . Who knows the director?' Hearing this Kaka immediately took the mic in his hands and announced, while pointing to Saawan, 'Meet him, he is Saawan Kumar . . . He has made this beautiful film.' Recalling this Saawan Kumar says, 'When he shows his humane side, no one can match his charm and generosity.'

Next on the mic, Rajesh followed up with one of the most popular dialogues of the film: *'Main woh bala hoon jo sheeshe se patthar ko todta hoon.'* [I am the one who can break a stone with glass]. This was Prem Chopra's dialogue in the film, but when Rajesh Khanna said it, the crowds erupted in thunderous applause. Nothing else could be heard.

His many fans had returned.

***

The huge success of *Avtaar* and *Souten* had brought him back in the reckoning. Then, in the same year, a semi-hit *Agar Tum Na Hote* completed his hat-trick. The icing on the cake was the mega success of *Disco Dancer* in which he made a famous guest appearance mouthing the popular song 'Goron ki Na Kaalon ki, Duniya Hai Dilwalon Ki'.

The year 1983 belonged to Rajesh Khanna.

Perhaps success irons out differences. After the success of these films Devyani Chaubal's column in the magazine *Star & Style* was titled: 'I Told You So: The Return of Rajesh'. He was nominated for the Filmfare Best Actor category, but missed out to Naseeruddin Shah, who won it for *Masoom*. *Avtaar* found its relevance years later in 2003, when the film *Baghban*, based on the same premise, was successfully remade—ironically, starring Amitabh Bachchan.

A close friend of Rajesh Khanna told me that in the 1970s, when he was hysterically successful, it was so unexpected that it took time to sink in. He couldn't enjoy it properly. Now when success came again, he was living it up. But in an interview to Harmeet Kathuri he said, 'I know over the past few years the lean patch in my career was attributed to my bad acting or bad habits. I was often advised to change. But I did nothing like that. What has actually changed is that over the last year I have been happy in my personal life. That is why I am not irritated any more. It has nothing to do with my films.'[1]

He did not take any names, but it was clear whom Rajesh was referring to. He had signed many films with Tina and both were very open about their relationship. In an interview given to Bharathi S. Pradhan he gave a very famous quote describing his comfort levels with Tina Munim, 'We share the same toothbrush.'[2]

CHAPTER 31

'I'm back on top,' Rajesh Khanna announced in a cover story by senior film journalist Meena Iyer of *Star & Style*. 'Yes,' she wrote, 'he did give Amitabh Bachchan a few sleepless nights in that phase.'

In the 1980s, the cold war that had developed between Rajesh Khanna and Amitabh Bachchan reached its zenith. The 1970s had been a game-changing decade for both the stars, and according to senior film journalist Rauf Ahmed, 'The two mega-stars, with their contrasting styles and predilections, shared the ten years almost equally.' While the average of Rajesh's hits dipped drastically, signalling an end to his superstardom, he still continued to deliver a few decent hits almost every year. Perhaps if he had chosen his films more wisely instead of acting in dozens of bad scripts, he might have been remembered for more than those four years only. Interestingly, out of the top fifty films of that decade, ten belonged to Rajesh Khanna, and ten to Amitabh Bachchan.

Now, ten years after *Namak Haraam*, Amitabh hit a lean phase with films like *Mahaan*, *Nastik* and *Pukar*, while Rajesh finally managed to make a proper comeback with three consecutive hits.

A comeback that he had eagerly anticipated, plotted and prayed for every day of the decade. Rauf Ahmed says, 'Star wars became more focused. It wasn't friendly rivalry any more as in the days of Dilip Kumar, Raj Kapoor and Dev Anand. The contenders scrambled for the top slot with a to-hell-with-ethics disposition.'

Targeting Amitabh's performance in the chartbuster song of the film *Laawaris*, Rajesh said in an interview, 'I will never compromise on my dignity and don a saree and do a "Mere Angane Mein" for all the money and all the applause in the world.'[1] When Ramesh Sippy's *Shakti* released in 1982, Rajesh Khanna was overheard taking a potshot at Bachchan, 'Wow, such a long queue outside movie halls for the man! Didn't know Dilipsaab is such a crowd-puller even at this age'[2]—thereby giving the entire credit of the film to veteran actor Dilip Kumar.

Another time, reacting to criticism on his mood swings and reputation for being one of the least punctual actors as compared to Amitabh's professionalism and punctuality, he said, 'Clerks are punctual. I'm not a clerk . . . I'm an artiste. I'm not a slave of my moods. My moods are my slaves.'[3] It must be said that Amitabh Bachchan has never retaliated or said anything about Rajesh Khanna in any of his interviews. In fact, for a large part of this decade, Amitabh Bachchan had put a self-restriction of sorts on the press. Politician Amar Singh, who was once very close to Amitabh Bachchan, told me, 'Rivalry is a strong sentiment. But Amitabh Bachchan takes on a stoic and imperturbable demeanour. He would behave as if the other person is non-existent. This is worse . . . At least if you speak against a person it's a form of acknowledgement. But if you completely overlook somebody, it's as good as them being dead . . . inconsequential.'

By the end of 1983, the stories of the one-upmanship between the two rival stars once again made headlines. Rajesh Khanna was shooting for Dasari Narayana Rao's *Aaj ka M.L.A. Ramavtar*. Around the same time *Inquilaab*, an Amitabh starrer, was in the making. Both the films had a similar subject, where a common man is trapped in the political system. So both star camps raced to be the early bird and release their film first.

It was alleged that Amitabh Bachchan used his proximity to the Gandhi family to get an early release of his film, while Rajesh Khanna's *Aaj ka M.L.A. Ramavtar* reportedly got stuck with the censor board. Bachchan's *Inquilaab* got cleared quickly despite its very violent climax. Journalist Coomi Kapoor wrote, 'In the *Inquilab* case, it was the chairman's decision that the film be cut drastically . . . The producer was desperate, having booked his film in 105 theatres on 17 January in the race to be ahead of the Rajesh Khanna-starrer *Aaj ka M.L.A. Ramavtar*. Bachchan stepped in, rushing to Delhi with the print . . . decision was overturned by higher-ups in the ministry in Delhi . . . The film was released on schedule all over the country.'[4]

Rajesh Khanna's film could only release a month later, in March 1984. Despite such controversy and real politics around the political-themed films, both the films flopped at the box office.

***

Riding high on the sudden return of love and popularity in his life, Rajesh Khanna felt vindicated. He had always strongly—and perhaps almost inanely—believed that the crowds that used to throng outside Aashirwad would return for him. For him, the crowds were always around the corner waiting for him to deliver huge blockbusters. With three hit films the elusive superstardom seemed to be somewhere near. Rajesh, without learning almost anything from the past, set out on the quest for his crowd-pulling blockbuster by signing as many films as he could, yet again. A number of these films were fronted by South Indian producers, usually poor remakes of the originals and complete misfits for Rajesh Khanna's image. In less than two years, between 1984 and 1985, there were a total of nineteen films starring Rajesh Khanna, vying for the audiences' attention. For some unknown reasons, Rajesh Khanna could never understand that releasing ten to eleven films in a year is akin to suicide. Being neck-deep in work seemed to be his raison d'être.

Out of these, some films like *Maqsad*, *Amrit*, *Rajput* and a few others were successful, but most of them, like *Paapi Pet ka Sawal Hai*, *Dharm aur Qanoon*, *Insaaf Main Karoonga*, failed miserably. In fact such was the oversaturation that theatres were running different films of his at the same time. The success of one film led to the failure of others as the audiences had to choose between many. Also, with the advent of VCPs and VCRs, the film business was beginning to be adversely affected by video piracy. Multi-starrer action films could still draw crowds to theatres, but social dramas like the ones Rajesh acted in were limited to home-viewing.

During this phase there was no one like Devyani Chaubal who could try to polish the image of the fading star and even praise his bad films. It is said that due to a complication involving her diet Devyani fell severely ill. Her health kept on deteriorating, culminating in a paralytic stroke in 1985. The stroke confined her first to a wheelchair and later to the bed. Her column was back after some time, but now unable to write, she used to dictate it. Clearly, the times were changing for Rajesh Khanna and his well-wishers.

***

As if sinking the money of his numerous producers wasn't bad enough, Rajesh set out to be a producer himself. The film was *Alag Alag*. Rajesh assembled all the goodwill that remained in the industry to make the film. He took on Tina Munim as the lead actress, his old associate Shakti Samanta became the director,

R.D. Burman was the music director, Kishore Kumar didn't charge money for the playback, Twinkle gave the clap for the first shot, Mohan Kumar's (*Avtaar* director's) wife broke the customary coconut for good luck, J. Omprakash's wife put the camera on and the director who directed the first shot was none other than Yash Chopra.

Alag Alag tanked, and with it vanished a lot of Rajesh's money and his credibility in the industry. Audiences had liked him with Tina in *Souten*, but the failure of films like *Alag Alag*, *Aakhir Kyon?* and *Adhikar* proved that their pairing was not working any more. With their on-screen relationship not going anywhere, Tina reportedly started asking for commitment in their off-screen personal relationship.

***

Around the same time news of Dimple's comeback to films had started making the rounds. Though they were separated, it seems that it was still very difficult for Rajesh Khanna to accept this fact. What was even more interesting was the fact that she was making her comeback opposite Rishi Kapoor, her hero from *Bobby*. The film was Ramesh Sippy's *Saagar*, and the obvious promotion strategy was to publicize the *Bobby* pair. Bharathi S. Pradhan told me, 'Before the shooting of *Saagar* commenced, Rishi Kapoor actually went to Rajesh Khanna's house, Aashirwad, to seek his permission before doing *Saagar* with his wife. A tipsy Rajesh had lectured Rishi on how he was responsible for breaking up a home, before showing him the gate.'

According to Pradhan, Rajesh's rants bore no fruit and *Saagar* finally brought Dimple back to the studios. After that, she signed a number of films. Among them were *Manzil Manzil* and *Arjun* with Sunny Deol as her co-star.

According to film historian Suresh Kohli, Rajesh Khanna never allowed any one of his paramours to enter the gates of his sanctum sanctorum, Aashirwad, after Dimple walked out of his life. 'He was dead against her working in films,' wrote Kohli, 'but there was precious little he could do to stop her. Even during his romantic dalliance with Tina Munim, he moved into [Munim's] Versova bungalow, spending a fortune getting it redone to his taste.'[5]

While Rajesh was adamant on not letting anyone take Dimple's place in his life, film magazines insinuated that Dimple's handsome co-star, Sunny Deol, had made a permanent place in her life. Stories of their involvement regularly did the rounds. In some reports it was even said that the much-married Sunny Deol had even given Dimple Kapadia the status of a wife. Bharathi S. Pradhan says, 'So close did Sunny get to Dimple that Twinkle and Rinke began to call him "Chhote Papa". Sunny took on the role of de facto husband to Dimple so completely that Simple became his costume designer, making Dimple and Simple a nightmare package that every Sunny producer had to endure and foot the bills for.'[6]

Like Rajesh Khanna, Dimple too was entitled to her decisions in life. But being a traditional conformist, Rajesh Khanna found it very difficult to evolve and accept the new man in his estranged wife's life. According to Dinesh Raheja, 'In the '80s, both the auburn-haired gorgeous Dimple as well as the yesteryear superstar wanted divorce, but when Rajesh Khanna began dodging Dimple's demand for financial security for her young daughters, the actress too refused to sign the divorce papers.'[7] Perhaps another fear that lurked in Rajesh's mind was that divorce meant losing his daughters to Chhote Papa Sunny Deol.

Prashant Kumar Roy told me, 'Once Tina Munim complained to Kakaji that we, the staff at Aashirwad, do not attend to her properly. Kakaji asked me why don't I listen to her? I said, "Kakaji, she is not Bhabhiji." He said, "So what, is she any lesser?" To this I replied, "But sir, Bhabhiji means Dimple.'"

***

Tina Munim wanted a commitment from Rajesh, which was nowhere in sight. Media commentator and author Shobhaa Dé wrote, 'In her company, Rajesh Khanna apparently discovered long-suppressed aspects of himself and she claimed she freed him from the countless hang-ups he'd harboured as a diffident young man . . . "I liberated Kaka from all his inhibitions," she laughed fondly at the memory.'[8] Rajesh himself said that Tina was a balm on the wounds inflicted upon him.

For a very long time, Tina Munim hoped that Rajesh Khanna would marry her after he divorced Dimple. But years kept passing by with no sign of Rajesh wanting to divorce Dimple. And as the pressure on their relationship kept mounting, Tina finally had to take a decision to break up with him.

Souten's director signed both Rajesh Khanna and Tina Munim for his next film *Souten ki Beti*. Saawan recalls, 'He had started living at Tina's house. I went there and we had lunch together. I gave them the signing amount. We did one shooting schedule with them. I spent 13 lakh on the shooting. Then the break-up happened.' As expected, this had huge repercussions on Saawan's film. Rajesh now did want to star in a film alongside Tina Munim. He apparently gave the director an ultimatum: 'Either she will work in the film or I will. You choose one.' Saawan had not forgotten the experience of his previous film. In the end, he decided to shelf the footage from the first shooting schedule and instead make the film from scratch with a new lead pair: Jeetendra and Jaya Prada.

Film journalist Ingrid Albuquerque, who had known Tina for years, wrote about this particular break-up, 'I asked her why she was doing it. She said that it was because he had promised her several times he would divorce Dimple, but [had] never got down to even speaking to Dimple about it. She did not want to continue with a relationship that was going nowhere; she left him though he wept and begged her not to go; her goodbye gift to him was to make copies of twenty of his best films and put them in velvet covers with the title name in gold threads—trust Tina to always do things in style.'[9]

After three consecutive unsuccessful relationships, Rajesh was left emotionally drained. As always, he remained a complex personality. He did not stand by the woman he committed to (Dimple), and did not commit to the women who stood by him (Anju and Tina).

Shobhaa Dé once asked Tina if she and Rajesh were truly in love, but she smiled and shook her head while saying, 'Kaka was incapable of loving anyone. He was only in love with himself.'[10]

CHAPTER 32

Film-maker Mahesh Bhatt once said that Rajesh Khanna was akin to the last Mughal emperor, Bahadur Shah Zafar. Like the delusional emperor, Rajesh had lost his kingdom, but still wasn't ready to accept that his time had passed.

In the 1980s the Hindi film industry was going through a striking change in terms of the content and style of film-making. The old guard made way for the new, and this period was marked by Rajendra Kumar's son Kumar Gaurav, who was launched in the musical smash hit *Love Story* and achieved overnight success. Many experts compare the stardom of Kumar Gaurav with that of Rajesh Khanna, but in Gaurav's case it was very short-lived. He ended up as a one-film wonder. Talented actors like Anil Kapoor, Sunny Deol, Sanjay Dutt and Jackie Shroff made their presence felt. After years of majorly bad films and an atrocious phase of cheap lyrics and forgettable music, better Hindi cinema and melodious music bounced back towards the end of the 1980s in the form of *Qayamat Se Qayamat Tak* (1988). It was produced by Nasir Hussain, who had given Rajesh one of his initial films *(Baharon ke Sapne)* almost two decades back. His latest smash hit gave the industry a new romantic star Aamir Khan. This was followed by another musical smash hit *Maine Pyar Kiya* (1989), launching scriptwriter Salim Khan's son Salman Khan.

More eminently forgettable films like *Woh Phir Aayegi* and *Mamta ki Chhaon Mein* always kept Rajesh Khanna busy during this period. But at the end of the day he was alone and defeated. Rajesh Khanna reached out to people he had once scoffed at because of his great ego. Yash Chopra came back to him in a nondescript role in his multi-starrer *Vijay*, which proved to be a mega flop.

Then, one fine day, according to film journalist and author Bhawana Somaaya, apparently Rajesh Khanna just picked up his phone and called up Anju Mahendroo and broke the ice. Reciprocating the gesture, Anju invited him over for a drink. He agreed, and then dropped by one evening at the same old bungalow on Juhu road that he had gifted to Anju—and later led his baraat past it to embarrass her. Bhawana wrote, 'When he parked his car outside the gate, it was as if time stood still. The Mahendroos recognized the honk and the old dog rushed to greet his master.'[1] That evening it was as if he had travelled back in time. With a cigarette in his hand, Rajesh Khanna settled down in his favourite chair and ordered his favourite drink. The evening went off smoothly and old ties were revived. From an ex-girlfriend, Anju transformed into his best friend and confidante, besides assisting him in his office. Anju said, 'When we spoke to each other for the first time after almost seventeen years, I admit that both of us felt a bit awkward. I didn't call him Jatin as I used to in the past and he didn't call me Nikki. I didn't call him Kaka either. It would have been too filmi!'[2]

The second step, perhaps, was to reach out to Dimple. He turned a leaf, and donned the hat of producer and started a film called *Jai Shiv Shankar*, with Dimple cast opposite him in the lead. For reasons unknown, the film was never released, although the shooting was completed. And apparently it had some 'torrid love scenes', according to film historian Suresh Kohli. Later Rajesh said in an interview, 'I had no problems about my wife working. But when I married Dimple I wanted a mother for my children . . . I had no idea about Dimple's talent . . . I wouldn't have stopped her. To curb talent is cruel. By the time I saw *Bobby* our first daughter was already born. But later, when I lived with Tina for seven years . . . I said, "Work, get it out of your system." I did not want to repeat the same mistake.'[3] He even offered to produce a film for his daughter Twinkle.

***

Many people in the industry believed that the film had been an attempt to get publicity via Dimple as she was a bigger news-making actor by now. Senior journalist and editor of Bollywood News Service, Dinesh Raheja, told me, 'At that time every film magazine was trying for a joint interview of Rajesh and Dimple.' Raheja has been a close witness to this phase of Rajesh Khanna's career. In the year 1990, as the editor of *Movie* magazine, Dinesh and senior journalist Nina Arora decided to 'try something different'—a joint interview of Amitabh Bachchan and Rajesh Khanna[4] 'despite knowing that they don't see each other or work together any more,' Dinesh recalled.

Nina was close to Rajesh, so it was decided that since Rajesh was senior, he should be approached first. Rajesh heard her and instantly said yes. Then Dinesh and Nina went to meet Amitabh. They told Amitabh that, as protocol, they had first asked Rajesh Khanna and he has said yes. Amitabh thought for a moment and also agreed. The deal was done.

But the journalists were now worried for a valid reason. The reason was that being a stickler for punctuality, Amitabh would reach the venue (Centaur Hotel, Mumbai) on time, while Rajesh had the reputation of being Mr Late. 'We were very scared. We had booked a room in Centaur. At the stipulated time my eyes were transfixed at the gate. At the decided hour, Amitabh made an entry. My anxiety heightened thinking how Amitabh will react if we had to wait long for Rajesh. But at that very moment magic happened. Rajesh Khanna entered the hotel lobby from the other gate. At the same instant two greatest superstars of Indian cinema were walking towards each other after almost seventeen years. It was a memorable visual,' recalls Dinesh Raheja. For perhaps the first time in his life, Rajesh Khanna was on time. What was he thinking? Why had he agreed to the joint interview?

Rajesh ordered whisky, and wine was ordered for Amitabh. Seventeen years of awkwardness filled the air. Amitabh was jittery with anticipation while Rajesh seemed to be overflowing with enthusiasm. 'The interview was not happening initially. The usual boring answers. They were answering in monosyllables,' Dinesh informs me. Such was Rajesh's enthusiasm that he almost hijacked the interview by cross-questioning Amitabh throughout the interview. He almost became the interviewer himself, like an emotional, inquisitive child. This made Amitabh cagey and he answered in monosyllables. But Rajesh had come prepared to show warmth and showered Amitabh with unhesitant praise. Rajesh said, 'After *Deewar* I always envied him. Only thing is I smiled each time he slipped because he made the same mistakes that I once made.' An admittance to jealousy seemed out of character for the ever-egoistic Rajesh Khanna. But perhaps after seventeen years, Rajesh had been able to come to terms with the epochal year of 1973. It was the same year he broke up with Anju, married Dimple, and his last films with Yash Chopra *(Daag)* and Amitabh *(Namak Haraam)* were released. It took Rajesh seventeen years to accept things and move on. Or did he?

In this interview Rajesh Khanna opened his heart in his own dramatic way. From his iconic superstardom to the dark alleys of failure, it was an emotional retelling. Rajesh Khanna admitted, 'I felt next to God! I still remember the exact moment when, for the first time, I became aware of how mind-blowing success can be. It psyches you totally—or you are not human? It was just after *Andaz* [in 1971], at a lottery draw held at the Vidhan Sabha in Bangalore . . . it was like a stadium from the time of the Romans. I wept like a baby . . . When I started slipping I hit the bottle.'[5]

Remembering the interview Dinesh goes back in time, 'He was one of his kind. Stars like them don't happen any more. He was enigmatic, he knew how to hook you in an interview. He used to talk from the heart . . . and yes, what a beautiful voice he had!' Throughout the interview most of Amitabh's answers sound politically correct, as if a lot of thought and planning went into them. Dinesh agrees: 'Amitabh Bachchan was more guarded in that interview and Kakaji was telling him "Come on! You must have got affected by success? How can you say you are not affected?" He was all heart. He was complimenting Amitabh. He said, "You took over me." They even spoke about their wives . . . Rajesh is such an incorrigible romantic at heart.'

Amitabh returned the compliments, confessing that Rajesh Khanna had been his inspiration to get into films and it was a dream come true to work with him in *Anand*. 'I got famous purely because I was working with Rajesh Khanna.' He said, 'Whether it was on the sets of *Anand* or *Namak Haraam*, we never ever bickered or argued or tried to upstage one another in any manner.'

Dinesh Raheja tells me that this issue of their magazine was a bestseller. The film industry couldn't believe that both the stars had given a joint interview. Later, when Dinesh had a chance meeting with Mahesh Bhatt, the latter shouted, 'You have created history!'

PART V

1991–2010

Zindagi ke safar mein guzar jaatey hain jo maqaam
Woh phir nahi aatey . . . woh phir nahi aatey . . .

(Song from *Aap ki Kasam*, 1974)

Question: What if you were the PM?

RK: I would rule the country romantically.

CHAPTER 33

'Film star Rajesh Khanna filed his nomination today as a Congress-I candidate from the New Delhi constituency.'

On 26 April 1991, news anchor Usha Albuquerque beamed this headline on the prime-time news bulletin of Doordarshan. A Friday is very important in an actor's life as films are released on this day of the week. April 26 was also a Friday . . . a new beginning in the life of actor Rajesh Khanna.

The Congress party needed a face who could be a star campaigner as well as contest elections if required. Rajesh Khanna fit the bill. Rasheed Kidwai, the author of Sonia Gandhi's biography, told me, 'It is correct that Rajiv Gandhi brought Rajesh Khanna . . . he wanted for people from different fields and thoughts to join his party. With Rajesh Khanna he had an excellent tuning.'

In Delhi Rajesh Khanna came to be in touch with Congress student leader Bhupesh Raseen. Bhupesh has been a huge fan of Rajesh Khanna. He is the person who remained closest to Rajesh in the last two decades of his life. He became a friend, adviser and like a younger brother to Rajesh Khanna. Today, a large portrait of Rajesh Khanna adorns his office in Malviya Nagar, south Delhi. Sharing the memories of Rajesh Khanna with me, Bhupesh told me, 'We were like brothers. Our fathers were both from Lahore. Kakaji used to travel with me. He was attached with the Congress since Sanjay Gandhi's time, then he got close to Rajiv Gandhi too. Kakaji used to tell Rajiv Gandhi, "You are so handsome . . . you look like a superstar." Rajiv Gandhi used to laugh and say, "I am your fan, you are the real superstar."'

Former political editor of *Hindustan Times*, Pankaj Vohra told me that Ambika Soni's name was almost finalized as the contestant for the New Delhi Lok Sabha seat. It is a Punjabi-dominated area. Then R.K. Dhawan and Brij Mohan Bhama suggested to Rajiv Gandhi that he bring in Rajesh Khanna to contest. Rajiv Gandhi instantly approved his name.

This seat was a fight against the BJP heavyweight Lal Krishna Advani. There was hardly any time to think and mull over the issue as Rajesh Khanna had to file his nomination in a day. At that time talking to the film journalist Nina Arora, he said, 'Ultimately, whenever I take a decision, it's always an overnight one. And I genuinely believe that the Congress-I alone can bring stability to the nation.' Overnight, Rajesh Khanna decided to take the plunge.

After the Ram Janma Bhoomi Aandolan, Advani's star was further on the rise. Everyone felt that Rajiv Gandhi was placing a big bet on Rajesh Khanna and that victory was going to be very tough. But Rajesh was thrilled with the faith and respect that the prime minister had reposed in him. Like a seasoned politician he mocked his opponent, 'Mr Advani has just rushed to Gandhinagar to file his nomination from a second constituency. That doesn't say much for his confidence in his New Delhi voters.'

Khanna was all excitement with this new responsibility. It was almost as if he was playing a new role of a politician in a film and was methodically preparing for it in all seriousness. But in politics there are generally no retakes.

The interview with Nina Arora happened when Rajesh Khanna went back to Bombay after filing his nomination from New Delhi. There was an air of excitement in his Bandra-Linking Road office. For the last few years, the office hadn't seen such a bevy of activity. According to Nina Arora, playing the perfect hostess was none other than Anju Mahendroo. Rajesh Khanna's face was brimming with the enthusiasm of beginning a new innings.

'This New Delhi constituency isn't going to be a cakewalk. Why did you agree?' asked Nina. In reply Rajesh Khanna was silent. He continued to purposely fidget with his spectacles. According to Nina, it was a familiar trick of Khanna's—pretending to look through, and if you didn't take the hint, he would ignore you. 'But I knew him well enough to know that this ruse is actually a defence mechanism used by the little boy who resides within, hiding behind the celebrated Khanna arrogance. That day, the little boy was highly excited, but nervous as hell too.'

Talking animatedly like a seasoned politician he said, 'Politics is a different ball game. It's not like films.'

Anju couldn't resist pulling his leg and commented, 'I wish we could all be in Delhi to see you campaigning in 45 degrees! *Yahan*, if even one air-conditioner conks out, you get so restless in spite of your portable fan.'

Everyone present there laughed at this, including Rajesh Khanna himself. But the obvious questions hung in the air. It was a second debut. The last time Rajesh had faced the future with such anticipation was perhaps before the release of *Aradhana*.

***

It was a dark night in 1991 in New Delhi. Gargi Parsai, who used to work with the *Hindustan Times*, was in peaceful slumber after a hectic day at work, when the phone started ringing. She picked up the phone to hear: *'Hello! Main Rajesh bol raha hoon.'* [Hello, this is Rajesh speaking.]

The clock showed it was a quarter past one in the morning. Stupefied, she asked, *'Kaun Rajesh?'* [Rajesh who?]

'Rajesh Khanna,' came the reply.

Hearing this name Gargi Parsai was jolted into wakefulness.

Gargi works with the *Hindu* now. Talking about that phone call twenty-two years ago, she still laughs about how her sleep vanished on hearing his name: 'His voice was slurring . . . perhaps he was drunk. I asked him what happened that you have called me so late?'

Rajesh Khanna started complaining like a kid, 'You people . . . the Delhi media is not supporting me. I have come from Bombay. I need a foothold and you people are not helping me. I know I am a first-timer, but at least give me a chance . . . You people are not giving a chance . . .' Gargi told me that he was speaking continuously without realizing that this was not an appropriate time to call a stranger. Gargi tried to reason with him, saying that the media is giving him as much coverage as it is to Mr Advani. But perhaps because he was inebriated, Rajesh Khanna was not in the mood to listen: 'I know Advaniji is a big leader. But if the media gives me good coverage, I can win.'

Gargi recalls the call was so long that her sleep vanished. 'It was only after the call ended that I realized I had received a call from the Superstar, the Phenomenon that girls would give their right arm to receive a smile from.'

The next morning Khanna perhaps realized his mistake. His secretary called Gargi and apologized for the late-night call.

For the film media of Bombay, he was the superstar, but here in the political game, he was a debutant player. His image as a politician was not as big as that of L.K. Advani. He was desperate to be on good terms with the Delhi media. Pankaj Vohra says, 'As a secretary general of the Press Club of India, I invited him for a "Meet the Press" programme.' He came wearing his trademark kurta-pyjama. He was accompanied by Bharat Upmanyu, a noted astrologer and one of his most trusted associates in Delhi.'

Initially, Rajesh Khanna used to live in the Som Vihar locality of Delhi, then he shifted to his friend Naresh Juneja's flat in Vasant Kunj in south Delhi. When he started campaigning, it became obvious why Rajiv Gandhi had brought him on this prestigious seat. There were huge crowds in his election rallies. Rajesh Khanna exuded superstardom and had a charisma that drew women of all ages to him instantaneously. Gargi Parsai covered his campaign. She told me that in the initial rallies, he came with a handful of affluent-looking women dressed in crisp white saris from Bombay who used to accompany him everywhere. It was very clear that nobody in his team had an idea about the Delhi crowds and political acumen/culture. 'But when he spoke—and he spoke little—he mesmerized people,' said Gargi. 'A smile and a wave of the hand was enough to make people pledge their vote to him.'

Bhupesh Raseen says, 'His charm was infectious. He used to say a few lines and would end his speech with a famous dialogue or *shayari*. Sometimes he used to call lyricist Anand Bakshi to write lines for his speech.'

A journalist who covered his rally in the Gol Market area of New Delhi told me that the audience there demanded him to utter his iconic dialogue from *Amar Prem*: 'Pushpa! I hate tears.' Rajesh immediately improvised according to the situation and said, crinkling his eyes, 'I'll wipe the tears of all the Pushpas and all the women present here because . . . Pushpa . . . I hate tears.' At that moment, only a thunderous applause could be heard. Like a seasoned performer, he knew how to impress his audience and get the right reaction in election rallies. But what were the problems the people were facing in his constituency? What were the election issues? He had little information about it.

In the last phase of campaigning, Rajesh's estranged wife, Dimple, and his daughter Twinkle also accompanied him. Rajesh Khanna even organized a press conference with them. A journalist who attended the conference says, 'Everyone felt that though Dimple must have come at his insistence, she looked quite uncomfortable in this whole scenario. But Twinkle was very charming. She answered the questions of the press.'

Pankaj Vohra told me that there used to be drinking sessions in the evenings and the starry tantrums used to be on full display, 'He was a nasty drinker . . . His baithaks mostly had his chamchas. To have fun, he used to target his chamchas, and sometimes if someone argued he used to get very angry. He was strangely temperamental.'

Gargi Parsai narrated another anecdote about him. Once, after one of his political press conferences, she went to speak to Rajesh in person. She waited outside his sanctum and he soon emerged to speak to her. But before she could speak, suddenly he turned around, raised his arm and showed her his kurta. Taken aback, the journalist gave an inquiring look. Smilingly, he pointed out a tear at the pocket. 'See I am wearing a torn kurta.' Gargi laughed at the way he said it. 'Why don't you get it mended or simply go in for a new one?' she asked. After all, he had so many people working for him. At that moment he simply went silent. Time seemed to stand still. Perhaps he didn't have an answer. Gargi told me, 'Despite being surrounded by so many people, he was perhaps too lonely . . . and too proud to admit his loneliness. It was a very poignant moment.'

CHAPTER 34

On 20 May 1991, Delhi went to vote. To cast their votes Rajiv and Sonia Gandhi reached the polling booth at 7.30 a.m. at Nirman Bhawan in New Delhi. Their daughter, nineteen-year-old Priyanka Gandhi, was with them too as she cast her vote for the first time. Rajesh Khanna accompanied them . . . talking and chatting . . . confident of his victory.

The next morning, 21 May 1991, almost all newspapers carried the picture where Rajiv and Sonia Gandhi can be seen casting their votes. This was incidentally also their last public photograph together. The same night, on 21 May, Rajiv Gandhi was assassinated in Sriperumbudur in Tamil Nadu, where he had gone for an election campaign rally.

No one expected Rajesh Khanna to actually be competition to senior leader L.K. Advani. But a surprise was in store on the counting day. The counting was being done at the UPSC Building on Shajahan Road, near India Gate. It was a time of manually counting votes, unlike today's EVM technology. The Advani camp had prepared for a party in advance, they had organized a band to celebrate once his victory was announced. But Rajesh Khanna was maintaining a lead from the very beginning. By afternoon seven rounds of counting had been completed and Rajesh was still ahead of Advani. This sent panic signals in the BJP camp. Bhupesh Raseen recalls, 'His lead sent shock waves in the BJP camp. The returning officer was Satbir Silas Bedi, who said that Kakaji was ahead till round seven. People close to Advaniji had started chanting the Hanuman Chalisa.'

But at this point Rajesh Khanna did something that can only be attributed to his political inexperience. Pankaj Vohra told me that even before the announcement of the results, thinking that Khanna's lead was decisive, Rajesh Khanna's supporters came out and went to buy garlands and sweets from the nearby Gauri Shankar temple, leaving the counting unwatched. 'Suddenly we heard loud noises from the BJP camp. Someone told me that Advaniji had won by 1500 votes. I remember that Jag Pravesh Chandra was the election officer, and Satbir Silas was the returning officer. So according to normal procedure Jag Pravesh should have demanded a recount . . . but he did not. He accepted the result.' Vohra further explained that it all happened so soon that no one had any clue.

Rasheed Kidwai also remembers the evening, 'The vigil that was needed till the last vote was counted, that was not there. Khanna's supporters were busy celebrating. Rajesh Khanna too had no idea . . . he was too inexperienced for the system and paid a heavy price.'

L.K. Advani defeated Rajesh Khanna by a meagre margin of 1589 votes. The political bigwig Advani had got 93,662 votes, and debutant politician Rajesh Khanna had notched up 92,073. Rajesh Khanna had fought very well indeed.

Despite almost tasting victory, Rajesh Khanna had lost. He was angry and felt cheated. So he created a scene at the counting booth. Once a bad loser, always a bad loser.

***

Post the results the Congress formed the government and India got P.V. Narasimha Rao as its new prime minister. Meanwhile, Advani who had contested from two Lok Sabha seats, left the New Delhi seat and opted for the Gandhinagar seat in Gujarat, since he had won there with a huge margin. The New Delhi seat was vacant again. Destiny had given Rajesh Khanna another chance.

This time BJP's contestant against Rajesh Khanna was another star from the Hindi film industry Shatrughan Sinha. According to Pankaj Vohra the by-election was expected to be a one-sided affair tilted towards Rajesh Khanna. But the campaign was very filmy and entertaining with both the stars quoting dialogues from their films.

This time Rajesh himself was worried, anticipating another defeat. He told his associates that his opponents might conspire to stop him from winning the elections again. In his mind, anyone who didn't toe his line was an enemy who should be punished.

***

Invariably, there were also those in New Delhi who did not have a favourable opinion of Rajesh Khanna, because their experiences of interacting with him were extremely unpleasant. One such person is a former commissioner of Delhi Police, who used to be the deputy commissioner of police (DCP) of the district from where Rajesh Khanna was contesting elections. According to him, Rajesh Khanna is a man 'who doesn't understand how things work in the government, who has no respect for the law, no respect for rules and regulations, and a person who was totally self-obsessed.'

The officer still remembers the terrible experience he had with Rajesh Khanna. He told me that during elections it is always considered better to meet the contestants, so that there is a certain amount of rapport and in the event of a law-and-order situation the police can always directly communicate with them. It's a regular practice in the police force.

'So I went to meet him at his residence in Vasant Kunj. He was extremely charming. Even though I have never been a great fan of his, I must say that I was totally charmed by his personality, by his talk and by the way he treated me.'

And there was more charm to follow. Two days later, Rajesh Khanna was at Hotel Ashok in south Delhi. The DCP's residence was very near to the hotel, in Chanakyapuri. Rajesh called him up and said that he had come to the hotel for some function and if the DCP was at home, Khanna would like to visit him. 'I asked him to please come. I thought he was returning my visit. So my children were very excited, my wife was very excited. Rajesh Khanna came, he posed for photographs. They were all charmed by him. He came across as a very humble and a very charming person.'

But then came the anticlimax.

About a week later, the DCP got a call from Rajesh Khanna. He said that there was a demolition party of the MCD which had come to the Lajpat Nagar police station which was under the DCP's charge. Rajesh Khanna demanded that the DCP should give instructions to the SHO (police station in-charge) that he should not provide any police force and support for the demolition party. (It was a building of someone known to Khanna.) Rajesh Khanna did not want the demolition to take place. The officer recalls, 'He wanted the demolition to be stopped. I told him that things don't work like this. It is the duty of the police to provide assistance to the demolition party. Now that you have brought it to my notice, I am going to ask the police station to make sure that the demolition party gets police assistance.' Rajesh Khanna lost his temper. Disagreement with his views in any form was unacceptable to him.

'Then he threatened me on the phone. He said, "This is not what I expected from you, the consequences will be very bad."

So I said, "You can do what you want and I will do whatever is required to be done." I even rang up the police station and asked them to carry out the demolition according to the procedure,' says the officer.

According to the officer, Rajesh Khanna took this snub to heart and went to the PM's house on the issue. He complained that the DCP of the area was anti-Congress, that he was anti-Rajesh Khanna, and pro-BJP. He even complained that the officer was a relative of Shatrughan Sinha, the rival candidate. The officer, it seems, also hails from Bihar, like Shatrughan Sinha. Rajesh demanded the officer's removal. Nothing came of this, but his tirade continued.

Then things got worse. The officer recalls, 'Mr Mukund Kaushal was the commissioner of the Delhi Police in those days. A drunk Rajesh called up the commissioner very late at night around 3 a.m. He asked the commissioner what was the worst posting a UT cadre officer could have, which was the farthest from Delhi and the most difficult? So Mr Kaushal—just to kind of ward him off, or maybe he wanted to go back to sleep—said there is a place called Saiha in Mizoram. Rajesh thanked him and finished the call.'

The next day, according to the officer, Rajesh started using his influence to get this man transferred to Mizoram, but did not succeed. 'There were demonstrations against me on the day of the polling,' claimed the officer. 'One of them, I clearly remember, was opposite the Lodhi Colony police station.'

The result of the by-election was totally on expected lines. On 8 June 1992 Rajesh Khanna defeated the BJP candidate Shatrughan Sinha and became a member of Parliament. The political journey that he started almost a year back had finally culminated in success.

With much disgust, the officer told me, 'We never met after that. Whatever respect I had for film people in general, and this person in particular, all of it was wiped away. I also realized that you could be self-centred, self-obsessed, but it is not necessary that you would be vicious, scheming, vindictive and want to harm someone just because he had not done what you had wanted him to do. So this was Mr Rajesh Khanna for me, may he rest in peace.'

***

After becoming an MP, Rajesh Khanna initially remained in the news courtesy his celebrity status. But apart from changing the political equations of the country, Rajiv Gandhi's death changed things for Rajesh Khanna too. Rasheed Kidwai says, 'Rajesh Khanna used to flaunt his closeness with Rajiv Gandhi a lot. After Rajiv's death it really harmed him.'

Journalist Vijay Simha, who covered Rajesh Khanna elections extensively, wrote, 'You could never catch Khanna by himself in Delhi. He always had about thirty to fifty people fawning over him. Some Congressmen didn't like it. They thought he was still acting it out.'

After Rajiv Gandhi it had become even more difficult to contact the high command. Khanna felt lost and confused. Politician Amar Singh says, 'The Congress is a monolithic organization. Even if you are an important leader, it is not necessary that you can get in touch with the party high command at your will. I remember there was a time when a senior leader like Sunil Dutt couldn't get a meeting with Rajiv Gandhi for two years. During election campaigning, the Congress used Rajesh Khanna and then he was discarded. Such things used to hurt him.'

It was widely reported that Rajesh Khanna was brought to settle scores with Amitabh Bachchan. But according to Amar Singh, even after leaving politics, Amitabh's relations with the Gandhi family were intact, 'The personal access that Amitabh Bachchan had to the Gandhi family was more than what Rajesh

Khanna enjoyed. Bachchan was like a family member while Rajesh Khanna was never considered more than just a party member. Rajesh didn't like that.'

As a politician no one took him seriously. As a member of Parliament his contribution was nothing to talk about. He couldn't even utilize his MP fund and couldn't do anything significant for his constituency. Accepting that the road of politics is not an easy one to travel, he said, 'Winning an election is one thing and then using that platform to get the actual work done for ordinary people runs into a whole new set of challenges . . . I did become a professional politician, but could not become a political superstar. *Kismet kahin to kum karegi.* [Fate has to hold something back.]'

In 1996 Rajesh Khanna lost his seat to BJP's Jagmohan by a margin of 58,315 votes. One of his close friends in Delhi told me that after this defeat, he lost the confidence to fight the elections again. He did try unsuccessfully for a Rajya Sabha seat for a few years, but his political career was over.

He had to go back to his city, Bombay, which had now officially changed its name and had become Mumbai. And along with the name of the city, the film industry too had changed and moved on.

CHAPTER 35

'I want to do something . . . I am not hungry for money . . . I've enough money by God's grace. But the actor inside me is restless,' said Rajesh Khanna to television producer and actor Dheeraj Kumar.

Rajesh Khanna was now disillusioned with politics and didn't have any films in hand. His last film with a prestigious banner had been Rishi Kapoor's directorial venture *Aa Ab Laut Chalen*, which had also flopped. Dheeraj still remembers the conversation that happened at Khanna's Linking Road office, 'I understood what he meant. How much can you eat or drink or try to bide your time in office? The pain he was feeling was of loneliness and neglect. He wanted to work, but the film industry was not ready to even touch him.'

Together they decided to make a television serial *Raghukul Reet Sada Chali Aayi*. This had Rajesh Khanna playing the head of a traditional family. The shooting started and Khanna surprised everyone with his professionalism. 'He used to sit even after pack-up, discussing the shoots. Kaka used to ask the director for the script for the next day. We used to laugh and tell him, *"Kakaji, yeh television hai . . . yahan kal ki script kal hi milegi"* [Kakaji, this is television. Tomorrow's script will be available tomorrow only],' recalls Dheeraj.

Rajesh Khanna as usual got excited with something new in his kitty and organized a trial show of his TV serial for prospective film producers. Dheeraj smiles, remembering the evening: 'I told him, "Yaar, there are no trial shows in television." He said the conference room of your office is like a theatre and you have a projector too. His enthusiasm was infectious. He called up some producers and when they watched it once, Rajesh said, "Please watch it once again." So everyone had to watch the episode twice. While they were watching the episode, I was watching Rajesh Khanna. He was sitting at the back, busy reading the faces of the producers.'

With such enthusiasm Rajesh Khanna worked in some TV serials like *Apne Paraye* (2001), *Ittefaq* (2002) and *Raghukul Reet Sada Chali Aayi* (2007). Each one of them was promoted in his name, but despite all efforts, neither the serials worked, nor did the producers line up at his door. Rajesh made a last desperate attempt at the elusive comeback. How far could he go? And since the big producers refused to even look in his direction, Rajesh ended up signing a C-grade flick called *Wafaa*. Playing the lead role of a business tycoon he romanced a pretty new starlet and even shot some cheap sex scenes. The film was widely panned and his fans hung their heads in shame. This was not something he would—or should—ever be remembered for.

***

This question always baffles Rajesh Khanna fans, that despite a commendable performance as a senior citizen in *Avtaar*, why did producers shy away from signing Khanna for important character roles? The years passed in waiting. People close to Rajesh Khanna remember that he kept on fighting his loneliness and frustration in the hope that the fans would return some day. The actor Sachin Pilgaonkar, who worked with him in *Avtaar*, told me, 'Our industry functions on image. If the image is bad, it is very difficult to change it. Rajesh Khanna towards the later phase tried to change, but perhaps it was too late . . . *Unka naam kharab ho gaya tha.* [His reputation was ruined.] While Bachchansaab's image is still of a very disciplined actor.'

Perhaps Sachin is right—Amitabh Bachchan introspected on the changed scenario and accepted it. He too had suffered various setbacks when his company, Amitabh Bachchan Corporation Ltd (ABCL), went bankrupt. After the ABCL debacle, he went to Yash Chopra to ask for work. Yash signed him for *Mohabbatein* which signalled a successful new innings for Amitabh Bachchan. In a way, this step initiated a turnaround for Bachchan with the iconic game show *Kaun Banega Crorepati* (KBC) following suit, marking his phenomenal comeback. The media also reported positively about his brave return to the limelight.

Nothing of this sort happened with Rajesh Khanna. Neither did he go to any producer to ask for work, nor did anyone come to him with good scripts. Dheeraj Kumar says, 'He wasn't a defeated man, but the media attached a "Loser" tag on him. Gradually he became disheartened . . . Till when you will wait? There were no friends or family who could share his sadness.'

Ashok Tyagi, the director of Khanna's last film, *Riyasat*, said in an interview to ABP News, 'His son-in-law Akshay Kumar worked with Amitabh Bachchan in many films where Amitabh played his father. Given Akshay's stature in the film industry and also when he co-produces many films, was it so difficult for him to manage a few good roles for Rajesh Khanna?'

With every passing day, what remained with Khanna was a deep loneliness residing within him, which had now manifested all around him.

Over time Khanna had let go of most of his office staff, including Prashant. But he remained close to Prashant, who had started working for Salim Khan. Prashant told me that often Rajesh Khanna would call him up and say, 'Prashant, when the older brother becomes poor, does the younger brother forget him?'

On being reassured that he wasn't forgotten, Khanna would reply, 'Who do I have, Prashant? I have nothing apart from this loneliness. *Zindagi kitna badal gaya hai re.* [Life has changed so much.]'

***

When the film industry realizes that the artist has played his innings, the Lifetime Achievement Awards follow. Generally, it is also a subtle hint to hang up one's boots. Rajesh Khanna was honoured with the Filmfare Lifetime Achievement Award in 2005. When the managing editor of *Filmfare*, Meera Joshi, went him to ask if he would come to receive the coveted trophy, Rajesh Khanna agreed, but asked for extra passes for the awards function. 'Even though he'd asked for extra passes, when he came to the venue there was no one with him. Already a shadow of the leading man he once was,'[1] said Meera Joshi.

In June 2006, an organization of some Indians in Trinidad was felicitating Rajesh Khanna and Zeenat Aman with Lifetime Achievement Awards. This was not particularly a favourable time for Rajesh as he had run into some tax problems with the income tax authorities. Senior journalist Meena Iyer was also in Trinidad to cover the event. Meena recalls, 'In fact Kaka and I sat next to each other in business class from Trinidad to London and spent a good six hours going down memory lane. In his head, he was still a superstar. He believed he was King. I didn't correct him.'

In India, Aashirwad had been attached by the tax authorities, so Rajesh Khanna was staying in his huge office on the Bandra-Linking Road above the Titan showroom. Meena told me, 'When he got very lonely in the evenings he would request his driver to take him to McDonalds on Linking Road for a chicken burger and a glass of strawberry milkshake.' There he would elicit the occasional recognizing stare or a passing smile as he sat eating his burger . . . alone.

During this phase Rajesh Khanna tried to stay more often in Delhi, where he had taken an apartment in Sarvapriya Vihar in south Delhi. Bhupesh Raseen, a close confidant of Rajesh's since his political days, told me that by this time the acceptance had started sinking in that his better days had been left far behind. He had resigned himself to fate. He could view his life from a distance as if it had been another man's. With a glass of his favourite Red Label scotch, he used to reminisce about his days of unseen superstardom.

Again, in June 2009, an emotional Rajesh Khanna was honoured with the International Indian Film Academy (IIFA) Lifetime Achievement Award from, ironically, Amitabh Bachchan, as the audience gave Bollywood's first superstar a standing ovation.

On this occasion Rajesh, now sixty-six years old, said, 'I have got this award after 180 films and a forty-year-long journey in the film industry . . . Look where the journey started and how it reached its destination. It is all the blessings of God and the public.' He went on to deliver his most memorable dialogue from *Anand*: '*Itna pyar achcha nahi, Babu Moshaye, ham sabhi rangmanch ki kathputliyan hai . . .*' [Too much love is not good, Babu Moshaye, we all are puppets in the world's theatre . . .]

***

Bhupesh Raseen once narrated a story about a side of Khanna that is not often talked about.

Rajesh's maidservant in Delhi once told him that her widowed sister had to undergo a heart-bypass surgery. Rajesh Khanna offered to take care of the entire expenses for the same. After the surgery, the doctor told him that the patient will have to rest and will not be able to work for the next three months. That day Rajesh Khanna returned home perturbed. Bhupesh told me, 'It was around midnight, and I had slept off. Suddenly I received a phone call from Kakaji. He said, "Bhupesh, bring the Gypsy [car] right now." Before I could ask anything else, he disconnected the call. I was surprised because that Gypsy was normally used during election campaigning. I took the car and reached Kakaji's place. Kakaji came out wearing a kurta-pyjama and said, "Call up Sonu General Store and ask him to urgently pack the rations for six months in new jars and boxes. Complete rations." Irritated, I said, "Kakaji, let's do it in the morning." He said, "No, let's do it right now." As always, when the mood struck him he had to act immediately. We delivered all the rations to the maid's house that very night. I remember while coming back driving, he was lost in his thoughts. He didn't say anything, but there was a smile on his lips.'

Bhupesh tells me this was not a one-off incident. Rajesh took great care of his staff, funded the education of their kids, took care of the marriage expenses of their daughters. 'He never cared for money. By heart he remained a superstar till his last breath,' he added.

Prashant Kumar Roy narrated one more incident when a car dealer came to show a new car to Rajesh Khanna at his house. Prashant asked him whether he was offering any discounts. Hearing this Rajesh Khanna called Prashant inside and told him, 'If you want to buy the car, then buy at the full price or else don't buy. Rajesh Khanna *kabhi discount nahi leta*.' [Rajesh Khanna never asks for or accepts discounts.]

Salim Khan told me that people judge a person on the basis of their experience with the person. If the experience is good, they say the person is good. If the experience is bad the person is branded as bad. But Salim Khan said he would always judge a person on the basis of his behaviour with his personal staff, servants and drivers—and Rajesh Khanna was really good in this aspect. He really helped his entire personal staff throughout their lives. The people who had worked closely with him, like Prashant Roy, his driver, Kabir, and some make-up men will vouch for this.

It is said that even now he commands incredible respect and fan following among his die-hard fans. Greta, who grew up in colonial Africa (Rhodesia, now Zimbabwe), is interestingly very fond of Hindi films and writes a very popular blog thememsaabstory.com, dedicated to Hindi films. One can see her passion for popular Hindi movies, particularly of the 1960s and the 1970s on her blog. She regularly interacts with the die-hard fans of erstwhile stars through her blog. But the craze of Khanna fans even in this era surprises her. Greta said to me, 'It has been my experience that Rajesh Khanna fans are indeed a bit more insane than some, although many stars have some strange devotees. He is deified in a way that amazes—and often amuses—me . . . They tend to be very defensive about him, too, but I think the perception that he's not been given his due for his part in cinema history is not entirely unwarranted.'

***

Bhawana Somaaya once wrote that Rajesh Khanna is 'doomed to be forever alone, in spite of the handful of people who have worked out the survival tricks of dealing with this sullen superstar, and are constantly around him.'[2]

In the loneliest phase of Rajesh Khanna's life, Bhupesh Raseen had become one of the few people whom Rajesh could trust. Bhupesh's son Harsh came to Mumbai with dreams of becoming a film director. Rajesh Khanna took him under his wing and invited him to live in Aashirwad till he could find his bearings in the city. For almost two years, between 2009 and 2011, Harsh stayed with him, receiving the rare privilege of observing Rajesh Khanna closely.

Harsh narrated several important and fascinating anecdotes. Rajesh Khanna had a mini theatre in his house where he organized a screening of *Amar Prem* for Harsh. Harsh recalls, 'It was an important and memorable moment for me when the superstar was sitting beside me, watching his best performance and sharing memories of its making. One hour into the film and he grew silent, lost in his thoughts—on a nostalgic trip into the golden days. Then he suddenly exclaimed to himself, "Wow, Rajesh Khanna! What have you done? It's a masterpiece . . . too good!!! *Kya acting kar gaya tu . . . waah*! [What an amazing performance you gave!]'

When Harsh told me that he had lived with Rajesh Khanna for two years, it took me to another controversy related to Rajesh Khanna that cropped up after his death: his relationship with a lady named Anita Advani, who had claimed to be Rajesh's last lover and live-in partner in the final decade of his life.

Anita Advani is originally from Jaipur, but lives in Bandra in Mumbai. She claims to be the niece of the former president of the Philippines Ferdinand Marcos. In an interview after Rajesh Khanna's death Anita said, 'I call myself his surrogate wife. I have lived-in with him at Aashirwad for around eight years. During this period, I took care of him like a wife would.'[3] She even questioned those people closest to him, demanding where they were when Rajesh Khanna was lonely and depressed. She claimed it was she who was by his bedside when he fell ill initially and was rushed to hospitals for his medical tests. 'I did a *karva chauth* for him. What more proof do I need to give?' claimed Advani emotionally.[4]

Anita Advani's claims had created a huge furore after Rajesh Khanna's death. But Rajesh Khanna's family, including his estranged wife Dimple and two daughters, never talked publicly on the issue. 'I won't talk about Anita Advani,' said Dimple clearly during a press interaction in 2013.

Regarding Anita's claim of living in with Rajesh Khanna, Harsh Raseen says, 'I have seen Anita Advani in Aashirwad. She was friends with Kakaji and used to come to Aashirwad quite often. But in my two years of staying with him, I have never seen her stay at Aashirwad, even for a night. She never ever stayed there like she claims. There was no live-in relationship.'

In fact, months before Rajesh Khanna's death and the subsequent controversy regarding Anita and his relationship, Mumbai-based newspaper *Mid-Day* had published Rajesh's pictures with Anita Advani. There was Anita's statement with the pictures that said, 'I feel very privileged to be very-very close to him. He is a very intelligent and romantic person. We hang out. We are at home together. We do go out for dinners and go on after-dinner drives.'[5]

She further elaborated, 'We are so close. We don't want any strings attached. I think we are very happy as we are. It's a very special, sacred relationship, and I truly cherish it. Unlike a normal relationship, there are no demands and expectations. This is much deeper.'[6]

Rajesh Khanna never commented on this article or the pictures; nor did he say anything on record about Anita Advani's claims published in the newspaper.

Bhupesh Raseen tells me that after the pictures and Anita's interview appeared in newspapers, Rajesh Khanna was very angry. Bhupesh says, 'He hated when someone tried to gain publicity using his name. He told me he had blasted her and even asked her to leave when she came that evening. I have also stayed extensively in Aashirwad whenever I used to visit Mumbai. I have never seen her living with Kakaji.'

Rajesh Khanna himself never spoke much about Anita Advani with anyone close to him; nor had he ever publicly acknowledged the relationship that Advani claims. The complete truth of this relationship may never come out now. However, after Rajesh was diagnosed with cancer, his family came to be at his side. Dimple and Rinke moved into Aashirwad for this purpose. This fact alone would further contradict any claims by Anita Advani that she was living there at the time.

In Aashirwad, Rajesh had become a friend, philosopher and guide to Harsh. Harsh recalls during those days that though he was no more the superstar, he continued to live life king-size with no change in his lifestyle. He would always ensure that his dinner table had an array of multiple dishes. Although he himself ate very little, he was very fond of making other people eat. They would often walk down to the nearby ice-cream parlour on Carter Road and Harsh would be inundated with tales from Rajesh's glorious past. Once a nostalgic Rajesh Khanna said, 'You know, Harsh, this very road we are walking upon used to be crowded with my fans . . . I had never been able to take a walk here in those times . . . Harsh! *Woh bhi ek daur tha . . . yeh bhi ek daur hai . . .* [Those were the glorious times . . .]'

There was a time when Harsh had been rather upset about how much he was having to struggle in Mumbai and how little he had been able to achieve. Rajesh noticed that the young man was troubled. One night, after dinner, he followed Harsh to his room and sat down next to him. Perhaps he had an inkling of what Harsh's troubles might be. After all, he knew how unforgiving and cruel the industry could be. He too had suffered and tasted defeat many times. Rajesh asked him how he was faring in the Hindi film industry. Immediately, the young man unburdened his troubles to Rajesh in a torrential outpouring.

With a knowing smile, Rajesh asked Harsh, 'Have you ever travelled in a train?'

Harsh was surprised at the tangential line of inquiry. What had struggling to find ground in the film industry got anything to do with travelling in trains?

But the ex-superstar had a sudden glow on his face. He continued, 'Just imagine . . . it's a dark night, you are in a second-class compartment and the train is running . . . *dhad-dhad-dhad-dhad-dhad* . . . Suddenly, the train enters a dark tunnel and there's darkness everywhere. You cannot see anything; there is no destination in sight. But despite the darkness, the train is still running on its tracks. It hasn't stopped. Then after some time you can see light at the other end of the tunnel. That light is this film industry. As a struggler you are in a dark tunnel, but do not ever leave the track . . . it will eventually lead you towards the light . . . Never leave hope. Never leave the track of hope and you shall reach your destination.'

Harsh stared at the ex-superstar. This was years of experience talking. The fire in his young belly was rekindled.

Just then the old man said, 'But, remember, this industry turns the best of men into selfish rats. Save the goodness and the love in your heart . . . Don't lose it here.'

CHAPTER 36

According to the theories of the evolution of the universe, there are the really massive stars and the low mass stars. A really massive star will burn out relatively quickly and end up as a supernova—a tremendous explosion that will leave a black hole in its wake. On the other hand, a low mass star, like our sun, may take billions of years to use up its fuel and then die relatively very quietly by slowly shedding its outer layers. In short, the more massive a star, the shorter its lifespan. It is not an exaggeration to apply this same analogy to a superstar like Rajesh Khanna.

Scientist and author Dr Seshadri Kumar says, 'The anomaly of the life of Rajesh Khanna is that although he was equivalent, at his peak, in astronomical terms, to a super-massive star, his descent into oblivion was characteristic of much smaller stars.'[1] He was a super-massive star that slowly disintegrated. He was indeed the fallen superstar.

Social commentator Santosh Desai wrote, 'It is not unusual for stars to burn brightly for a short time and then fade away, but in Rajesh Khanna's case, this pattern played out with such intensity so as to become uncomfortable . . . He lived the rest of his life in reverse, seeing it recede through the wrong end of the binoculars, beginning with his heydays, till he was barely a distant speck in our consciousness.'[2]

Once, before granting an interview to veteran film journalist Rauf Ahmed, Khanna insisted on writing the headline of the piece: 'Rajesh Khanna: A King in Exile'. He had accepted his failure at a comeback, but he still believed himself to be a king. 'He [Khanna] once told me, "I didn't have the reference point. Today Amitabh has me as the reference point. There was never a star before me. I admit that I made mistakes. But you can't blame me. I thought that the kind of success I enjoyed could never ever end,"' recalled Ahmed.

Did the professional mistakes he made cost him his career, or was it something more deep-rooted inside his personality and subconscious? Senior journalist and film-maker Khalid Mohamed once described his first meeting with Rajesh Khanna towards the late 1970s: 'I met Rajesh Khanna on the sets of *Dhanwan*, when he was just about doing okay in showdom. A rookie reporter, when told about his mood swings, I wasn't disappointed. Before I could ask the first question, he played a drum beat on the table between us. It could have been for two minutes but felt like twenty. A year later I saw his other side: super affable and chatty . . . He grinned, ordering a virtual bakery of cakes to go with a cup of tea.'

People couldn't understand this strange and often inane behaviour of Rajesh Khanna. He was the typical large-hearted Punjabi one minute, and a cold, egoistic and moody man the next. Most of those who had known the superstar at close quarters always have one or the other story to narrate that pointed towards his complex personality. Even his oldest confidante, Anju Mahendroo, could never understand him completely. According to Anju this personality trait was present in Rajesh from the very beginning. She once said, 'I know it's a contradiction, but then Rajesh Khanna is like that. Confusion was a part of our relationship. If I wore a skirt, he'd snap, "Why don't you wear a sari?" If I wore a sari, he'd wrinkle his nose and say, "Why are you trying to project a *Bhartiya nari* look?" Things became worse when stardom found Rajesh Khanna.' Under pressure from his stardom, Khanna's coping mechanism brought the two personalities living in him to a stark foreground. Writer Salim Khan said to me, 'He was an altogether different kind of man. Good or bad I cannot judge, but definitely different. What he would do the very next minute nobody could tell. He was the most unpredictable man.'

According to film journalist Bhawana Somaaya his cruel moods alternated with his gentle nature. His perverseness was the other side of his generosity. She recounts an interesting example from the sets of his film *Janta Hawaldar*. In a foul mood, Rajesh Khanna had strictly ordered not to be disturbed even in the eventuality of an earthquake: 'No calls, no visitors, no snacks, no tea!' But unawares of the order a unit boy happened to enter his room to announce a visitor. Rajesh screamed at the boy, 'I told you not to disturb me! Who the hell gave you permission to enter the room?' The boy emerged ashen-faced and was scared of losing his job. Others knew better than to be near the superstar when he was in a bad mood. About an hour later Rajesh comes out, spots the unit boy and charmingly says, 'Wasn't too hard on you, was I? When I say don't disturb me, I mean don't disturb me. Now run along and get tea for me. I've got a headache.' Bhawana Somaaya sums this well: 'He's a closed book to most people, but there are flashes of a warmer human being trapped in his star image.'[3] Interestingly this wasn't a once-in-a-blue-moon episode. It was his everyday personality, but his critics wrote it off as part of the infamous Superstar Khanna Tantrums.

According to Film Historian Suresh Kohli, 'A sadistic trait was part of the Rajesh Khanna persona, it was like a Jekyll and Hyde act. What Mr Khanna said or did was spontaneous, he wouldn't even know the hurt his words had caused, though sensitivity was another of his hallmarks.'[4] This of course resulted in him being a bad interpersonal communicator. As everyone around him left him and he became the lonely man he eventually turned out to be, Khanna had no clue of the harm he had inflicted. Things became worse when Rajesh Khanna's films started flopping. Khanna withdrew into his own shell, unable to comprehend what he did wrong. In his own eyes, he remained the perpetual victim. He could never see his own actions from the viewpoint of a third person. According to Dimple, 'He neither shared his happiness nor his sorrow, and I was too frightened of giving him any kind of support. All I could do was wait in attendance just in case he needed me.'[5] At the same time Dimple was completely in awe of her superstar husband, 'When he wants to charm you, he always succeeds. He is very generous—both with his purse and his heart. Anyone who comes into close contact with him will vouch for this.'[6]

At the peak of his stardom he kept himself perpetually surrounded with chamchas. The biggest grouse the film industry had with him (especially the producers) was that he wanted to turn them into his yes-men. But as Anju said, 'He needed them'. Perhaps it was a loneliness that resided in him throughout. Journalist Sudhir Gadgil recounts that Khanna would often stand alone on the terrace of Aashirwad for hours at end. Alone, staring at the setting sun, lost in his own thoughts, with the vast expanse of sea in front of him. What was he looking for?

'My first impression of him is that he's a cold, proud man. My second, that his pride is a defence mechanism held between him and the rest of the world because he doesn't want anyone to know he's lonely . . . damn, damn, damn lonely,'[7] wrote Bhawana Somaaya towards the late 1970s. Even during his heyday Rajesh was known to often retreat into himself and be unapproachable on film sets. 'We are on the sets of *Aanchal*. Between shots, Rajesh is like an iceberg. He sits miles away from everybody. He makes no attempt to be friendly or talk. He's sulky, peevish, a little starry. And he expects a lot of tolerance from others, when he creeps into his shell.'[8] Adds Bhawana to me, his long-time co-star Mumtaz also agrees that 'he wasn't the overfriendly sort'. Hema Malini called him 'a temperamental man, and someone who kept to himself. There was this distance he'd maintain.' Zeenat Aman narrates that in their first film, *Ajanabee*, Rajesh was reserved and had turned 'introspective' by their last film together. Asha Parekh, who has seen the length of Khanna's career, makes interesting observations: 'When we did our first film, *Baharon ke Sapne* [in 1968], he wasn't THE Rajesh Khanna. I remember him as a shy, reserved man. By the time we did *Aan Milo Sajna*, success had brought him confidence and he was more expressive. When we did our last film, *Dharm aur Qanoon*, in 1984, he had turned aloof and introverted. We hardly spoke after that.'[9] Perhaps his leading ladies were still quite expressive while Khanna had turned quiet with the years, but he had always been guarded and remote from the beginning.

A telling tale was once tweeted by actress Dia Mirza, 'I saw him [Rajesh Khanna] one day standing alone in a white kurta pyjama by the gate [of Aashirwad] . . . a nation that was crazy about him was now just passing him by . . . [sic],' very poignantly summing up the last few years of Rajesh Khanna's life.

PART VI

2011–12

Maut tu ek kavita hai . . .
Mujhse ek kavita ka vaada hai milegi mujhko . . .

(Poem from *Anand*, 1971)

Question: When was the last time you cried?

RK: A minute ago, when it was raining; I cry when it rains, so nobody notices.

CHAPTER 37

'*Toh aap hamare saath film banana chahte hain?*' [So you want to make a film with me?] asked Rajesh Khanna over the phone.

'At that moment I felt that *"shareer boodhe ho jaate hain par awaazein boodhi nahi hotien"* [The body may grow old, but the voice doesn't],' said film director Ashok Tyagi to whom this question had been posed. Ashok Tyagi had earlier made some films like *Return of Jewel Thief* with Dev Anand, and *Bharat Bhagya Vidhata* with Shatrughan Sinha in the lead. He was now trying to make a film with Rajesh Khanna based on the Hollywood classic *The Godfather*. The film, *Riyasat*, became the last film of Rajesh Khanna, released after his death in 2014 to dismal reviews and an unpromising box office response.

Rajesh Khanna asked his astrologer friend, Bharat Upmanyu, to study his *kundli*; he strongly believed his good days would soon be back. According to journalist Pankaj Vohra he sold one of his properties in Tamil Nadu and used the money from it to free his bungalow Aashirwad from the tax authorities and started its renovation with a new enthusiasm. *Riyasat* went on the floors

251

on 25 February 2011. Ashok recalls, 'Amitabh Bachchan had played a similar role in *Sarkar*. Kakaji asked me to get the DVDs of *Sarkar* and *The Godfather* and watched both films. When he came on the sets he was a different Rajesh Khanna. You will be surprised to see his performance. He had completely changed his mannerisms to get into the skin of a gangster.' Over 90 per cent of the shoot was wrapped up in the next three months. One schedule for the film climax remained.

In June 2011 Rajesh Khanna suddenly fell very ill and was bedridden. About a month later, Ashok Tyagi went to meet him and was shocked at Khanna's appearance. Within a single month Rajesh Khanna had lost an abnormal amount of weight and looked very weak and fragile. The super massive star had begun deteriorating. Ashok tells me, 'That day I teased him and said, "Kakaji, today you are having tea with us." After a little thought he said slowly, "Complete your film." I assured him, "Don't worry, Kakaji, we will finish the film, but first you get better." I didn't know it at the time, but I believe Kakaji knew that he had surpassed the point of getting well again.'

Ashok Tyagi recalls an incident when Khanna sat with him on the benches on Carter Road, overlooking Aashirwad (when it was still with the tax authorities), and reminisced about the days when fans and onlookers would sit on those very benches awaiting a single glimpse of Khanna. To this Tyagi would say, 'Don't worry, Kakaji; after our film those fans will be back.' To this Khanna would smile feebly in response. And now he was giving the same smile again as he urged Tyagi to finish his film quickly. His last hidden wish remained the return of the crowds outside his bungalow, and perhaps he didn't want to leave this world without seeing that wish fulfilled.

***

'Agar Ghalib daaru peekar mar sakta hai, toh main kyun nahi?'[1]
[If Ghalib can die of drinking alcohol, then why can't I?] said
Khanna to senior journalist Ali Peter John.

True to his word, he had consumed so much alcohol in his
life that finally his liver gave up. Once he hit the bottle, he could
never stop. After a series of tests and examinations, his doctors
diagnosed him in the advanced stages of cancer.

When Rajesh Khanna was informed about the diagnosis,
the superstar went silent for some time, recalled his oncologist,
Dr P. Jagannath of Lilavati Hospital in Mumbai. It took
him a few moments to internalize what had perhaps been a
nagging fear. Then he collected himself together and bravely
looked straight at Dr Jagannath and said with a weak smile,
'I am destined to live like Anand.'[2] After the diagnosis, many
doctors were consulted in India and abroad. But the answer
was unanimous—Rajesh Khanna had little time left.

Dr Jagannath said that Rajesh Khanna fought cancer for
about eighteen months, but kept his spirits high till the end.[3]
The character of Anand that Rajesh had passionately lived for
the screen and rendered immortal . . . that same character had
now come out from the realms of the script and had become flesh
and bones. Anand and Rajesh Khanna had become one and the
same . . . inseparable.

Bhupesh Raseen recalls the changes that came in Khanna's
personality during this phase. 'Yes, he lived like Anand during this
last phase of his life. The fear of death approaching every moment
can scare anyone, but I never saw him crying. He had changed.
He wanted to live these moments and initially would joke a lot.
But all of us knew he was acting . . . because when he was left
alone he was another man . . . He had stopped taking phone calls.'

Bharat Upmanyu tells me, 'Initially Kakaji hoped for a miracle
for some time. Then gradually it dawned upon him that the time

had come.' It was as if he had been set free from the burden of loneliness, and he embraced this inevitability.

A close friend of Khanna remembers that he would smilingly ask the doctors, 'When is my visa expiring?'

***

In these difficult times his family returned to stand by him. Dimple, his daughters and son-in-law actor Akshay Kumar all kept him company. Dimple and Rinke had even moved back to Aashirwad to be at his side.

Dimple's close friend, politician Amar Singh told me, 'She always used to say, "He is the father of my children." As the father of her kids, she always respected him.'

Bhupesh Raseen told me that Rajesh Khanna now wanted to spend more and more time with his daughters. A few months later, the family decided to go to Goa to celebrate Rajesh Khanna's sixty-ninth birthday (on 29 December 2011). It was a family picking up the pieces of almost two decades of lost years and putting together memories for posterity. Before leaving, Rajesh Khanna called up Bhupesh and invited him to join the family in Goa. Bhupesh still remember the conversation, 'Kakaji told me, "Yaar Bhupesh, the kids want to celebrate my birthday and the New Year in Goa. You should also reach there." Not wanting to intrude on his family time, I said, "Kakaji, you know that I celebrate the New Year with my family." But he was adamant and became angry at my excuses. In a trembling, upset voice he said, "Bhupesh how can you behave like this . . . you know everything. This might be my . . . my last birthday." He almost choked on his words and disconnected the call.' After almost two hours Rajesh Khanna called up once again and said that he had become very emotional and hadn't been able to speak. This time a guilt-ridden Bhupesh agreed to go to Goa.

In Goa the entire family focused on Khanna. Everyone would party together and have family dinners. Bhupesh says those moments spent with Rajesh Khanna were priceless, 'This was supposedly his birthday celebration, but we all knew the reality: that he was not going to be with us for a long time. Sometimes, while talking to him, our eyes would brim with tears.' Khanna too enjoyed the love and company, but would often retreat into his own world, lost in his own thoughts.

With time he became bedridden and would rarely go out of Aashirwad, except for his medical check-ups. He kept to his family and a few close friends. He was in acute pain, and his body had been reduced to a skeleton almost.

Around this phase, Salim Khan saw him at an awards function and was shocked, 'Those days I was living at my farmhouse in Panvel, so I used to come to Mumbai less frequently. So I saw him after a long time at a function and couldn't recognize him at all. He was not looking like the Rajesh Khanna we knew. I felt I should meet him. Whatever the ailment was, he never used to tell anyone. It was clear that slowly and slowly he was deteriorating and would not survive for long. I am not a doctor, but just felt it instinctively. I strongly felt I should meet him and resolve any problem related to me in his heart. I had to go to Panvel the next morning, but I stayed back. Prashant Kumar Roy, who worked with him for twenty years, now works in my office. I asked Prashant to go to Rajesh's house and tell him that I want to meet him. He went and told him that Salimsaab wants to meet him. Rajesh asked, "Why?" The meeting could never happen. Maybe he was not in that state of mind.'

Actor Prem Chopra, who has worked with Khanna in more than twenty films, met him around the same time. He said, 'I met him at a party. Being an old friend I hugged him, but he gave me a cold reaction. I felt really bad, not because he ignored me, but I felt sad at the fact that he was sad with himself.'[4]

***

Rajesh Khanna had distanced himself from the world. But then around this time, came an offer from the famous advertising agency Lowe Lintas. This was an ad for Havells fans, with a novel concept. Rajesh had never worked in ad films even in his heyday, so there was little chance of doing it now at a junction when he had given up on life and cut himself off.

The well-known ad-film-maker and director of the award-winning movie *Paa*, R. Balki, came on board to direct the ad. Balki strongly felt that there was no other person who could match the profile of Khanna to suit the concept they had in mind.

The storyboard of the ad film was shared with Khanna. It was about a man who was surrounded by a huge fan following and ended with the star reminiscing about his glory days with the punch line: 'My "fans" can never leave me', with a special emphasis on the word 'Fans' as a pun with an obvious reference to the Havells fans in the background. For the shoot they needed a huge stadium and the organizers had been able to book this in Bangalore.

Surprisingly, Rajesh Khanna agreed to do the ad. Against all odds and against medical advice, Rajesh confirmed his availability and willingness to travel to Bangalore. Why did Khanna want to do an ad film for Havells fans in the worst of health?

When the production team called Rajesh Khanna to confirm the shooting dates, his condition had further worsened. But the bigger problem was that he had suffered a hairline fracture in his leg. There was so much pain and swelling that he couldn't even wear his shoes. It was near impossible for him to even stand. Bhupesh recalls, 'I asked Kakaji, "Would you be able to do it?" He said, "Now that I have committed, I will do it. You give him a date after two days." I said, "Kakaji, this is impossible, you can't even stand." He replied, "Bhupesh, this fracture will not recover at home. Take me to Nanavati Hospital." So we took him to the hospital. For two days he was on heavy painkillers and complete bed rest. After two days, he didn't go home from Nanavati, but straight to the airport to catch the next flight for Bangalore where the shoot had to take place in the stadium.'

What was it about the ad film and the shoot in Bangalore that the ex-superstar surprisingly couldn't say no to? Bhupesh Raseen accompanied Khanna to Bangalore for the shoot. Rajesh Khanna went fully prepared and had taken along a hairstylist and helper boy. Director R. Balki reached Bangalore the same night. Post dinner they sat down to discuss the script. It was decided that Khanna would use his trademark mannerisms to the chorus of the famous song 'Yeh Shaam Mastani' (from his movie *Kati Patang*) playing like an anthem in the background. Rajesh Khanna loved the idea.

In a way the ad film was a salute to Rajesh Khanna's magical superstardom. It very movingly took the viewers down memory lane when Rajesh Khanna was the uncrowned king of the film industry, and ended with the superstar stating what he always believed—that his fans would never leave him. Khanna very sportingly took the tongue-in-cheek humour in the right spirit. Before leaving for his room a limping Khanna showed Balki his famous walk that was to be used in the film. Seeing his courage Balki just said, 'Hats off to him.'

Limping from a fracture injury, not being able to stand up straight and constantly fighting cancer with every ounce of remaining energy, the ghost of a superstar was preparing for his last shoot in Bangalore's stadium with the same enthusiasm as he had for perhaps his first shoot. What was it about the city that almost called out to him?

The next day was the shooting. Khanna came to his vanity van and got ready, put on make-up and donned a tuxedo with a white collared shirt and bow. The shoot was to take place inside the stadium and his vanity van was parked at the gates.

As it was difficult for him to walk, he travelled the distance on a wheelchair.

As he entered the stadium a smile played on his lips. In these moments perhaps he was transported back to the day in Bangalore when the godly might of his stardom had dawned on him. He had said then, 'I still remember the exact moment when, for the first time, I became aware of how mind-blowing success can be. It was just after *Andaz* (1971) . . . in Bangalore . . . and there was just one echo of the voices—"Haaaaa" . . . You know, it was like a stadium from the time of the Romans. I wept like a baby.'[5]

Almost four decades later fate had brought him back for his last shoot to this place. During the making of the ad film Rajesh said, *'Jahaan pehli baar meri pehchaan bani . . . mere audience ne mujhe sweekaar kiya, main yeh mehsoos kar raha hoon ki aaj main ussi hisse mein aaya hoon . . . unke saath aaya hoon . . . unke liye aaya hoon . . . unke pyaar ki khaatir. Woh sammaan jo main chahta tha, unhone mujhe dono haathon se diya.'* [The place where I found my identity as a superstar . . . my audience accepted me . . . I have the feeling that today I have come to the same place . . . I have come with them . . . I have come for them . . . for the sake of their love . . . they gave me the respect that I always wanted with both hands.]

Perhaps this was why he had agreed to and hurried for the shoot of this ad film. With his failing health he wished to give his last shot at the place where it all had started for him.

The circle of destiny was complete.

***

'Light, sound, camera, action!' These words echoed in the stadium all through the day. R. Balki recalled, 'In front of me was the man who has seen stardom like nobody else . . . He knows the grammar of the camera in and out.'

In the beginning of the ad film his silhouette is seen walking in the dark towards a light at the other end of a door with the soundtrack creating a nostalgic ambience. A montage in sepia follows, recreating his crazy fans . . . some running after his car . . . some asking for autographs . . . many waving his posters . . . interspersed with shots from his old films. With a din of fans crying out for him, Rajesh enters the stadium and looks around, recreating the amazement of being washed over by the warmth and love of his fans. The stadium is full of 'fans' standing on every seat and in every corner. The catch in this ad film is that it is literally Havells fans that are placed on the seats filling out the huge stadium.

Khanna shows no hint of physical pain on screen . . . as he mouths the dialogue, *'Fans kya hote hain mujhse poocho . . . pyaar ka woh toofaan . . . mohabbat ki woh aandhi . . . woh jazbaat . . . woh junoon . . . hawa badal sakti hai . . . lekin fans . . . yeh sab mere rahenge. Babu Moshaye. . . mere fans mujhse koi nahi cheen sakta.'* [Ask me what are fans . . . that storm of love . . . that flurry of adoration . . . those emotions . . . that passion . . . the winds might change . . . but fans . . . these will remain mine. Babu Moshaye, nobody can take away my fans.]

Around seven in the evening, director R. Balki's voice pronounced, 'Pack up!' The entire unit gave a standing ovation to Rajesh Khanna as he waved his hands in his unique style. Balki said, 'He loved the camera and was a completely different man once it was switched on. He was very sharp and knew exactly what he was doing. Some portions of the commercial that could not be used had Kaka doing a small jig on the song 'Achcha Toh Hum Chalte Hain' as if he was bidding goodbye to the camera.'

Amidst the applause, Khanna reached his wheelchair. Then he turned around for a last look at the stadium and his eyes seemed to be looking at a time long past.

His last shooting had been packed up.

CHAPTER 38

The Havells ad film, released in April 2012, elicited lots of reactions from both fans and the media. While many criticized the ad film for being a 'joke' at the superstar's cost by referencing his constant efforts to regain his fandom, others were shocked at the appearance of the superstar. There was a direct contrast between the old footage and the present-day Rajesh Khanna in the ad. He hardly resembled himself any more. Weak, wrinkled, fragile, white-bearded, in heavy glasses, with his suit lying loose on his skeletal frame, Rajesh drew sympathy from all those who saw him. Very few understood the good humour and willpower he exhibited by having the courage to appear on screen again in this way. Many of his contemporaries are known to go into a virtual exile from the cameras in order to not be remembered at their worst.

With each passing day, Rajesh Khanna was being slowly consumed by cancer. The end was approaching faster than anticipated. The superstar could all but wait helplessly for the inevitable. In these aching moments of wait he used to appear lost, as if living in a different world. He wanted his daughters to be always around. The politician Amar Singh told me, 'Dimple took really good care of him in his last days. Dimple is my friend and during the last one year of my life I went to meet and spend time with Rajesh Khanna many times at his house. I felt he was always asking for Twinkle and Rinke. When the question of his will came up, he looked at Dimple questioningly. Dimple said, "I don't want anything. Whatever you want to give, give it to your children."'

According to Bharat Upmanyu, Twinkle was pregnant those days, so it was difficult for her to spend much time with Rajesh Khanna, but Rinke was constantly by his side. 'Tina [Twinkle] and Kaka's attachment was very strong, but in his last days he became very close to Rinke. The last time I met him in Mumbai, he told me in his weak voice, "If Chaaiji was alive, she would have been very happy to see how Dimpi is taking great care of me."'

In the initial days of his illness, Rajesh Khanna had put on a brave front and tried to live the *Anand* philosophy. He would smile and laugh with the family and play the doting father. But gradually as his condition further deteriorated, he had almost stopped talking. His sparkling voice had lost its touch. He aged drastically and was withdrawn. His stubborn belief that he would come back with a bang, his perpetual fight to achieve this dream— it all seemed to have finally been proved to be just that . . . a dream. And now it was as though he had ceased to even put up a fight.

Amar Singh told me, 'He became silent, just looking around at the people gathered around him. Then maybe he would say a sentence or two in a weak voice. He had come to terms with the fact that the film industry would pay obeisance only to the rising sun.'

***

Then one day, about a month later, Rajesh Khanna was admitted to Lilavati Hospital in Mumbai. The news of Rajesh Khanna's worsening health leaked into the media. Suddenly, everyone wanted to know what exactly had happened to the ex-superstar? Rajesh Khanna, the man everyone had forgotten, had come back into public consciousness thanks to the same ad film that people had been giving mixed reactions to. 'It had brought back a frail Rajesh Khanna and . . . it got people talking about the brand,' said a senior advertising professional. The noise and conversations around the ad did one more thing—it brought Rajesh Khanna to the top of people's minds. His fans, who had been shocked at his appearance, started wondering about what had become of their beloved superstar.

But the family members maintained their silence and secrecy on the whole matter. Many people close to him, including Anju Mahendroo, was seen visiting the hospital, but nobody was ready to say anything publicly. In the newspapers and on TV news channels, many stories about his worsening health continued to circulate. Every story was pointing towards his illness, insinuating that he was in the last stages of cancer and anything could happen any time.

And then on the morning of 16 June 2012, suddenly there were reports that Rajesh Khanna was on his deathbed. In fact, social media sites like Twitter and Facebook were abuzz with rumours of his death. It was surprising that initially no family member or doctor released any official statement on the matter. Perhaps nobody anticipated any furore around his death . . . A few other yesteryear actors had passed away recently without much media hype, and Rajesh was the forgotten superstar—or was he? Outside the hospital there was heightened media frenzy. Everyone wanted confirmation on Rajesh's death or some news that he was okay—anything that would afford them even a glimpse of the ex-superstar.

***

Bharat Upmanyu told me about an odd incident: 'Before he fell ill we were discussing an idea of a television serial on Lord Krishna. It was supposed to be a different take on Lord Krishna's struggles.' Then Kakaji's health started failing. Bharat used to meet him at his house in Mumbai. At one of these meetings Rajesh said dejectedly that they may not be able to make the serial. To make him feel better, Bharat promised that they soon shall. This time Rajesh went silent for some time and then thoughtfully added, 'Bharat, let's change the setting of the serial to the New Age world—a character based on Lord Krishna, who is born of one mother, but is lovingly raised by another. He has immense talent and power, but this is the Kaliyug and he has to face difficult conflicts. The entire universe is stopping him from achieving his goal, but he defeats everyone to claim his kingdom. Let's make a serial on this subject.'

Before leaving this world, this was perhaps the last story that Rajesh Khanna wanted to tell the world. A story that was perhaps very close to his heart . . . running in his blood. A story that he had possibly tried to hide from all throughout his life . . . but a story that had nevertheless often peeked out in the different facets of Rajesh Khanna . . .

To unravel this story, we will have to go back in time sixty-nine years to the day when a baby named Jatin Khanna was born . . .

PART VII

1942–2012

Kuch toh log kahenge
Logon ka kaam hai kehna

(Song from *Amar Prem*, 1972)

Question: Tell us a secret?

RK: Never tell a secret.

CHAPTER 39

On 29 December 1942, in the undivided Punjab province of Lahore, a baby boy was born to Nandlal Khanna and Chandraani Khanna. At birth he was given the name Jatinder or Jatin. He was the second son—and third child—of his parents. People close to the Khanna family say that Nandlal Khanna and his elder brother, Chunnilal Khanna, were railway contractors with work spread across Lahore. As the freedom struggle gained momentum and rumours of an impending partition loomed large upon the Punjab province, the Khanna family temporarily shifted base to the old city of Amritsar. The late Dunichand Khanna, a relative who lived in the house right opposite to the ancestral house of Rajesh Khanna in Amritsar, said, 'The family had migrated from Lahore and after a brief stay here, they went to Mumbai. Later on, the ancestral house where the extended Khanna family lived was given to a committee running a temple. This temple is still adjoining the house and the pujari of the temple and his family live there.'

In Amritsar, I spoke to Varun Khanna, the son of the late Dunichand Khanna of Gali Tiwarian. His father had shared stories with him, reminiscing about the time he spent playing with young Jatin in this very lane. Varun tells me that Jatin was remembered as a very fair-complexioned kid, with tiny eyes that became small slits when he smiled. Rajesh's childhood friend the late Faqirchand Sharma in Gali Tiwarian recalled, 'I still remember that during childhood we played together in the street. He was smart then also and it was always said that he might become a hero one day. But he never returned after attaining stardom.'[1] Sharma's son Sunil still lives in the house adjoining Rajesh's ancestral house. Sunil told me, 'My father's face used to light up whenever he watched Rajesh Khanna's songs or movies on TV. They played together as kids.'

During the little time he spent in Amritsar, Jatin was a happy child.

Post Independence in 1947, his father's elder brother, Chunnilal Khanna, established his work in Bombay and settled there permanently. He and his wife Leelawati had no offspring of their own. On the other hand, Nandlal Khanna had six children: the eldest was a son, Narinder Khanna, followed by an elder daughter, Chanchal Khanna; the third was Jatin, followed by three more daughters: Vijay, Kamlesh ('Kamli') and the youngest, Manju Khanna.

In a twist of fate, Jatin was put under the foster care of Chunnilal and Leelawati Khanna. Little has been mentioned on the precise reasons for this change of hands vis-à-vis Jatin's adoption, but inferences can be made. In traditional Punjabi households, the eldest brother is usually given the respect and status accorded to the patriarch of the family. And Chunnilal, as the head of the house, had no sons. Was this a possible reason why he was given custody of baby Jatin? Perhaps. After all, there is also a traditional preference for male children among Punjabi families, and Nandlal already had two sons. But even so, it is impossible to determine whether the suggestion for this adoption came from Chunnilal or Nandlal. All we can say for certain is that it happened, and Jatin travelled to Bombay with a new set of parents and towards a new life.

This must have had a profound effect on young Jatin's psyche. Although he knew that Chunnilal and Leelawati loved him dearly, he must have wondered how it was possible for his biological parents to give him up. Did they not love him? Was there something unlovable about him? He might have felt abandoned and neglected on account of the sudden disappearance and prolonged absence of his own parents and siblings. Such intense, disturbing feelings would have been extremely difficult for a young child to process or grapple with. It would have left him hurt, vulnerable, lost. How far was the distance between Bombay and Amritsar in the heart and mind of young Jatin? The answer to this can perhaps be inferred from Rajesh Khanna's interviews later in life.

The exact flow of events that transpired between Lahore, Amritsar and Bombay remains buried in the Khanna family's memory vault. Rajesh Khanna never spoke openly on the matter and neither did any of his close relatives. Till date, they remain elusive on this particular subject. I tried to speak with some members of his biological family, but they clearly refused to throw light on the matter, citing a privacy code.

Different versions are recorded in various interviews and reports. Some reports suggest his place of birth to be Amritsar in India; others suggest that he was born in the Pakistani town of Burewala rather than Lahore. The secret and guarded nature of this matter makes one wonder about the deep impact it must have had on the young child. He was too young to deal with the emotional conflict arising out of suddenly having two sets of parents. According to a senior psychiatrist at the Institute of Human Behaviour and Allied Sciences in New Delhi, such situations can sometimes culminate into conflicting emotional confusion. The child can grow up wondering what his life with the biological parents might have been like. Sometimes the blame game for having been given up on never ceases. Or sometimes this may lead to trust issues, insecurities and extreme fear of loss. Perhaps Rajesh went through a similar gamut of conflicted emotions as a child—and these could well be the building blocks of his personality. Characteristic traits like extreme possessiveness and the tendency to build walls around oneself (as seen in the sense of loneliness that always enveloped Khanna even in his heyday) often mark such personalities. Rajesh Khanna himself carried such traits. Was this the result of the events of his childhood or his experience of struggle during later years? To understand this better, we would have to closely examine what we do know about the life and times of Rajesh Khanna.

***

It is important to note that Rajesh Khanna himself never made any mention of his biological parents in any recorded interviews. In an old interview given to senior film journalist Bhawana Somaaya, the superstar shared some interesting stories from his childhood. In it he mentions he was born after eighteen years of his parents' marriage. They already had three daughters and his parents wanted a son. To this effect his mother organized a havan before his birth. So after Rajesh was born he was the most loved of all his siblings. He was always dressed in garbs of silk by his mother.

What makes these lines interesting is the very nature of facts presented in them. Bhupesh Raseen sheds light on this topic by speaking with Rajesh's biological younger sister, Chanchal Khanna, in my presence. She clearly mentions six siblings: four sisters and two brothers, of whom Rajesh was the third child. She makes no mention of foster siblings. This does not match

Rajesh Khanna's account of his birth and siblings. Did he present a tweaked version of his childhood in accordance with what better suited his superstar image or was it a complete denial of the hurt he associated with his childhood?

In his version of his childhood, Rajesh Khanna constantly fails to identify which set of his parents he is referring to. His version was always shown through rose-tinted, nostalgic lenses. It is also interesting to note a reference to Pakistan made in this same interview, 'My naming ceremony was performed in Dhapalpur, a small village in Karachi inside our *kuldevta*'s temple. Even today, when I pray, I am somehow mentally communicating to the God inside that temple. My parents named me Jeetendra, but nobody ever called me by that name. In the house, I was always referred to as Kaka. "Kaka", up north, is a very common pet name for the youngest child in the family.'[2]

In his interview, he further says, 'The only time my mother yelled at me was when I refused to drink milk. I hated drinking milk and looked for ways to avoid the tall glass coming my way. Every day, my line of excuse changed. One day I felt nausea. One day giddy. One day it was a stomach ache and on another a headache. Each time, however, my mother was one up on me. "You think you can fool Leelavati, do you?" she would say. Holding me tight by the arm, she'd clasp my nose and force it all down my throat.'[3] This remains one of the few interviews of Rajesh Khanna where he mentions the name of his mother. The name is Leelavati, his foster mother. No reference is ever made to his biological parents, or to any incident that would indicate their existence. It seems Rajesh Khanna had undone his past in his mind. Easier said than done, perhaps?

Did he want to wipe out the memory of his real parents completely? Maybe he was so badly hurt that he decided that they had no right to be a part of his present life? This follows from the fact that they had initially chosen to give him up. Perhaps young

Jatin interpreted this as them not caring enough to keep him? Veteran scriptwriter Salim Khan who had worked with Rajesh Khanna and known him closely during his superstar days told me, 'If I want to describe Rajesh Khanna in one word that would be "unpredictable". He was too unpredictable and extremely possessive. There must have been a childhood problem because his possessive streak was not normal.'

Later his biological parents also came to live in the Churchgate locality of Bombay. His elder brother, Narinder Khanna, was very active in the local and college theatre scene in Bombay. Although Rajesh Khanna never accepted this fact, his love for theatre and acting was also inspired by watching his brother Narinder Khanna. While growing up, he would see Narinder applying greasepaint and portraying characters on stage. Since the Khanna family constantly refused to divulge any details, I tried to look in other directions and reached a close friend of Narinder Khanna. This friend is seventy-two-year-old Kailash Advani, a resident of Meera Road, Mumbai.

Kailash Advani worked at length with the famous producer-director Ramanand Sagar as his chief assistant director for many years, and even directed a movie, *Ikraar* (1979). Kailash was very close to Narinder Khanna. He shared some interesting information about the two brothers. He recounts acting with Narinder in the plays of Begum Zaidi and Zohra Sehgal in the early 1960s. Kailash has fondly maintained an album of the photographs of their plays together. He also shared some pictures of Narinder Khanna with me.

Kailash remembers that Narinder would often visit Rajesh Khanna. What was peculiar is the fact that he was never referred to as a real sibling by Rajesh. Kailash reminisces, 'Though as a close friend of Narinder, I knew from him that Rajesh was his real brother. But Rajesh Khanna always mentioned Narinder as his cousin. Never ever as a real brother.'

Many other veterans from the film fraternity who knew Rajesh Khanna recount the visits of a 'cousin' to his house and film sets. But few knew Narinder to be Rajesh's actual brother. Those who were aware of the fact do not want to comment upon it now. Striking similarities in facial features can be noted between Narinder Khanna and Rajesh (Jatinder) Khanna in the photographs sourced from Narinder's wedding in Bombay. Of course, Rajesh Khanna is missing from the frame, though in later years Rajesh did become close to Narinder. Prashant Kumar Roy recounts, 'All of us knew that Narinder Khanna was his real brother. He used to come to Aashirwad. We used to call him Khanna Papa. Kakaji often sent money for his real sisters through me. He told me not to tell Khanna Papa about it. We all knew that there was a biological family connection, but we never heard any mention of the real parents or saw any photographs in the house.'

Talking about his real family, Prashant recalled another incident, 'I remember Kakaji used to send money to his sisters Kamli-behen and Manju-behen. I used to carry the money for them with instructions from Kaka that Narinder Khanna should never know of this gesture. Manju-behen was married into a family in Delhi. When Manju-behen passed away Kakaji didn't share the news with anyone and went to Delhi for her funeral. When he came back in the night, I was there along with two to three servants. He quietly sat in his office in Aashirwad and his tears started rolling uncontrollably, and in a low voice he wailed, "Manju . . . my sister . . . Manju!" It was a long, low, mournful cry. Perhaps he hadn't cried at the funeral itself.'

There are various loose ends to this story of Rajesh Khanna's childhood. The family's tight-lipped stance on this matter makes it all the more complicated. Also, all interviewers only report what the superstar said and do not cross-question him. Unlike him, other superstars like Raj Kapoor, Dilip Kumar, Dev Anand and even Amitabh Bachchan took pride in talking about their childhood and parentage. Rajesh Khanna, on the other hand, had made scarce references to his childhood and eventually what little he did say can well be disputed.

Senior journalist and film-maker Khalid Mohamed wrote about how in the early 1980s Rajesh Khanna had agreed to be interviewed on one condition: 'As long as you don't ask about my early days, I'm fine.'

The childhood of Rajesh Khanna was akin to a warped film script with various indistinguishable layers. But what remains the core truth is that the events of his early childhood had a huge bearing on his heart and mind and eventually shaped the personality of the man he became. Says a male co-star, 'Kaka loved to play the martyr both in his real and reel life.' Possibly, he never could outgrow his feelings of having been wronged. While fighting these mixed emotions, little did young Jatin know of the big turn his life would take in Bombay. Fate had bigger plans for him and his aspirations had only to put their Midas finger on the dream of his choosing. But as history tells us now, the dream run was not for long.

Dinesh Raheja says, 'I think he was very nice till the point life was nice to him. When life turned, he also turned bitter.' Was this bitterness only a consequence of the sudden end of his success? Or did it run deeper? Could this have been a case of past emotions catching up with him . . . or, in fact, never having left him?

Both Anju and Dimple in their interviews talk about him being an insecure person and how this, in turn, affected their relationships with him. Bhawana Somaaya once insightfully wrote, 'Maybe it's got something to do with the man that makes women involved with him feel insecure. Maybe in their insecurity, Khanna seeks his security.'[4] Both Anju and Dimple also had the same problem—Khanna wanting absolute attention from them. Were these signs of Khanna seeking absolute loyalty? Maybe this was not just in the case of his women. Perhaps only in the complete loyalty of everyone—loved ones, friends, co-workers and even fans—did Khanna feel fully loved and secure, and not as though he'd been left in 'foster care'. Was the feeling of 'being left alone' the reason for his possessiveness and insecurity that, eventually, alienated everyone around him, leaving him a bitter, lonely man? Deep inside, had he always remained the lost, vulnerable Jatin Khanna of long ago?

Probably the answer to these questions will never surface. Towards the end Rajesh Khanna seemed to have found a peace within him. He had patched up with most of the important people in his life. But till the very end, Rajesh Khanna tried staging a comeback—a chance to win back his many fans who had once shown him the greatest love and devotion of all.

But even this longing for his fans' love can perhaps be traced back to the unfulfilled yearning of the young Jatin Khanna. After all, whose love and devotion is the greatest for a child?

CHAPTER 40

The rumours pertaining to Rajesh Khanna's ill health were still afloat in the media and film industry even a few days later. The family was still with him at Lilavati Hospital. Remembering those days Bharat Upmanyu told me, 'When he was admitted to Lilavati I went to meet him. He asked everyone to leave us alone. We used to talk about spirituality and astrology. That day we discussed the Bhagwad Gita for long. Then I asked him, *"Kakaji, darr lag raha hai?"* [Kakaji, are you scared?] He went silent for a few moments as if lost somewhere, then looked at me and replied, *"Nahi yaar . . . darr-varr nahi lag raha"* [No, my friend, I am not scared], but I wanted to do some more good work. Good times were about to come; financially, better times had already come . . . I wanted to make some good films . . . but what to do . . . it's time to go . . . I'll have to go."'

Bharat remembers that while saying this there was a strange tenderness on his face. It seemed to speak of unfulfilled dreams—of a comeback before he left for good, of regaining his superstardom, if only for just a day, for his fans to return.

It was as if this deep wish that had been held on to for so long was being heard somewhere up in the heavens. What can better explain the sudden, rapidly growing frenzy in the media which had long forgotten him and which now camped outside Aashirwad and Lilavati Hospital?

***

'I remember a day in June when the rumour started that he had passed away. It was totally wrong and irresponsible,' said Bhupesh Raseen. According to him Rajesh Khanna had become so weak that he used to lose consciousness quite often. That day, 20 June, when he regained his consciousness, the family was with him. Bhupesh recalls, 'Rinke was holding his hand, Dimple was standing near his head; Akshay, Aarav and Anju Mahendroo were also there. Towards his feet were Harsh and I. Kakaji looked at all of us. He had no clue that rumours of his death had started outside. But there was still some life left in him.'

In his low voice he said to Dimple, 'I want to go home . . . to my room. I don't want to stay here,' and the family started preparations to shift him back to Aashirwad.

The homecoming of the superstar was greeted with the same frenzy on Carter Road that he had generated in his prime. Thousands of people thronged there just to catch a glance of the actor. Fans were accompanied by television cameras. History was being repeated. Aashirwad was swarmed again. Everyone wanted to know about Rajesh Khanna.

Akshay Kumar and Dimple spoke with the media and assured them that Rajesh Khanna's health was better and that he had been discharged from the hospital. But strange rumours were still in the air.

Finally, on the afternoon of 21 June 2012, laying to rest all rumours, there emerged a frail old man wearing black sunglasses over a white kurta, a light shawl on his drooped shoulders and the familiar charming smile. Rajesh Khanna gave a brief appearance for the crowds from the same famous terrace of Aashirwad. Standing beside him were Dimple, Akshay Kumar and Bhupesh Raseen. The fans and camera crews became hysterical. A softly smiling Rajesh Khanna waved at them with great style, his eyes surveying the crowds.

Yes, they had returned.

In those moments, forgetting all others, every news channel was beaming these pictures of Rajesh Khanna . . . LIVE. It seemed to be a matter of personal joy and happiness for everyone as they joined the chorus: the superstar Rajesh Khanna is alive and kicking. The rumours proved to be baseless. An ecstatic media started replaying his famous songs and dialogues. Television anchors gave short capsules of Rajesh's life. People from the film industry jumped in to wishing him the best of health and gave sound bites about his good old days. It was a celebration of his classic charm and nostalgia.

The scene was playing out exactly in the manner that Rajesh Khanna had dreamed about for many years. His wish had been granted. It was like rewinding to the old days of superstardom, only the King had aged many a decade. He was smiling, weak but exuberant, and made a V-for-victory sign with his fingers. It marked the victorious return of a king from exile.

***

The next morning, every newspaper carried the iconic picture of Rajesh Khanna standing on his terrace showing the victory sign and quotes from Khanna assuring the world that he was fit and fine. But the very next day, 22 June 2012, his health started failing again. He stopped eating completely. On 23 June he was admitted again to Lilavati Hospital.

With each passing day the pain became worse. The medicines ceased to work. Rajesh Khanna was collapsing. The beautiful voice had almost extinguished. Amar Singh told me, 'He used to stare at a point in space. He was in acute pain and even speaking aggravated it. He used to appear drowsy, maybe because of his medication.'

Dramatically, for almost the next three weeks Rajesh Khanna was continually in and out of hospital, giving everyone ample time to come to terms with the undeniable fact that his end was near. Khanna himself embraced this fact. Bhupesh says, 'His family wanted him to remain in the hospital. But he was adamant that he will die in his bedroom.'

As per his wish he was discharged from Lilavati Hospital for the last time on 17 July, and taken to Aashirwad. Rajesh Khanna had become so weak that he would lose consciousness at regular intervals. He was short of breath and his body was finally giving up its long-drawn battle against cancer. To raise his spirits, his family members reassured him that he will be all right—anything to encourage him to hold on to life. In response, Rajesh Khanna opened his eyes, looked at everyone around him and announced in a delicate voice, '*Time up ho gaya* [My time is up] . . . Pack up!'

Question: What would you like inscribed on your tombstone?

RK: 'Died without regrets, played his innings well.'

EPILOGUE

Grandson Aarav lights Rajesh Khanna's pyre

ABP News bureau
Thursday, 19 July 2012

Mumbai: Nine-year-old grandson Aarav lit Rajesh Khanna's pyre on Thursday at the Vile Parle crematorium, said a close family friend.

'Aarav lit the pyre and Akshay Kumar (Rajesh Khanna's son-in-law) assisted him,' the late superstar's close friend Vijay Zaveri said.

The legend's final journey started around 10 a.m. from his residence, Aashirwad, in Bandra. His body, in a transparent casket, was placed on a mini-truck decorated with white flowers. With him on his last journey were his estranged wife, Dimple Kapadia, who took care of him in the last days, his younger daughter, Rinke, and son-in-law, actor Akshay, who is married to his elder daughter, Twinkle.

Thousands of fans waiting outside Rajesh Khanna's house broke barricades just to get a glimpse of him. Despite the heavy rainfall, thousands of fans took part in his last journey. Braving the rain, thousands of people gathered to pay tribute to Bollywood's first superstar Rajesh Khanna. Amitabh Bachchan, Abhishek Bachchan, Raj Babbar, Manoj Kumar, Karan Johar and Rani Mukherji were also there

Bollywood's original superstar Rajesh Khanna, who charmed his way into the hearts of millions of swooning women in the 1960s and '70s, died on Wednesday.

Here was a man who debuted at the young age of twenty-four and became the biggest superstar of Hindi cinema at the age of twenty-eight. He ruled the roost, becoming the first one-man industry. Then he lost his throne by thirty-two. He kept delivering hits for the next decade and a half, but had been written off; with rapidly diminishing popularity, he slowly faded into oblivion. And after that came an excruciatingly long wait of almost forty years for the same mass hysteria to come back. For the fans did come back, and how!

Rajesh always had a penchant for enacting death scenes. He always believed that death gave him his biggest hit films. Alas, this proved to be true even in his real-life death. That was how his life was always, reel to real, real to reel.

Rajesh Khanna appeared in more than a hundred and sixty films with a high success ratio—a staggering achievement by any standards. He actually got a special Filmfare award in 1991 for achieving the unique feat of playing the main lead in 101 films, as he had continued to do solo-hero films even when multi-starrers were reigning at the box office. He was nominated for the Filmfare

Best Actor Award as many as fourteen times, and won it three times, along with a Lifetime Achievement Award.

The frenzy of Rajesh Khanna's fans on his death proved that the charisma of the superstar actually never faded. It was destiny that perhaps determined everything: the meteoric rise, the shocking downfall, the lost loves, the agony, the frustration and the king-size life Rajesh Khanna lived, despite everything.

The 'fallen superstar' had perhaps been granted lesser room for fallibility than he deserved. As long as Kaka burned brightly, he lit up the world, making millions smile, laugh and cry. 'An artist must always be judged by his best work,' said the great Satyajit Ray. Rajesh Khanna too should be remembered for his better works and not for the string of films that were unworthy of his calibre. Yes, he made some bad choices. But it would be harsh to crucify him for wanting to keep working always. In any case, his best films far outshine most others and are still regarded as an intrinsic part of cinematic history.

Somewhere from a distant heavenly star, he must have watched the massive procession of fans that accompanied his funeral bier. Perhaps, in his unique style—batting his eyelashes, flashing his disarming smile, slightly tilting his head—he would have looked upon the frenzy and said, '*Rajesh Khanna mara nahi, Rajesh Khanna marte nahi.*' [Rajesh Khanna did not die. Rajesh Khannas do not die.]

In an interview given about twenty-two years ago, Rajesh Khanna had said: 'A king dies a king! He might not have a following. He might be dying alone, lost in a desert, but he will still be a king, whether on the throne or in exile!'

Perhaps he was right.

RIP Rajesh Khanna Sahib.

NOTES

Prologue

1. Ingrid Albuquerque, 'In Love and Death We Cry', *Times of India*, 22 July 2012; available online at: http://lite.epaper.timesofindia. com/getpage.aspx?edlabel=BGMIR&pubLabel=MM&pageid=6 &mydateHid=22-07-2012.
2. Ibid.

Chapter 1

1. Bhawana Somaaya, 'Echoes of an Era', *Junior G*, July 1991.
2. Bunny Reuben, 'My Life and Loves', interview with Rajesh Khanna, 1975; available online at: http://cineplot.com/rajesh-khanna-my-life-and-loves/.
3. Ibid.

Chapter 2

1. Bhawana Somaaya, 'Echoes of an Era', *Junior G*, July 1991.

2. Ramesh Bhatlekar, interview with Rajesh Khanna, *Indian Express*, 21 July 2012; available online at: http://archive.indianexpress.com/news/rajeshs-mother-could-not-stand-even-his-onscreen-death/977527/2.
3. Bhawana Somaaya, 'Echoes of an Era', *Junior G*, July 1991.
4. Ibid.
5. Ibid.

Chapter 3

1. *Filmfare*, January 1970.
2. Bhawana Somaaya, 'Echoes of an Era', *Junior G*, July 1991.
3. Devyani Chaubal, 'Frankly Speaking', *Star & Style*, December 1971.

Chapter 5

1. Rajesh Khanna in an interview to *Filmfare*, 2 January 1970.
2. Ibid.

Chapter 6

1. Devyani Chaubal, 'Frankly Speaking', *Star & Style*, December 1971.
2. Ibid.
3. *Filmfare*, January 1970.
4. Bhawana Somaaya, 'Echoes of an Era', *Junior G*, July 1991.
5. Bhawana Somaaya, 'Echoes of an Era', *Junior G*, July 1991; also based on a recorded interview of Ramesh Talwar with the author.

Chapter 7

1. Bhawana Somaaya, 'Echoes of an Era', *Junior G*, July 1991.
2. Ibid.
3. Interview with Ketan Anand, *Indian Express*, 16 November 2007.

Chapter 8

1. Bhawana Somaaya, 'Echoes of an Era', *Junior G*, July 1991.
2. Aniruddha Bhattacharjee and Balaji Vittal, '"Woh Phir Nahi Aate": Things You Didn't Know about the Rise and Fall of Rajesh Khanna', IBNLive.com, 19 July 2012; available online at: http://ibnlive.in.com/news/woh-phir-nahi-aate-things-you-didntknow-about-the-rise-and-fall-of-rajesh-khanna/272284-3.html.

Chapter 9

1. Shaikh Ayaz, 'How *Aradhana*, *Kati Patang* Were Made', Rediff.com, 26 June 2012; available online at: http://www.rediff.com/movies/slide-show/slide-show-1-shakti-samanta-the-director-with-a-keen-ear-for-music/20120626.htm.
2. Ibid.
3. 'Golden Boys: The Dev–Kaka Connection', *Times of India*, 20 July 2012; available online at: http://timesofindia.indiatimes.com/entertainment/hindi/bollywood/news/Golden-boys-The-Dev-Kaka-connection/articleshow/15043708.cms.

Chapter 10

1. 'Bollywood Blockbusters: The Success of Aradhana', interview aired on CNN-IBN, 29 October 2011.
2. Rakesh Rao, 'Heart-throb of an Era', *Frontline*, vol. 29, no. 15, 28 Jul.–10 Aug. 2012; available online at: http://www.frontline.in/static/html/fl2915/stories/20120810291510700.htm.
3. Bhawana Somaaya, 'Echoes of an Era', *Junior G*, July 1991.

Chapter 11

1. Avijit Ghosh, 'Rajesh Khanna: The God of Romance', *Bollywood's Top 20: Superstars of Indian Cinema*, ed. Bhaichand Patel (New Delhi: Penguin Books India, 2012), p. 173.

2. Bhawana Somaaya, 'Echoes of an Era', *Junior G*, July 1991.
3. *Love Story*, interview of Meena Iyer with Yasser Usman, ABP News, July 2012.
4. Uma Rao, 'End of a Seven-Year Romance', *Stardust*, May 1973.
5. Ibid.

Chapter 12

1. Dilip Chitre, 'The Charisma of Rajesh Khanna', *The Best of Quest*, eds Laeeq Futehally, Achal Prabhala and Arshia Sattar (New Delhi: Westland Books, 2011).
2. Bhawana Somaaya, 'Echoes of an Era', *Junior G*, July 1991.
3. Ibid.
4. Bharathi S. Pradhan, 'Champagne Star Who Gave My First Bottle', *Telegraph*, 19 July 2012; available online at: https://in.news.yahoo.com/champagne-star-gave-first-bottle-214205771.html.
5. Bhawana Somaaya, 'Echoes of an Era', *Junior G*, July 1991.
6. Amitabh Bachchan, 'Day 1552', Bachchan Bol: Amitabh Bachchan's Official Blog, 18 July 2012; available online at: http://srbachchan.tumblr.com/post/27501033560.
7. Ibid.
8. Patcy N., 'When Rajesh Khanna Apologised to *Anand* Director', Rediff.com, 24 January 2013; available online at: http://www.rediff.com/movies/slide-show/slide-show-1-when-rajesh-khanna-apologised-to-anand-director/20130124.htm.
9. Pallavi Kharade, 'I Felt Nervous to Work with Superstar, Rajesh Khanna: Ramesh Deo', *DNA*, 19 July 2012; available online at: http://www.dnaindia.com/pune/report-i-felt-nervous-to-work-with-superstar-rajesh-khanna-ramesh-deo-1716968.
10. Aniruddha Bhattacharjee and Balaji Vittal, *R.D. Burman: The Man, the Music* (New Delhi: HarperCollins India, 2011).
11. Nirmala George, 'Rajesh Khanna Dead: Bollywood Superstar Dies at 69', *Huffington Post*, 18 July 2012; available online at: http://www.huffingtonpost.com/2012/07/18/rajesh-khanna-dead-bollywood-actor_n_1681996.html.

Chapter 13

1. Ali Peter John, 'Rajesh Khanna's Bungalow Aashirwad Was Haunted', *Mumbai Mirror*, 25 July 2012; available online at: http://timesofindia.indiatimes.com/entertainment/hindi/bollywood/news/Rajesh-Khannas-bungalow-Aashirwad-was-haunted/articleshow/15116861.cms.

2. Namita Gokhale, 'Super Days: A Remembrance of Bollywood Past', *The Popcorn Essayists: What Movies Do to Writers*, ed. Jai Arjun Singh (New Delhi: Tranquebar Press, 2011).

Chapter 14

1. Nina Arora, 'The New Dimple', *Super*, September 1978.

2. 'Bollywood Babes and Cricketers', *Times of India*, 7 May 2009; available online at: http://timesofindia.indiatimes.com/entertainment/hindi/bollywood/news/Bollywood-babes-and-cricketers/articleshow/4490924.cms.

3. Uma Rao, 'End of a Seven-Year Romance', *Stardust*, May 1973; available online at: http://memsaabstory.files.wordpress.com/2010/02/rajesh-anju.pdf.

4. Ibid.

5. Nina Arora, 'Star Craze', *Super*, May 1978.

Chapter 15

1. Amitabh Bachchan, 'Day 1552', Bachchan Bol: Amitabh Bachchan's Official Blog, 18 July 2012; available online at: http://srbachchan.tumblr.com/post/27501033560.

Chapter 16

1. Dilip Chitre, 'The Charisma of Rajesh Khanna', *The Best of Quest*, eds Laeeq Futehally, Achal Prabhala and Arshia Sattar (New Delhi: Westland Books, 2011).

2. Shekhar Gupta, 'Creating the Angry Young Man Was Not a Conscious Decision', *Indian Express*, 25 May 2013; available online: http://archive.indianexpress.com/news/creating-the-angry-young-man-was-not-a-conscious-decision/1120627/3.

3. Nina Arora and Dinesh Raheja, 'Face to Face: For the First Time Superstars Share—The Agony after the Ecstasy!', interview with Rajesh Khanna and Amitabh Bachchan, *Movie*, May 1990; a version is available online at: http://www.hindustantimes.com/entertainment/bollywood/i-m-not-scared-of-death-rajesh-khanna-in-a-1990-interview/article1-892017.aspx.

4. Sunaina Kumar, 'The After Shadow of the Star', *Tehelka*, vol. IX, no. 30, 28 July 2012; available online at: http://archive.tehelka.com/story_main53.asp?filename=hub280712After.asp.

5. Interview with Navin Nischol, *Star & Style*, Sept.–Oct. 1980.

6. Malavika Sangghvi, 'Original Superstar', *Business Standard*, 30 June 2012; available online at: http://www.business-standard.com/article/beyond-business/original-superstar-112063000003_1.html.

7. Shekhar Gupta, 'Creating the Angry Young Man Was Not a Conscious Decision', *Indian Express*, 25 May 2013; available online: http://archive.indianexpress.com/news/creating-the-angry-young-man-was-not-a-conscious-decision/1120627/3.

Chapter 17

1. Devyani Chaubal, 'Frankly Speaking', *Star & Style*, December 1971.

Chapter 18

1. Bunny Reuben, 'My Life and Loves', interview with Rajesh Khanna, 1975; available online at: http://cineplot.com/rajesh-khanna-my-life-and-loves/.

2. Uma Rao, 'End of a Seven-Year Romance', *Stardust*, May 1973.

3. Gautam Kaul, 'The Darker Side of Rajesh Khanna', *New Indian Express*, 22 July 2012; available online at: http://www.newindianexpress.com/entertainment/gossip/article573866.ece.

4. Uma Rao, 'End of a Seven-Year Romance', *Stardust*, May 1973.
5. Ibid.

Chapter 19

1. In *Movie* magazine (published in February 1994, a month after Pancham's death).
2. Santosh Desai, 'Remembering the Poetic Masculinity of Rajesh Khanna', *Times of India*, 22 July 2012; available online at: http://blogs.timesofindia.indiatimes.com/Citycitybangbang/remembering-the-poetic-masculinity-of-rajesh-khanna/.
3. Patcy N., 'Rajesh Khanna Did Not Care for Anyone', Rediff.com, 27 July 2012; available online at: http://www.rediff.com/movies/slide-show/slide-show-1-rajesh-khanna-did-not-care-for-anyone/20120723.htm.
4. *Stardust*, September 1976.

Chapter 20

1. In an interview with the author for a show on ABP News.
2. Devyani Chaubal in the BBC documentary *The Bombay Superstar* by Jack Pizzey.
3. Ingrid Albuquerque, 'In Love and Death We Cry', *Times of India*, 22 July 2012; available online at: http://lite.epaper.timesofindia.com/getpage.aspx?edlabel=BGMIR&pubLabel=MM&pageid=6&mydateHid=22-07-2012.
4. Harish Kumar Mehra, 'Khanna: The Cult of the Super Personality', *Star & Style*, vol. XXIV, no. 17, August 1975.
5. Ibid.
6. Sudeshna Banerjee, 'Superstar Friend in Need with Friends Too Few', *Telegraph*, 22 July 2012; available online at: http://www.telegraphindia.com/1120722/jsp/calcutta/story_15748318.jsp#.VDpakvmSxPo.

7. Devyani Chaubal in the BBC documentary *The Bombay Superstar* by Jack Pizzey.
8. Bhawana Somaaya, 'Echoes of an Era', *Junior G*, July 1991.

Chapter 21

1. Harish Kumar Mehra, 'Khanna: The Cult of the Super Personality', *Star & Style*, vol. XXIV, no. 17, 15 August 1975.
2. Uma Rao, 'End of a Seven-Year Romance', *Stardust*, May 1973.
3. Ibid.
4. Bunny Reuben, 'My Life and Loves', interview with Rajesh Khanna, 1975; available online at: http://cineplot.com/rajesh-khanna-my-life-and-loves/.
5. Uma Rao, 'End of a Seven-Year Romance', *Stardust*, May 1973.
6. Bunny Reuben, 'My Life and Loves', interview with Rajesh Khanna, 1975; available online at: http://cineplot.com/rajesh-khanna-my-life-and-loves/.

Chapter 22

1. Uma Rao, 'End of a Seven-Year Romance', *Stardust*, May 1973.
2. Bhawana Somaaya, 'Echoes of an Era', *Junior G*, July 1991.
3. Mohan Bawa, 'How the Stars Ate a Reporter for Breakfast!', *Super*, vol. II, no. 4, April 1978.
4. Ibid.

Chapter 23

1. Mohan Bawa, 'How the Stars Ate a Reporter for Breakfast!', *Super*, vol. II, no. 4, April 1978.
2. Bharathi S. Pradhan, 'The End of the Sister Act', *Telegraph*, 22 November 2009; available online at: http://www.telegraphindia.com/1091122/jsp/7days/story_11770224.jsp.

Chapter 25

1. Subhash K. Jha, 'Gulzar on His Long Association with Hrishikesh Mukherjee', Santabanta.com, 31 August 2006; available online at: http://www.santabanta.com/bollywood/11717/gulzar-on-his-long-association-with-hrishikresh-mukherjee/

2. Susmita Dasgupta, 'Zindagi Badi Honi Chahiye, Lambi Nahin . . . Ha, Ha, Ha', Bargad: Enlightened Prattles, 19 July 2012; available online at: http://bargad.org/2012/07/19/rajesh-khanna/.

3. Hrishikesh Mukherjee, 'Salute to the Legend', Screen; available online at: http://www.screenindia.com/old/fullstory.php? content_id=13412.

4. Nina Arora and Dinesh Raheja, 'Face to Face: For the First Time Superstars Share—The Agony after the Ecstasy!', interview with Rajesh Khanna and Amitabh Bachchan, Movie, May 1990.

5. 'Director's Diary', Super, June 1978, p. 29.

Chapter 26

1. Bijal Kaji, 'Rajesh Khanna: Unveiling of an Enigma by Directors Closest to Him', Picturpost, April 1987, p. 9; available online at: https://www.flickr.com/photos/asli_jat/2877192576/in/photostream/.

2. Interview with Yash Chopra, Picturpost, April 1987, p. 13.

3. Monojit Lahiri, Stardust Annual, 1973, p. 81.

Chapter 27

1. Sumit Mitra, 'Dimple Kapadia: The Second Coming', India Today, 1985; available online at: http://indiatoday.intoday.in/story/from-bobby-to-saagar-dimple-kapadia-has-come-along-way/1/354728.html.

2. Interview with Randhir Kapoor, Super, February 1978.

3. Chunnibhai Kapadia quoted in Nina Arora, 'Jaya Is Back . . . Dimple to Follow Suit?' Super, November 1980.

4. Bhawana Somaaya, Screen, July 1987.

5. Ibid.
6. Uma Rao, 'End of a Seven-Year Romance', *Stardust*, May 1973.
7. Ingrid Albuquerque, 'In Love and Death We Cry', *Times of India*, 22 July 2012; available online at: http://lite.epaper.timesofindia. com/getpage.aspx?edlabel=BGMIR&pubLabel=MM&pageid=6 &mydateHid=22-07-2012.
8. Nina Arora, 'The New Dimple', *Super*, September 1978.
9. Ibid.
10. Ibid.
11. Ibid.
12. Bhawana Somaaya, 'Echoes of an Era', *Junior G*, July 1991.
13. Bhawana Somaaya, *Screen*, July 1987.
14. Nina Arora, 'The New Dimple', *Super*, September 1978.

Chapter 28

1. As told to Harmeet Kathuri in an interview, 1983.
2. Chunnibhai Kapadia quoted in Nina Arora, 'Jaya Is Back . . . Dimple to Follow Suit?', *Super*, November 1980, p. 17.
3. Bhawana Somaaya, *Salaam Bollywood: The Pain and the Passion* (Hartford: Spantech & Lancer, 2000), 83–84.
4. Nina Arora and Dinesh Raheja, 'Face to Face: For the First Time Superstars Share–The Agony after the Ecstasy!', interview with Rajesh Khanna and Amitabh Bachchan, *Movie*, May 1990; a version is available online at: http://www.hindustantimes.com/ entertainment/bollywood/i-m-not-scared-of-death-rajesh-khanna-in-a-1990-interview/article1-892017.aspx.
5. Ibid.
6. Bhawana Somaaya, 'Echoes of an Era', *Junior G*, July 1991.

Chapter 29

1. Bhawana Somaaya, *Screen*, July 1987.
2. Bhawana Somaaya, *Salaam Bollywood: The Pain and the Passion* (Hartford: Spantech & Lancer, 2000).

Chapter 30

1. Rajesh Khanna in an interview with Harmeet Kathuri.
2. Bharathi S. Pradhan, 'Champagne Star Who Gave My First Bottle', *Telegraph*, 19 July 2012; available online at: https://in.news.yahoo. com/champagne-star-gave-first-bottle-214205771.html.

Chapter 31

1. R. Sriram, 'Rajesh Khanna: Bollywood Mourns as India Loses Its Superstar', *Economic Times*, 19 July 2012; available online at: http://articles.economictimes.indiatimes.com/2012-07-19/ news/32747499_1_rajesh-khanna-haathi-mere-saathi-namak-haram.
2. Anil Thakraney, 'Remembering Devyani Chaubal', MxM India, July 2012; available online at: http://www.mxmindia.com/2012/07/ anil-thakraney-remembering-devyani-chaubal/.
3. Bhawana Somaaya, *Salaam Bollywood: The Pain and the Passion* (Hartford: Spantech & Lancer, 2000).
4. Coomi Kapoor, 'Censorship: Dual Standards', *India Today*, 15 April 1985; available online at: http://indiatoday.intoday.in/ story/film-makers-face-the-brunt-of-censor-board-whims-and-fancies/1/354035.html.
5. Suresh Kohli, 'Rajesh Khanna: Alone in the Multitude', *Uday India*; available online at: http://www.udayindia.in/english/ content_04%20august 2012/cine-buzz.html.
6. Bharathi S. Pradhan, 'The End of the Sister Act', *Telegraph*, 22 November 2009; available online at: http://www.telegraphindia. com/1091122/jsp/7days/story_11770224.jsp.
7. Seema Sinha, 'Complicated Relationships!', *Times of India*, 12 March 2011; available online at: http://timesofindia.indiatimes.com/ life-style/relationships/man-woman/Complicated-relationships/ articleshow/6525606.cms.
8. Shobhaa Dé, 'The Loneliness of a Superstar', *Mumbai Mirror*, 19 July 2012; available online at: http://www.mumbaimirror.com/mumbai/

cover-story/The-loneliness-of-a-superstar/articleshow/16224309.
cms.

9. Ingrid Albuquerque, 'In Love and Death We Cry', *Times of India*,
22 July 2012; available online at: http://lite.epaper.timesofindia.
com/getpage.aspx?edlabel=BGMIR&pubLabel=MM&pageid=6
&mydateHid=22-07-2012.

10. Shobhaa Dé, 'The Loneliness of a Superstar', *Mumbai Mirror*, 19 July
2012; available online at: http://www.mumbaimirror.com/mumbai/
cover-story/The-loneliness-of-a-superstar/articleshow/16224309.cms.

Chapter 32

1. Bhawana Somaaya, *Screen*, July 1987.
2. Ibid.
3. Nina Arora and Dinesh Raheja, 'Face to Face: For the First Time
Superstars Share—The Agony after the Ecstasy!', interview with
Rajesh Khanna and Amitabh Bachchan, *Movie*, May 1990.
4. Ibid.
5. Ibid.

Chapter 35

1. Meera Joshi, 'To Kaka with Love . . .', *Filmfare*, 19 July 2012;
available online at: http://www.filmfare.com/features/to-kaka-with-
love-885.html.
2. Bhawana Somaaya, 'Rajesh Khanna 1979', Rajesh Khanna Fan
Club, take 25, excerpt 9, 4 January 2009; available online at:
http://rajeshkhannafanclub.blogspot.in/2009/01/rajesh-khannna-
1979.html.
3. Meena Iyer, 'I Call Myself Rajesh Khanna's Surrogate Wife: Anita
Advani', *Times of India*, 1 September 2012; available online
at: http://timesofindia.indiatimes.com/entertainment/hindi/
bollywood/news/I-call-myself-Rajesh-Khannas-surrogate-wife-
Anita-Advani/articleshow/16060995.cms.

4. Ibid.
5. 'Rajesh Khanna's Live-in Love: Who's Anita Advani?', IBNLive.com, 24 July 2012; available online at: http://ibnlive.in.com/news/rajesh-khannas-livein-love-whos-anita-advani/273833-8-66.html.
6. Ibid.

Chapter 36

1. Seshadri Kumar, 'Death of a Superstar: Remembering Rajesh Khanna', Leftbrainwave.com, 26 July 2012; available online at: http://www.leftbrainwave.com/2012/07/death-of-superstar-remembering-rajesh_8505.html.
2. Santosh Desai, 'Remembering the Poetic Masculinity of Rajesh Khanna', *Times of India*, 22 July 2012; available online at: http://blogs.timesofindia.indiatimes.com/Citycitybangbang/remembering-the-poetic-masculinity-of-rajesh-khanna/.
3. 'Salute to the Legend', *Screen*; available online at: http://www.screenindia.com/old/fullstory.php?content_id=13412.
4. Suresh Kohli, 'Rajesh Khanna: Alone in the Multitude', *Uday India*; available online at: http://www.udayindia.in/english/content_04%20august2012/cine-buzz.html.
5. Bhawana Somaaya, *Screen*, July 1987.
6. Ibid.
7. 'Rajesh Khanna: The Heart is a Lonely Hunter', *Super*, October 1978.
8. Bhawana Somaaya, 'Rajesh Khanna 1979', Rajesh Khanna Fan Club, take 25, excerpt 9, 4 January 2009; available online at: http://rajeshkhannafanclub.blogspot.in/2009/01/rajesh-khannna-1979.html.
9. 'Rajesh Khanna's Leading Ladies Share Their Memories', *Times of India*, 19 July 2012; available online at: http://timesofindia.indiatimes.com/entertainment/hindi/bollywood/news/Rajesh-Khannas-leading-ladies-share-their-memories/articleshow/15039228.cms.

Chapter 37

1. Patcy N., 'Rajesh Khanna Did Not Care for Anyone', Rediff.com, 27 July 2012; available online at: http://www.rediff.com/movies/slide-show/slide-show-1-rajesh-khanna-did-not-care-for-anyone/20120723. htm.

2. Y. Mallikarjun, '"Rajesh Khanna Lived like Anand"', *The Hindu*, 18 August 2012; available online at: http://www.thehindu.com/todays-paper/tp-national/tp-newdelhi/rajesh-khanna-lived-like-anand/article3787708.ece.

3. Ibid.

4. Interview of Prem Chopra, BBC Hindi, July 2012; available online at: www.bbc.co.uk/hindi/.

5. Nina Arora and Dinesh Raheja, 'Face to Face: For the First Time Superstars Share—The Agony after the Ecstasy!', interview with Rajesh Khanna and Amitabh Bachchan, *Movie*, May 1990; a version is available online at: http://www.hindustantimes.com/entertainment/bollywood/i-m-not-scared-of-death-rajesh-khanna-in-a-1990-interview/article1-892017.aspx.

Chapter 39

1. Aseem Bassi, 'Rajesh Khanna Leaves Amritsar Heartbroken', *Hindustan Times*, 18 July 2012; available online at: http://www.hindustantimes.com/india-news/punjab/rajesh-khanna-leaves-amritsar-heartbroken/article1-891239.aspx.

2. Bhawana Somaaya, 'Echoes of an Era', *Junior G*, July 1991.

3. Ibid.

4. Bhawana Somaaya, *Screen*, July 1987.

LIST OF SOURCES

During the course of my research, I interviewed several people who knew Rajesh Khanna or worked closely with him. Some of them wish to remain anonymous, and I respect their decision. The others, whose insights and anecdotes were crucial to helping me understand Rajesh Khanna better, are as follows:

- Ashok Tyagi
- Amar Singh
- Bharat Upmanyu
- Bharathi S. Pradhan
- Bhupesh Raseen
- Harsh Raseen
- Dinesh Raheja
- Hanif Zaveri
- J. Omprakash
- Prashant Kumar Roy
- Saawan Kumar Tak
- Salim Khan
- Sagar Sarhadi

- Sachin Pilgaonkar
- Sudhir Gadgil
- Kailash Advani
- Pankaj Vohra
- Gargi Parsai
- Dheeraj Kumar
- Ramesh Talwar
- Rasheed Kidwai
- Haridutt
- Suparna Sharma
- Greta
- Varun Khanna
- Raju Karia

I also gathered a wealth of information, not only about Rajesh Khanna but also about Bollywood in the 1970s and 1980s, from a variety of secondary sources—journals, articles, published interviews and fan blogs. In particular, the short questions at the beginning of each part in this book were taken from an interview of Rajesh Khanna (1990), which was compiled by his official fan club on the following forums:

- https://www.facebook.com/permalink.php?story_fbid=3849 92278220140&id=236136926439010
- http://www.topix.com/forum/who/rajesh-khanna/ T1KHRQRLA8I7LO3L6/p15
- https://www.facebook.com/pages/Rajesh-Khanna/ 236136926439010?fref=nf

The remaining sources are as follows:

- ABP News Bureau, 19 July 2012.
- *Love Story*, interview of Meena Iyer with Yasser Usman, ABP News, July 2012. Ramesh Bhatlekar, interview with Rajesh

Khanna, *Indian Express*, 21 July 2012; available online at: http://archive.indianexpress.com/news/rajeshs-mother-could-not-stand-even-his-onscreen-death/977527/2.
- Interview in *Filmfare*, 2 January 1970.
- *Love Story*, interview of Rauf Ahmed with Yasser Usman, ABP News, July 2012. Bhawana Somaaya, 'Echoes of an Era', *Junior G*, July 1991.
- Bunny Reuben, 'My Life and Loves', interview with Rajesh Khanna, 1975; available online at: http://cineplot.com/rajesh-khanna-my-life-and-loves/.
- Devyani Chaubal, 'Frankly Speaking', *Star & Style*, December 1971.
- Ketan Anand's interview, *Indian Express*, 16 November 2007.
- Aniruddha Bhattacharjee and Balaji Vittal, '"Woh Phir Nahi Aate": Things You Didn't Know about the Rise and Fall of Rajesh Khanna', IBNLive.com, 19 July 2012; available online at: http://ibnlive.in.com/news/woh-phir-nahi-aate-things-you-didnt-know-about-the-rise-and-fall-of-rajesh-khanna/272284-3.html.
- Shaikh Ayaz, 'How *Aradhana*, *Kati Patang* Were Made', Rediff.com/movies, 26 June 2012; available online at: http://www.rediff.com/movies/slide-show/slide-show-1-shakti-samanta-the-director-with-a-keen-ear-for-music/20120626.htm.
- 'Golden Boys: The Dev–Kaka Connection', *Times of India*, 20 July 2012; available online at: http://timesofindia.indiatimes.com/entertainment/hindi/bollywood/news/Golden-boys-The-Dev-Kaka-connection/articleshow/15043708.cms.
- 'Bollywood Blockbusters: The Success of Aradhana', interview aired on CNN-IBN on 29 October 2011.
- Rakesh Rao, 'Heart-throb of an Era', *Frontline*, vol. 29, no. 15, 28 Jul.–10 Aug. 2012; available online at: http://www.

frontline.in/static/html/fl2915/stories/20120810291510700. htm.

- Avijit Ghosh, 'Rajesh Khanna: The God of Romance', *Bollywood's Top 20: Superstars of Indian Cinema*, ed. Bhaichand Patel (New Delhi: Penguin Books India, 2012), p. 173.
- Uma Rao, 'End of a Seven-Year Romance', *Stardust*, May 1973.
- Aniruddha Bhattacharjee and Balaji Vittal, *R.D. Burman: The Man, the Music* (New Delhi: HarperCollins India, 2011).
- Amitabh Bachchan, 'Day 1552', Bachchan Bol: Amitabh Bachchan's Official Blog, 18 July 2012; available online at: http://srbachchan.tumblr.com/post/27501033560.
- Pallavi Kharade, 'I Felt Nervous to Work with Superstar, Rajesh Khanna: Ramesh Deo', *DNA*, 19 July 2012; available online at: http://www.dnaindia.com/pune/report-i-felt-nervous-to-work-with-superstar-rajesh-khanna-ramesh-deo-1716968.
- Nirmala George, 'Rajesh Khanna Dead: Bollywood Superstar Dies at 69', *Huffington Post*, 18 July 2012; available online at: http://www.huffingtonpost.com/2012/07/18/rajesh-khanna-dead-bollywood-actor_n_1681996.html.
- Ali Peter John, 'Rajesh Khanna's Bungalow Aashirwad Was Haunted', *Mumbai Mirror*, 25 July 2012; available online at: http://timesofindia.indiatimes.com/entertainment/hindi/bollywood/news/Rajesh-Khannas-bungalow-Aashirwad-was-haunted/articleshow/15116861.cms.
- Namita Gokhale, 'Super Days: A Remembrance of Bollywood Past', *The Popcorn Essayists: What Movies Do to Writers*, ed. Jai Arjun Singh (New Delhi: Tranquebar Press, *2011*).
- 'Bollywood Babes and Cricketers', *Times of India*, 7 May 2009; available online at: http://timesofindia.indiatimes.com/entertainment/hindi/bollywood/news/Bollywood-babes-and-cricketers/articleshow/4490924.cms.

- 'Rajesh Khanna's Leading Ladies Share Their Memories', *Times of India*, 19 July 2012; available online at: http://timesofindia.indiatimes.com/entertainment/hindi/bollywood/news/Rajesh-Khannas-leading-ladies-share-their-memories/articleshow/15039228.cms.
- Nina Arora, 'Star Craze', *Super*, May 1978.
- Dilip Chitre, 'The Charisma of Rajesh Khanna', *The Best of Quest*, eds. Laeeq Futehally, Achal Prabhala and Arshia Sattar (New Delhi: Westland Books, 2011).
- Shekhar Gupta, 'Creating the Angry Young Man Was Not a Conscious Decision', *Indian Express*, 25 May 2013; available online: http://archive.indianexpress.com/news/creating-the-angry-young-man-was-not-a-conscious-decision/1120627/3.
- Interview with Navin Nischol, *Star & Style*, Sept.–Oct. 1980.
- Nina Arora and Dinesh Raheja, 'Face to Face: For the First Time Superstars Share—The Agony after the Ecstasy!', *Movie*, May 1990; a version is available online at: http://www.hindustantimes.com/entertainment/bollywood/i-m-not-scared-of-death-rajesh-khanna-in-a-1990-interview/article1-892017.aspx.
- Malavika Sangghvi, 'Original Superstar', *Business Standard*, 30 June 2012; available online at: http://www.business-standard.com/article/beyond-business/original-superstar-112063000003_1.html.
- Gautam Kaul, 'The Darker Side of Rajesh Khanna', *New Indian Express*, 22 July 2012; available online at: http://www.newindianexpress.com/entertainment/gossip/article573866.ece.
- Debasish Mahapatra, 'Musical Amar Prem', *Telegraph*, 18 August 2012; available online at: http://www.telegraphindia.com/1120818/jsp/odisha/story_15867677.jsp#.VEQGK_mUdPo.

- Santosh Desai, 'Remembering the Poetic Masculinity of Rajesh Khanna', *Times of India*, 22 July 2012; available online at: http://blogs.timesofindia.indiatimes.com/Citycitybangbang/remembering-the-poetic-masculinity-of-rajesh-khanna/.
- Sunaina Kumar, 'The After Shadow of the Star', *Tehelka*, vol. 9, no. 30, 28 July 2012; available online at: http://archive.tehelka.com/story_main53.asp?filename=hub280712After.asp.
- Patcy N., 'Rajesh Khanna Did Not Care for Anyone', Rediff.com, 27 July 2012; available online at: http://www.rediff.com/movies/slide-show/slide-show-1-rajesh-khanna-did-not-care-for-anyone/20120723.htm.
- Jack Pizzey, *The Bombay Superstar*, documentary, directed by James Kenelm Clarke and Harry Weisbloom (United Kingdom: BBC, 1973).
- Ingrid Albuquerque, 'In Love and Death We Cry', *Times of India*, 22 July 2012; available online at: http://lite.epaper.timesofindia.com/getpage.aspx?edlabel=BGMIR&pubLabel=MM&pageid=6&mydateHid=22-07-2012.
- Harish Kumar Mehra, 'Khanna: The Cult of the Super Personality', *Star & Style*, vol. XXIV, no. 17, August 1975.
- Sudeshna Banerjee, 'Superstar Friend in Need with Friends Too Few', *Telegraph*, July 22 2012; available online at: http://www.telegraphindia.com/1120722/jsp/calcutta/story_15748318.jsp#.VDpakvmSxPo.
- *Super*, April 1978.
- *Super*, June 1978.
- Bijal Kaji, 'Rajesh Khanna: Unveiling of an Enigma by Directors Closest to Him', *Picturpost*, April 1987, p. 9; available online at: https://www.flickr.com/photos/asli_jat/2877192576/in/photostream/.
- Interview of Randhir Kapoor, *Super*, February 1978.

- *Super*, November 1980.
- Bhawana Somaaya, *Screen*, July 1987.
- Nina Arora, 'The New Dimple', *Super*, September 1978.
- Rajesh Khanna's interview with Harmeet Kathuri, 1983.
- Bhawana Somaaya, *Salaam Bollywood: The Pain and the Passion* (Hartford: Spantech & Lancer, 2000).
- Coomi Kapoor, 'Censorship: Dual Standards', *India Today*, 15 April 1985; available online at: http://indiatoday.intoday. in/story/film-makers-face-the-brunt-of-censor-board-whims-and-fancies/1/354035.html.
- Bharathi S. Pradhan, 'The End of the Sister Act', *Telegraph*, 22 November 2009; available online at: http://www. telegraphindia.com/1091122/jsp/7days/story_11770224.jsp.
- Suresh Kohli, 'Rajesh Khanna: Alone in the Multitude', *Uday India*; available online at: http://www.udayindia.in/english/ content_04%20august2012/cine-buzz.html.
- *Filmfare*, September 1998.
- Subhash K. Jha, 'Gulzar on His Long Association with Hrishikesh Mukherjee', Santabanta.com, 31 August 2006; available online at: http://www.santabanta.com/bollywood/11717/gulzar-on-his-long-association-with-hrishikesh-mukherjee/.
- 'Salute to the Legend', *Screen*; available online at: http://www. screenindia.com/old/fullstory.php?content_id=13412.
- Seema Sinha, 'Complicated Relationships!', *Times of India*, 12 March 2011; available online at: http://timesofindia. indiatimes.com/life-style/relationships/man-woman/ Complicated-relationships/articleshow/6525606.cms.
- Sharmila Tagore, 'Last Goodbye from Pushpa as Bollywood Loses Rajesh Khanna', *Hindustan Times*, 19 July 2012; available online at: https://in.news.yahoo.com/last-goodbye-pushpa-bollywood-loses-rajesh-khanna-183000660.html.
- Shobhaa Dé, 'The Loneliness of a Superstar', *Mumbai Mirror*, 19 July 2012; available online at: http://www.mumbaimirror.

com/mumbai/cover-story/The-loneliness-of-a-superstar/
articleshow/16224309.cms.

- Susmita Dasgupta, 'Zindagi Badi Honi Chahiye, Lambi
  Nahin . . . Ha, Ha, Ha', Bargad: Enlightened Prattles;
  19 July 2012; available online at: http://bargad.org/2012/07/19/
  rajesh-khanna/.

- Rajesh Khanna's interview with Nina Arora, May 1991.

- Meera Joshi, 'To Kaka with Love . . .', *Filmfare*, 19 July 2012;
  available online at: http://www.filmfare.com/features/to-kaka-
  with-love-885.html.

- Interview of Anita Advani to ABP News with Umesh
  Kumawat.

- Meena Iyer, 'I Call Myself Rajesh Khanna's Surrogate
  Wife: Anita Advani', *Times of India*, 1 September 2012;
  available online at: http://timesofindia.indiatimes.
  com/entertainment/hindi/bollywood/news/I-call-
  myself-Rajesh-Khannas-surrogate-wife-Anita-Advani/
  articleshow/16060995.cms.

- 'Rajesh Khanna's Live-in Love: Who's Anita Advani?',
  IBNLive.com, 24 July 2012; available online at: http://
  ibnlive.in.com/news/rajesh-khannas-livein-love-whos-anita-
  advani/273833-8-66.html.

- Anita Advani's interview, *Mid-Day*, 17 May 2011.

- Suresh Kohli, 'The Rise and Fall of a Superstar', *Deccan Herald*,
  28 May 2011; available online at: http://www.deccanherald.
  com/content/164705/rise-fall-superstar.html.

- Y. Mallikarjun, '"Rajesh Khanna Lived like Anand"', *The Hindu*,
  18 August 2012; available online at: http://www.thehindu.com/
  todays-paper/tp-national/tp-newdelhi/rajesh-khanna-lived-like-
  anand/article3787708.ece.

- Susmita Dasgupta, 'Rajesh Khanna Was Never Anything
  Except an Illumination', *Economic Times*, 26 July 2012;
  available online at: http://articles.economictimes.indiatimes.

com/2012-07-26/news/32869710_1_rajesh-khanna-anand-and-bawarchi-kati-patang.

- Interview of Prem Chopra, BBC Hindi, July 2012; available online at: www.bbc.co.uk/hindi/.
- 'Rajesh Khanna Havells AD—The Making', YouTube.com, 30 April 2012; available online at: https://www.youtube.com/watch?v=4tr8errgbgE, https://www.youtube.com/watch?v=g9Me2Zxf0K4 and https://www.youtube.com/watch?v=fhfRruJ7KDY.
- Bhawana Somaaya, 'Rajesh Khanna 1979', Rajesh Khanna Fan Club, take 25, excerpt 9, 4 January 2009; available online at: http://rajeshkhannafanclub.blogspot.in/2009/01/rajesh-khannna-1979.html.
- Seshadri Kumar, 'Death of a Superstar: Remembering Rajesh Khanna', Leftbrainwave.com, 26 July 2012; available online at: http://www.leftbrainwave.com/2012/07/death-of-superstar-remembering-rajesh_8505.html.
- 'Rajesh Khanna: The Heart Is a Lonely Hunter', *Super*, October 1978.
- Aseem Bassi, 'Rajesh Khanna Leaves Amritsar Heartbroken', *Hindustan Times*, 18 July 2012; available online at: http://www.hindustantimes.com/india-news/punjab/rajesh-khanna-leaves-amritsar-heartbroken/article1-891239.aspx.
- Dinesh Raheja, 'The Magic of Rajesh Khanna, Sharmila and *Amar Prem*', Rediff.com; available online at: http://www.rediff.com/movies/2002/oct/16dinesh.htm.

FILMOGRAPHY

Year	Film	Role
1966	*Aakhri Khat*	Govind
1967	*Raaz*	Kumar/Sunil
1967	*Baharon ke Sapne*	Ramaiya
1967	*Aurat*	Suresh
1968	*Shrimanji*	Himself
1969	*Aradhana*	Arun/Suraj Prasad Saxena (dual role)
1969	*Ittefaq*	Dilip Roy
1969	*Doli*	Amar Kumar
1969	*Bandhan*	Dharmchand 'Dharma'
1969	*Do Raaste*	Satyan Gupta
1970	*Khamoshi*	Mr Arun Choudhury (Patient #24)
1970	*The Train*	CID Inspector Shyam Kumar

Year	Film	Role
1970	*Sachaa Jhutha*	Bhola/Ranjit Kumar (dual role)
1970	*Safar*	Avinash
1971	*Kati Patang*	Kamal Sinha
1971	*Anand*	Anand Saigal
1971	*Aan Milo Sajna*	Ajit
1971	*Andaz*	Raj
1971	*Maryada*	Raja Babu/Rajan Ram Bahadur
1971	*Chhoti Bahu*	Madhu
1971	*Haathi Mere Saathi*	Raj Kumar 'Raju'
1971	*Guddi*	Himself
1971	*Mehboob ki Mehndi*	Yusuf
1971	*Badnam Farishte*	Lawyer
1972	*Dushman*	Surjit Singh/Dushman
1972	*Amar Prem*	Anand Babu
1972	*Apna Desh*	Akash Chandra
1972	*Dil Daulat Duniya*	Vijay
1972	*Bawarchi*	Raghu (Bawarchi)
1972	*Joroo ka Ghulam*	Rajesh
1972	*Mere Jeevan Sathi*	Prakash
1972	*Maalik*	Raju
1972	*Shehzada*	Rajesh
1972	*Anuraag*	Gangaram
1973	*Raja Rani*	Raja
1973	*Daag: A Poem of Love*	Sunil Kohli
1973	*Namak Haraam*	Somnath (Somu)/Chander Singh

Year	Film	Role
1973	*Bombay Superstar*	Bombay Superstar
1974	*Aavishkar*	Amar
1974	*Humshakal*	Ram/Laxman (dual role)
1974	*Aap ki Kasam*	Kamal Bhatnagar
1974	*Prem Nagar*	Chhotey Kunver Karan U. Singh
1974	*Ajanabee*	Rohit Kumar Saxena
1974	*Roti*	Mangal Singh
1975	*Prem Kahani*	Rajesh Kamleshwar Narain
1975	*Aakraman*	Karnail singh
1976	*Sawa Lakh Se Ek Ladaun*	Qawwali singer
1976	*Maha Chor*	Raju Khan/Rajeshwar A. Singh/Johnny Fernandes (dual role)
1976	*Bundalbaaz*	Rajaram 'Goku' 'Raja'
1976	*Ginny aur Johnny*	Inspector
1976	*Mehbooba*	Prakash/Suraj
1977	*Tyaag*	Chetan
1977	*Karm*	Arvind Kumar
1977	*Chhailla Babu*	Babu Chhailla
1977	*Chalta Purza*	Amar Gupta
1977	*Anurodh*	Arun Choudhury/Sanjay Kumar/Pritam Nath Ghayal
1977	*Aashiq Hoon Baharon Ka*	Ashok Sharma
1977	*Aaina*	Ashok J. Rao
1977	*Hatyara*	Special appearance
1977	*Tinku*	Special appearance

Year	Film	Role
1977	*Palkon ki Chhaon Mein*	Ravi Raj Sinha (Dak Babu)
1978	*Chakravyuha*	Amit Narayan
1978	*Bhola Bhala*	Ram Kumar Verma/Nathu 'Nathiya' Singh
1978	*Naukri*	Ranjit Gupta 'Ronu'
1979	*Naya Bakra*	Person visiting coutesan
1979	*Muqabla*	Qawwali Singer
1979	*Janta Hawaldar*	Janta Prasad/Jantu/Janta Hawaldar
1979	*Shaitan Mujrim*	Special appearance
1979	*Amar Deep*	Raja/Sonu
1979	*Prem Bandhan*	Kishan/Mohan Khanna
1980	*Phir Wohi Raat*	Dr Vijay
1980	*Bandish*	Kishan
1980	*Thodisi Bewafaii*	Arun Kumar Choudhary
1980	*Red Rose*	Anand
1980	*Aanchal*	Shambhu
1981	*Kudrat*	Mohan Kapoor/Madho
1981	*Sundara Satarkar*	Special appearance
1981	*Dhanwan*	Vijaykumar Saxena
1981	*Dard*	Deepak Srivastav/Vikas 'Vicky' (dual role)
1981	*Naseeb*	Himself
1981	*Fiffty Fiffty*	Kishan Singh
1981	*Khoon aur Paani*	Special appearance

Year	Film	Role
1982	*Dil-e-Nadaan*	Anand
1982	*Ashanti*	Police Inspector Kumar Chandra Singh
1982	*Suraag*	Qawwali singer
1982	*Rajput*	Dhirendra Singh
1982	*Dharam Kanta*	Ram/Shanker
1982	*Ayaash*	Special appearance
1983	*Jaanwar*	Raju
1983	*Souten*	Shyam Mohit
1983	*Avtaar*	Avtaar Krishen
1983	*Agar Tum Na Hote*	Ashok Mehra
1983	*Disco Dancer*	Master Raju
1984	*Dharm aur Qanoon*	Justice Diwan/Rajan
1984	*Awaaz*	Advocate Jayant
1984	*Aaj ka M.L.A. Ramavtar*	Ram Avtaar
1984	*Asha Jyoti*	Deepak Chander
1984	*Maqsad*	Rajeshwar
1984	*Naya Kadam*	Ramu
1985	*Oonche Log*	Rai Bahadur Rajdev Singh/Raju/Jagdev Singh/
1985	*Zamana*	Inspector Vinod S. Kumar
1985	*Hum Dono*	Raja/Dr Shekhar (dual role)
1985	*Masterji*	Masterji
1985	*Insaaf Main Karoonga*	Captain Ravi Khanna
1985	*Durgaa*	Advocate
1985	*Aakhir Kyon?*	Alok Nath

Year	Film	Role
1985	*Bewafai*	Ashok Nath
1985	*Alag Alag*	Neeraj
1985	*Babu*	Babu
1985	*Aar Paar*	Special appearance
1985	*Awara Baap*	Raj
1986	*Shatru*	Inspector Ashok Sharma
1986	*Mohabbat ki Kasam*	Krishna
1986	*Angaaray*	Ravi
1986	*Amrit*	Amrit Lal Sharma
1986	*Adhikar*	Vishal
1986	*Anokha Rishta*	Robert Bob
1987	*Sitapur ki Geeta*	Ramu
1987	*Nazrana*	Rajat Verma
1987	*Awam*	Captain Amar Kumar
1987	*Goraa*	Goraa
1988	*Woh Phir Aayegi*	Raju
1988	*Vijay*	Ajit Bhardwaj
1989	*Main Tera Dushman*	Shankar
1989	*Mamta ki Chhaon Mein*	Special appearance
1989	*Ghar ka Chiraag*	Kumar
1989	*Paap ka Ant*	Special appearance
1990	*Swarg*	Mr Kumar
1990	*Dushman*	Special appearance
1991	*Rupaye Dus Karod*	Ravi Varma
1991	*Begunah*	Jeevanlal 'J.V.'
1994	*Khudai*	Raj Anand

Year	Film	Role
1996	*Sautela Bhai*	Master Tulsiram
1999	*Aa Ab Laut Chalen*	Balraj Khanna
2001	*Pyaar Zindagi Hai*	Hridaynath
2002	*Kyaa Dil Ne Kahaa*	Siddharth
2006	*Jaana . . . Let's Fall in Love*	Hamid
2007	*Om Shanti Om*	Special appearance
2008	*Wafaa: A Deadly Love Story*	Amritlal Chopra
2010	*Do Dilon ke Khel Mein*	Joginder Singh
2012	*Jaanleva Black Blood*	CID Officer
2014	*Riyasat*	Saheb

Source: IMDb.com and Wikipedia.com.

INDEX

Conversations with Waheeda Rehman

Nasreen Munni Kabir

'Insightful . . . Rehman speaks with honesty and humour'
India Today

In this highly acclaimed book of conversations with Nasreen Munni Kabir, Waheeda Rehman speaks about her life and work with refreshing honesty, humour and insight: from detailing her personal triumphs and tribulations to giving enthralling accounts of working with cinematic personalities like Guru Dutt, Satyajit Ray, Raj Kapoor and Dev Anand. Against all odds, she successfully made a life in cinema on her own terms. Filled with compelling anecdotes and astute observations, this is a riveting slice of film history that provides a rare view of a much-adored and award-winning screen legend.

'An engaging and revealing account'
Rajeev Masand

Cinema
Rs 499

Ten Years with Guru Dutt: Abrar Alvi's Journey

Sathya Saran

'The best book ever written on a film personality in India'
Deccan Herald

Guru Dutt is probably the only Indian film-maker who, within the parameters of the box office, made a personal statement with his cinema. In this page-turning account, Sathya Saran looks at the tumultuous yet incredibly fecund relationship between the mercurial director and his equally talented albeit unsung writer, Abrar Alvi—a partnership that evolved over a decade till Guru Dutt's tragic death in 1964. Starting his career as a driver and chaperone to Guru Dutt's producer on the sets of *Baaz*, Abrar soon caught the attention of the director with his sharp ear and understanding of film dialogue. The two went on to collaborate on masterpieces like *Aar Paar*, *Mr and Mrs '55*, *Pyaasa* and *Kaagaz Ke Phool*, before Abrar donned the director's mantle with great success in *Sahib Bibi Aur Ghulam*. Brimming with lively anecdotes—about how Abrar honed his skills by writing over 300 love letters; how an accident involving a buffalo led to the discovery of Waheeda Rehman; Guru Dutt's visit to a kotha to get the ambience right for *Pyaasa*—this acclaimed book is a warm and insightful look at two remarkable artistes who inspired each other to create movie magic.

'This book is for every film-goer who has been enchanted
by the magic of Guru Dutt'
The Hindu

Cinema
Rs 299

Romancing with Life: An Autobiography

Dev Anand

**'The only major autobiography to come out of the
Hindi film industry'**
Outlook

With the death of Dev Anand in December 2011, Bollywood lost its
most passionate, most charismatic romantic hero. In *Romancing with
Life*, Dev Anand tells his remarkable life story—no less dramatic and
gripping than any of his films—as only he could. Here are tales from
Dev's youth in 1930s' Gurdaspur and Lahore; his years of struggle in
1940s' Bombay; his doomed romance with Suraiya; his marriage to
co-star Kalpana Kartik; and his relationship with many luminous heroines.

Romancing with Life is the quintessential Dev Anand—a book chock-
full of bittersweet reminisces, written in a pacy, effervescent style that
carries the reader through sixty of Bollywood's most interesting years.

'A vivid . . . well-written account of a wonderful life'
Times of India

Memoir
Rs 399